Praise for A

'Anyone who reads Dr Arian's rem[...]
inspired by the immense power and resilience of the human will.
Spanning from war-wracked Kabul to the lecture halls of Cambridge,
Dr Arian tells a riveting story of loss, exile and rebirth. At a time
when displacement has become increasingly politicized, this book is
a gift, a dazzling testimony to the extraordinary contributions that
refugees make to the host communities that welcome them.'
KHALED HOSSEINI

'A thrilling and absorbing read from first to last.
What a life and what an inspiration.'
STEPHEN FRY

'A phenomenal story of a boy's realization that saving others was
the way to help himself. From war in Afghanistan to refugee camps
and escaping to Britain, he understood that by educating
himself he could benefit the world.'
THE TIMES

'A powerful, heart-warming account of a young man's escape from
war and deprivation to extraordinary success in serving the people
of his new country. His is a book which thoroughly deserves to be
read and celebrated. I was moved and delighted by it.'
JOHN SIMPSON

'An immensely powerful and moving account of a child who
endured war, trauma, displacement and racism, yet who never
faltered in his passion to help others through becoming a doctor.
Dr Arian's journey, resilience and heart are truly remarkable.'
DR RACHEL CLARKE

'One of the most incredible life stories . . .
A lesson to be drawn for others.'
JAMES O'BRIEN

'A remarkable story. I thought this book was brilliant.'
NAGA MUNCHETTY, *BBC Breakfast*

www.penguin.co.uk

In *the* Wars

From Afghanistan to the UK and Beyond –
A Refugee's Story of Survival and Saving Lives

Dr Waheed Arian

PENGUIN BOOKS

TRANSWORLD PUBLISHERS
Penguin Random House, One Embassy Gardens,
8 Viaduct Gardens, London SW11 7BW
www.penguin.co.uk

Transworld is part of the Penguin Random House group of companies
whose addresses can be found at global.penguinrandomhouse.com

First published in Great Britain in 2021 by Bantam Press
an imprint of Transworld Publishers
Penguin paperback edition published 2022

A CIP catalogue record for this book
is available from the British Library.

ISBN
9780552177641

Typeset in 10.12/13.86pt Minion Pro by Jouve (UK), Milton Keynes.
Printed and bound in Great Britain by Clays Ltd, Elcograf S.p.A.

The authorized representative in the EEA is Penguin Random House Ireland,
Morrison Chambers, 32 Nassau Street, Dublin D02 YH68.

Penguin Random House is committed to a sustainable
future for our business, our readers and our planet. This book
is made from Forest Stewardship Council® certified paper.

*For my dear parents: my father, Taj Mohammad, and my
late mother, Bibi Aminah, who never gave up.*

For my cherished family, Davina, Zane and Alana.

And for all those who strive to make our world a better place.

Contents

Illustrations

Author's Note

THIS IS A PERSONAL story. Naturally, some of my childhood experiences overlap with those of other members of my family. Some are mine alone. In this book our early family life is inevitably recalled from my perspective but we all suffered, as have the millions of people in Afghanistan, and in other countries around the world, whose lives have been blighted by conflict, displacement, poverty and oppression. Many have suffered, and still suffer, far worse than we did.

Every one of us has our own story, and the individual stories of my relatives are not mine to tell. Out of respect for the privacy of my sisters and their families, I have changed their names. My parents and my brothers are referred to by their real names.

While memories from our early childhoods tend to be random and fragmented, significant episodes leave a deeper impression and many of my recollections remain striking. Some have been pieced together from the collective family memory bank and with the particular help of my parents. Amid the confusion and trauma of war, it is hard to keep track of time, place and an ordered sequence of events, especially since Afghanistan follows a different calendar from Western countries.

Details of some events have been withheld, for legal reasons and to protect confidentiality. But everything I have recounted happened and has been recounted truthfully.

The troubled history of Afghanistan is extremely complex and the brief coverage given here is not intended to offer a complete over-view. Afghanistan's story is touched on only where it provides a context to my own childhood and in terms of the impact on my life of some of its key moments.

As a humanitarian, my mission is to improve and save lives, in the land of my birth, my adopted home, the UK, and across the world, irrespective of nationality, ethnicity, culture or religion. I make no apology for maintaining an impartial stance in describing the conditions, past and present, faced by Afghanistan and other countries.

The political battles are for others to fight. My purpose in telling my story is to show how standing shoulder to shoulder and working together can change the world for the better and how every one of us has a contribution to make to society. Above all, it is to inspire others to pursue their dreams.

Part One

1

Home

THE BOY WAS YOUNG, about my age. Skinny, thin, pale face, sharp nose, short, blondish hair. His blue eyes were watchful but not unfriendly. His name was Ryan, and he was my cellmate.

'Why are you here?' I asked him.

'I steal things, mate.' He seemed surprised by the question.

I was dismayed.

I'd been brought to this place, called Feltham, from Heathrow Airport and had spent my first couple of nights billeted with a different cellmate: a muscle-bound man-mountain who had seemed a lot older than me, though as we were, I'd been informed, in a prison for juvenile offenders, he must have been younger than he looked. He was here because he had got into a fight and beaten someone up. We hadn't spoken much: he was a man of few words and I was struggling to make sense of what was happening to me.

Ryan was more open and approachable. We talked a bit and exchanged potted life histories. He lived with his mum, who had a clerical job. It was clear this wasn't the first time he had been at Feltham.

I didn't really understand why I was here. It certainly hadn't been part of the plan three days earlier, when I'd boarded a flight in Peshawar, carrying my hopes, and those of my family, for a new beginning. I had left with a brand-new UK passport, a visa and the assurance that I would be welcomed in London with open arms as a refugee. I was fifteen years old.

Instead I had been held in a cell overnight at Heathrow and told that I could expect to be in prison for a year, maybe a year and a half, before being sent home. After two days in Feltham, I'd been taken in a van to some kind of courtroom and then brought back again. My attempts to explain myself had so far been ignored by everyone I had met. I just couldn't reconcile this response with the impressions I had formed of Britain and the British who, I believed, were compassionate and fair-minded, horrified by the suffering of the people of Afghanistan and ready to accept those willing to work and make a contribution to society. It was like being in the middle of one of those bad dreams where you're urgently trying to tell someone something and they just can't hear you.

I had been given this one chance to save myself from the brutal Taliban regime and ensure the survival of my family in Kabul. All the hopes invested in me were crumbling to dust; all the money scraped together, the huge sacrifice made to get me to a place of safety, where I could work to help support my mum, dad and ten brothers and sisters, pursue an education that, because of all the disruptions to our lives, had barely got off the ground and make something of myself. And the worst of it was it was my fault. The burden of self-blame weighed heavily on my shoulders. I was convinced that this would break my parents and if I couldn't get out of here I would never see them again. They would both have heart attacks and die while I languished in an English prison.

I was in a pit of despair. I told one of the prison officers if I had to stay in this place for a year I would kill myself. I meant it, too, in that moment. I'd always found a way over or, more often, round the daunting obstacles I'd faced but this time I just could not see past the prison walls.

As I went over and over it all in my mind in the cold light of day, I knew that, whatever suffering I might face, taking my life wasn't the solution. I was the eldest son. If something happened to my parents, I would be responsible for the family. Who would take care of them then? There had to be another way, if only I could get someone to listen. I lay awake at night deliberating how best to try to tell my story and asked for a pencil and paper to write everything down.

It seemed the staff took my suicide threat seriously because they sent a social worker to the cell to see me. She was a lovely, motherly woman in her forties, about the same age as my own mum. Clutching my notes, I told her everything, in my halting English, and she listened. My tears splashed down on to the paper. She gave me a hug, the first warm human contact I'd had since saying goodbye to my dad in Peshawar. She suggested perhaps it might help if I could talk to an imam.

I was taken to a room to see a young imam after Friday prayers. He, too, listened quietly and patiently. He said God was with me, I should keep my hopes up, keep praying. I must make sure that my behaviour was exemplary and that I obeyed the rules.

These were the only people to offer me comfort and sympathy. But comfort and sympathy were not what I was looking for. I was looking for answers.

While I obsessed over how to make my voice heard to someone in authority, I kept myself to myself. There was a games room with pool tables, table football and a TV but I wasn't interested in those. I wasn't interested in food, either, but I ate because I knew I must.

It was the summer of 1999, and Feltham Young Offenders Institution was overcrowded and understaffed. It meant vulnerable teenagers were sharing cells with hardened criminals and we all spent prolonged spells under lock and key. In the same week I arrived, the crisis at Feltham was being debated in the House of Lords after a report from Her Majesty's inspector of prisons declared that his recent unannounced visit had been without doubt the most disturbing that he'd had to make in his three years in the post. The following year, a nineteen-year-old boy was to be battered to death here by his cellmate in a racist attack.

I knew nothing of this, or of what was considered acceptable or unacceptable in HM Prisons. I didn't witness any violence or sense any threatening undercurrents and I was not afraid of my fellow inmates. I had already survived relentless war, poverty, hunger and disease. I was used to being self-sufficient and this was in most respects a safer environment than anything I was accustomed to. In an Afghan prison, I would have been knocked about, or worse, as a matter of course. My one real fear was that I might remain locked up here.

Through the windows I could see cars outside and indications of a whole different world beyond those walls. I wanted to find out as much as I could about it and pestered Ryan for information about his life.

'Why don't you work? Your mum works. Why do you steal when you could work? You are not a good boy if you steal. Why would you do that when it means you end up back in here? How many hours does your mum work? How much does she get paid?'

I think Ryan found me slightly baffling, but he tolerated the barrage of questions with a combination of irritation and good grace. He busied himself during lockdown with a mysterious communal activity which involved inmates passing stuff to each other through the windows using bedsheets. I have no idea what it was: they communicated using a system of whistles and a private language that was lost on me. It was one thing I thought it wiser not to ask about.

I passed my time in our cell doing push-ups, sit-ups and practising my Taekwondo. I prayed. Ryan was bemused.

'What are you doing, mate?'

'Praying.'

'*Praying?* Who to?'

I had identified what I saw as my one shot at presenting my case. I'd been told I would be going back to court to answer the charges against me and I wanted to be physically and mentally ready for it. Work, study, faith and exercise were what had kept me going so far, and two of those coping mechanisms were still available to me here.

Subconsciously, I understood that life is not about what happens to you, it's about how you respond to what happens to you. I may not have expressed it that way back then, but it was a lesson I had been learning for as long as I could remember.

I was born in Kabul at the height of the Soviet–Afghan war, my parents' fifth child and their first boy. It is customary among some tribes to greet the birth of a son with a volley of rifle shots into the air, but I doubt this was considered advisable in the volatile streets of the Afghan capital in 1983.

Kabul sits high in a narrow valley in the snow-capped Hindu Kush mountains of Afghanistan, a country often described as the crossroads of central Asia. Its rich and ancient heritage bears the influences of northern India, Mongolia, Greece, Persia, Arabia and China. The population is composed of a variety of ethnicities, among which Pashtuns, Tajiks, Hazaras and Uzbeks predominate.

Bordered by Pakistan to the east and south, Iran to the west and in the north by Turkmenistan, Uzbekistan and Tajikistan (all part of the USSR at the time of my birth), the unique strategic position of our landlocked country has, throughout recorded history, entangled it in the shifting allegiances and agendas of its immediate neighbours and on the world stage. Since the nineteenth century, it had been shaped by the competition for supremacy between the British and Russian empires.

In the 1950s and 1960s big strides had been made towards democratic reform, balanced with a respect for the more conservative factions. In Kabul, where there were good schools and hospitals, middle-class women went to university, worked in the professions and held government positions. In the provinces, people lived peacefully according to their own local traditions. The country was a tourist destination, popular with adventurers and hippies, and visitors were amazed by its beauty.

My parents had grown up under the rule of Mohammed Daoud Khan, a member of the royal family who had been prime minister for twenty years when, in 1973, he seized power from King Zahir Shah and established Afghanistan as a republic for the first time in its history. This sea change fractured the political order. The new president's progressive policies of gradual modernization did not sit well with the government of neighbouring Pakistan and they began to encourage resistance among Afghan Islamic leaders.

Afghanistan was becoming increasingly reliant on another, more powerful neighbour, the USSR, while the USA vied with the Soviets to invest in the country. The president's attempts to steer an independent course sidelined the communists and alienated traditionalists, and in 1978 former allies of Douad Khan's in the People's Democratic Party of Afghanistan (PDPA), backed by the military, overthrew his government and assassinated him.

The PDPA forged ahead with its more radical socialist agenda, which included abolishing arranged marriages and a drastic reform of land ownership. The party may have been in control in the cities but its policies were strongly opposed by Islamic leaders in the countryside, where they were perceived as undermining the traditional tribal order. People from all walks of life joined the resistance. Continued in-fighting within the ranks of the PDPA and uprisings against the new government resulted in Soviet tanks rolling into Kabul the following year. The invasion was intended to be a brief intervention to support regime change but it was to last for a long, hard decade and light the fuse of the complex armed struggle that persists in Afghanistan to this day.

Red Army special forces stormed the Presidential Palace and assassinated the new president, Hafizullah Amin, who was replaced with Babrak Karmal, a rival from another PDPA faction. The Soviets took over key government installations in Kabul, occupied the cities and controlled the main highways in and out of the country. There were curfews, travel bans and mass incarcerations. They met with fierce retaliation from the Mujahideen, a coalition of guerrillas drawn from disparate groups united in their opposition to the secularization of the country.

The Mujahideen, which had grown out of the religious rebellion against Douad Khan, had the international support of the USSR's rivals, including the USA, Pakistan, Saudi Arabia, China and the UK, each motivated by their own reasons for wanting to keep the Soviet influence at bay. In essence, the Cold War was now being enacted on our soil.

By the time I was born, the war had been raging for three and a half years. Our home was in the heart of Kabul, on a main thoroughfare in Shahre Naow, the major administrative and commercial district of the city, close to the Presidential Palace. My parents, Taj Mohammad and Bibi Aminah, had bought the house jointly with my dad's elder brother, who ran an electrical store in the city centre. We occupied one side and my uncle's family lived separately in the other. At the front were some shops they rented out. My uncle had his own shops, and ours were a shoe shop, a kebab shop, a carpenter's and a repair shop where a guy mended old fridges and assorted broken electrical appliances.

My dad had had a tough childhood. He was four years old when he lost his mother and had been brought up in Kabul by a stepmother with his brother, sister and step-siblings. He had barely any formal education. When he asked his father for money to go to school, he was told, 'If you want to go to school you need to earn the money to pay for it.'

As a result, although he had a quick, sharp mind, and was a deep and independent thinker, his literacy was poor. Afghan Muslims absorb Arabic almost by osmosis – we learn enough at home, and from the mullah at the mosque, to enable us to read the Holy Quran – so he could read a little, but he couldn't write. His mental arithmetic was impressive, though. Even now, he will have added up a column of figures while the rest of us are still reaching for our calculators.

As a small boy he sold chewing gum and cigarettes in Pul-e Khishti, the marketplace near the central mosque in old Kabul, a warren of vintage houses and narrow streets. Then he went into partnership with a Sikh who made herbal preparations. The herbalist would concoct them in his house while Dad sold them out front. By the time my sisters began arriving, he was buying and selling currency at Sarai Shahzada, Kabul's financial and trading market, which consists of hundreds of small shops dealing in money, gold and precious stones.

My parents were both from Pashtun families with their roots in rural Logar province, to the south of the city. My mother's family had a certain standing because her father was educated and worked in an office. My mum had grown up in Logar and, like most country girls, was not sent to school as her brothers were but was brought up to be a housewife and mother, and she could not read or write.

My father and mother were determined that their children should have the education they had been denied. They strongly believed that education, for girls as well as boys, was the key to a better life, not only for us as individuals but for the whole country. My two eldest sisters, Nageenah and Nazifa, were enrolled in school, although concerns for their safety during the war meant their attendance was intermittent. They would often be exhausted in the mornings after lying awake all night, terrified by the noise of the bombs.

The military used air power to deal harshly with rebels and civilians alike. Most of the combat took place in the mountains and the country areas, where they laid landmines on the Mujahideen's supply routes from Iran and Pakistan and levelled villages to prevent their inhabitants giving shelter to the guerrillas. On the main roads, the Mujahideen, covertly armed and trained by their powerful supporters, would attack tanks and convoys bringing in equipment and provisions. At night we would hear the screams of jets taking off from Bagram Air Base on the outskirts of Kabul and the distant explosions as planes and helicopters were shelled by the resistance with American surface-to-air missiles. From time to time, bombs would suddenly crash from somewhere between the mountains on to a market or a row of houses. But in general the closest the Mujahideen fighters came to Kabul was the Surobi Dam, about 70 kilometres away. They would fire off a series of rockets from here and then retreat back into the hills.

It was nothing like the constant bombardment we would suffer a few years later during the civil war. And it felt somehow as if it wasn't personal, because we were not the targets – or at least, it did until one of them destroyed a building or killed somebody.

My parents kept us close to them, and at home, for our own safety. Our house, built of clay bricks and vintage wood, was an old-fashioned dwelling with interconnecting rooms, cosy and comfortable. It was connected to mains electricity (sometimes – the supply was unreliable) and running water, and lit after the sun went down by the warm glow of oil lamps. Mum cooked on a metal stove fuelled by coal and wood and heated oil or made tea on our Russian-made plug-in hotplate.

We had a small garden at the back of the house where I would play, usually with my third sister, Zari. Nazifa and Perveen, sisters two and four, were quieter and more self-contained, whereas Zari was outgoing and exuberant, and we would get into mischief together. My eldest sister, Nageenah, was about eight years my senior. Calm, perceptive and mature for her age, she was Mum's right-hand woman, and helped her to run the household. Maternal and affectionate, she also took care of us little ones. It was Nageenah who taught me the Arabic alphabet and my numbers.

My dad was the extrovert, the talker and idealist. Mum, the practical one, was the realist. She was quiet, watchful and did the worrying for both of them. She was also very protective and incredibly strong. She may not have said much, but what she did say was succinct and potent and often extremely blunt. Some of her one-liners were very funny, too, and are still quoted as the punchlines to many family stories. How she coped with everything life threw at our family is astonishing. Her instincts were so razor-sharp it sometimes seemed as if she had a sixth sense. She could anticipate danger before anyone else had the slightest inkling of it.

Mum fed the family on what we could afford: *shola*, the sticky rice that is a staple of the Afghan diet, sometimes made with *maash* (mung beans) or *quroot* (dried curd), lentil *dhal* and bread and vegetables brought into the city by the farmers, usually potatoes, pumpkins and beans, from which she made soup. We did not have meat – that was too expensive. When you opened the front door, the scent of sizzling lamb would sometimes waft through up the alleyway from the kebab shop: a delicious torture. If we were hungry, Mum gave us tea and bread dipped in oil and sugar.

After we ate, she would often help Dad, clearing a space on the table, laying out a cloth and painstakingly repairing torn banknotes with a glue she made herself. He would then be able to exchange them at the bank or sell them on at a small profit.

The summers could be hot in Kabul but it was the kind of crisp, dry heat typical of desert climates and high altitude, with low humidity, and perfectly comfortable. I can still remember the magical surprise of the first snow of winter, so pure, sparkling and beautiful. I would have snow fights with my cousins in our back garden. My excitement was always short-lived. Within a day, the cold would have seeped into our bones. We didn't have enough clothes to keep us warm for long outside. The men would wear jumpers bought at the market over their usual *perahan tunban*, the Afghan *shalwar kameez*, often in garish colours, and perhaps a jacket, if they had one. The jumpers came from Russia or China and there wasn't much choice: you just had to take whatever colour they had. And more often than not, they were full of holes. We kids stayed inside, wrapped in blankets.

At night we had Afghan central heating: the *sandeli*, a traditional wood or coal stove located in the middle of the room, consisting of a brazier of hot coals placed beneath a low table or upturned box, with a quilt or blanket over the top. Families might sit round the *sandeli* in the late evening to drink tea or to eat, with their feet close to the heat source and the cover over their legs to keep them warm, or lie down around it for the night when it is time to sleep. Needless to say, it is not the safest domestic appliance. Many a household accident is caused by a *sandeli*.

My dad was a great storyteller, with a real knack for painting a picture, and as we dozed off under our blankets he would recount tales of ancient Islamic wars, or stories adapted from the plots of Bollywood movies he had seen or which he made up himself. They always featured feats of great courage and heroism and had a moral to them. If Perveen or I were woken by the sound of shelling my mother would soothe us back to sleep. 'Hush, there's nothing to worry about. It's just fireworks.'

It has been estimated that a million civilians were killed during the brutal nine-year Soviet–Afghan conflict, along with 90,000 Mujahideen, 18,000 Afghan troops and 14,000 Soviets. Most of the casualties were outside the capital. If you talk to anyone who lived in Kabul at the time of the invasion about their experiences, you will get a wide range of responses. For the middle classes, and those who worked for the government, daily life went on pretty much as normal. Hafizullah Amin had been distrusted by many and some saw the Soviet presence as a good thing. Others, those who were imprisoned or tortured, or whose relatives were killed for political or religious reasons, would tell a different story. Some supported the government, others the Mujahideen, often without a full understanding of the motives and political manoeuvrings involved, and families were torn apart by conflicting loyalties. Many, like my dad, tried to stay neutral and keep their heads down. Everyone felt the loss of their freedom of speech. Afghanistan may have been historically poor and under-developed, but it had never before known political repression. Now nobody dared to discuss the new regime publicly.

The biggest threat posed to our family by the Soviet–Afghan war was to my father. We had relatives, friends and neighbours in the Afghan army and others among the Mujahideen, but he had no alle-giance to any side or splinter group. He always had a clear-sighted grasp of politics and saw something of the light and shade, the com-plexities and the underlying agendas involved. He listened to the news every night, on his little battery-operated radio, from our neighbouring countries and the BBC World Service, when he could pick it up, rather than to the slogans and patriotic anthems served up by the government in Kabul.

But the authorities were forcing all able-bodied men under forty into military service. Nobody was exempt apart from those who worked for the government or in a handful of other key occupa-tions. All men had to carry documentation recording their military status, and if they couldn't produce it, they could be seized on the spot and inducted into the army. The government relied heavily on press gangs of Soviet and Afghan soldiers who combed the streets for men of fighting age, some just boys, as young as fifteen years old, and simply bundled them into trucks.

When the army had first attempted to call up reserves in 1980, some 100,000 men fled Kabul, reducing the city's population by 20 per cent. A lot of them went to Pakistan or joined the rebels. Not surprisingly, the desertion rate remained huge throughout the war and beyond – somewhere between 10,000 and 30,000 every year.

While my much older uncle next door was safely past the age limit, my father had a target on his back. Like so many others, he was not willing to take up arms against his fellow countrymen at the bidding of any government, let alone one controlled by a foreign power. Nevertheless, while he remained in Kabul, it was inevitable that one day the authorities would catch up with him. That day finally came and he was duly conscripted.

My memories of this time come in fragments, snapshots without context or sequence, as memories of our early childhood tend to do. Sometimes it is hard to know whether they are true memories, or have been constructed retrospectively from the stories told and retold by my family. But one in particular remains vivid. I was devoted to my dad, and used to wait every evening for him to come home. One day he appeared at the door with a present for me: a huge kite.

Kite-fighting is a big thing in Afghanistan, and indeed across the Indian subcontinent. The object is to liberate your opponent's kite. Sometimes their fine strings used to be coated with powdered glass to slice through the string of a rival kite. The convention is that a loose kite can be kept by the person who captures it and droves of children chasing drifting kites are a common sight. Kite-running can be a dangerous pastime. Focused on the brightly coloured prize whirling in the sky, kids may run into traffic or fall from trees or rooftops trying to reach it. The strings are a hazard to birds and humans, causing cuts, or becoming entangled in electricity cables. But there is something poignantly joyful in the sight of these vibrant spots of crimson, orange, sapphire, yellow dancing free, high in the air, above the so often grim existence below.

This one was a beauty. It was bigger than I was, all the colours of the rainbow and hardly damaged at all. My father must have either found it somewhere or reached up to grab it over the heads of the children chasing it. We did not have toys, or presents – it was tough enough for my parents to provide our basic essentials – and I was thrilled.

I can still picture my dad standing there holding it out to me, beaming, in his drab, brown army uniform and military boots, before bending down to give me a hug.

And then, all of a sudden, he disappeared.

2

After the Next Mountain

FOR MONTHS I WAITED every day for my dad to come home. He never did. I soon learned not to ask questions about where he had gone. My mum remained tight-lipped. She just told me not to worry, we would see him soon, and that if ever anyone asked us where he was, we must always, always say we didn't know. It was drummed into us that we must never answer the door to anybody, but leave it to Mum or Nageenah. We were rarely allowed to go out, not even to play with the neighbourhood children, for fear a careless word might be dropped and repeated.

I can remember only one proper outing in the whole of that time, when my mother and aunt took me, with my cousins, to the nearby Shahre Naow park. I played with my cousins on the slide and we clambered and swung on the climbing frame. Even there, my mum watched me like a hawk all the while. The attractions were modest, but for me it was as exciting as an afternoon at a theme park. And before we went home we were allowed a special treat: an ice cream. This was so rare I can still recall to this day how wonderful it tasted.

There were whispered conversations with Nageenah. Mum discussed everything with her and involved her in all the family decisions. Nageenah was entrusted to collect the rent from the shopkeepers and would return with wood shavings and offcuts from the carpenter to fuel the fire. My mum had plenty on her plate: at some point around this time she took herself off to the Malalai

Maternity Hospital, where my sisters and I had all been born, and returned with another baby sister, Gululai.

That summer Mum took us all to visit our relatives in Logar. The main highway from Kabul to Khost runs through the province and there was a bus there from Kabul, which came in from Logar on the same day every week, bringing the farmers to sell their produce in the markets, and made the return journey the day after.

The pick-up point was at Balahissar, near the old fort, in the old part of Kabul. My mum and Nageenah would shepherd us all through the streets, past the manicured lawns of the imposing Presidential Palace and the giant tanks, steering clear of the gun-toting Russian and Afghan government soldiers lounging watchfully, smoking, on every corner. The Logar–Kabul service was operated for years by the same guy, Shamsai, who always drove the bus himself. As he was considered trustworthy by both sides, it was a relatively safe mode of transport. There were checkpoints, and the bus would be searched for deserters and Mujahideen, but it was a familiar sight on the road and at least never the target of attacks.

On reaching Logar province, the elderly bus chugged through beautiful scenery with breathtaking views, impossibly green fields, tiny villages dotted in the foothills of the enormous mountains and the river glinting in the sunlight. The scent of flowers and forest trees – cedar, pine, walnut, juniper – drifted in on the breeze. To me, gazing saucer-eyed out of the bus window, it seemed like paradise. My father's family village, Kotobkhil, was in the Baraki Barak district, about 80 kilometres from Kabul. We would be greeted there by a throng of grandmas and aunties, who all made a huge fuss of me, my dad's precious son.

The Logar villages consisted of a cluster of maybe six or seven houses, surrounded by thick mud walls. The houses were built to withstand the cold winters, also with thick mud walls and roofs of dense, robust wood, which retained the heat. There was no electricity but they were always warm, thanks to the strategically placed ovens: the traditional Afghan clay bread ovens were, in Logar, sunk into the centre of the floor to keep the whole home heated. There would be farm workers coming in and out all day. We stayed in a farmhouse guest room above the stable where the cows lived.

The family were cattle farmers, so in Logar there was meat, milk and yogurt. In the city dairy products were a luxury, because of the difficulty of keeping milk from spoiling. Here it came fresh from the cow. There were sweets made with fruit and nuts and the best cornbread I have ever tasted before or since. The villagers lived mainly on what they produced. Some villages had a small shop. For other supplies, such as a new tyre for your bike or some fabric, you went to the market in Baraki Barak, the district's main town.

That summer, as we were welcomed into the farmhouse, a handsome, well-built figure jumped to his feet. I couldn't believe my eyes. It was my dad. I threw myself into his arms. 'How you've grown, Waheed!' he exclaimed. We were all in tears as he held us close in a big bear hug.

We spent several weeks in Logar. My dad would take me to visit other relatives, who somehow always had a fresh batch of cornbread ready to offer us, or to the mosque. I whiled away days outside with the local kids, playing marbles, making little models of cars out of mud clay and learning how to use a catapult. My sisters and I stroked the cows and tried to sit on the donkeys. We invariably lost our balance and fell off, to the amusement of the village children.

Looking back, it seems perverse that my recollections of Logar can be so idyllic, given that the area was one of the main theatres of the war and far more dangerous at that time than Kabul. In truth, my memories are a mosaic of the good and the horrific. There are perhaps various reasons why the good prevails: Logar was the backdrop to the happiest of the remembered moments of my early childhood, on the surface a serene landscape where I had the freedom to play outside and was spoiled by my relations. During the Soviet occupation, I was too young to properly understand the savage realities of life there. And later, during the civil war that followed the withdrawal of the Red Army, the battle lines changed and it was a genuine sanctuary. At that time it was Kabul that became a hell on earth. Maybe, above all, it was because, as a small child, it was here that I knew I would see my dad.

In the 1980s, government forces were conducting a cat-and-mouse war with the Mujahideen in rural Afghanistan. On the ground, the army would monitor large areas from high vantage points that gave them a panoramic view of the fields and villages below. Planes and helicopters would be deployed to target rebels and deserters. The killing was indiscriminate. They would carpet-bomb entire villages if they suspected they were harbouring Mujahideen. Villages in the Baraki Barak district were razed to the ground several times and had to be rebuilt by the communities. All the farmers had rifles. The military thought nothing of killing anyone, freedom fighter or civilian, on sight, and women and children were not exempt from their cruelty.

The slaughter in Logar was so ferocious at some stages that the province was nicknamed Bab al-Jihad – the Gates of Jihad. There were many stories of atrocities. One of the most shocking took place early on in the Soviet war, in 1982, the year before I was born, when 105 villagers, including a dozen children, were massacred in the Logar valley. They had been hiding in a covered irrigation canal. Witnesses reported that soldiers had poured an inflammable liquid into the trench and fired incendiary bullets into it from AK-47 assault rifles to set it alight.

The government's tanks and helicopters were stationed on the flatlands of Baraki Barak, which had previously been the provincial capital. Kotobkhil was on higher ground, and during the day we would watch their troops observing us through binoculars from

Mir Abdul Mountain. The attacks would come in the early morning or early evening, when we could see the fighting going on below us. But mostly they would come in the middle of the night: the noise of tanks echoing around the mountains, the horrible, deafening whine of jets, the loud throbbing of helicopters and the whole sky ablaze with blinding lights.

Soldiers would descend on a village and search every house. I can remember them striding in and asking for bread, or helping themselves to our milk and yogurt, before investigating each room. The locals would quietly provide food for army and rebels alike. They didn't want to invite trouble. If there was enough warning of an impending raid, men would leave their homes at sundown and melt away into the trees and bushes. They knew this territory like the backs of their hands and would move from house to house, village to village, along hidden paths.

When there wasn't time to escape, they would disappear into secret holes and tunnels or into cellars, creeping behind the bread ovens. In the family farmhouse in Kotobkhil there was a hole dug in the floor of the stable, covered over with straw. My dad remembers having to take refuge there once squashed in with my grandfather, my mum's dad, who also happened to be visiting at the time. If the soldiers spotted any of these hiding places, sometimes they didn't bother searching them. They simply lobbed in a grenade to deal with anyone who might be concealed there.

My parents did everything they could to shield us from what was going on: the bombs, they told us, were the same as the fireworks we heard in Kabul, just closer here; the aircraft merely flying low over the village on their way to somewhere else. But we still woke in the night screaming with terror, and there was no disguising the bombshells we saw sticking out of fields or accounting for the sons of relatives and neighbours who vanished overnight and were never seen again.

When the time came for us to return home that summer, I couldn't understand why my dad was not coming with us. The bus set off early, about 4am. Shamsai would honk his horn at each village to announce its arrival. It was always so cold at that time in the morning, and my toes were freezing as we waited to clamber aboard among the farmers and their sacks of potatoes and corn. I sobbed as my father hugged us all goodbye.

My mother said nothing, except to warn me not to talk about my dad any more, on the bus or anywhere else. It was some time before I made sense of his sudden disappearance and continued absence and, like so many of the events of my childhood, I pieced it together gradually over the years from different stories and reminiscences. In their desire to protect us and spare us from fear – and, during the Soviet war, because it was safer for everyone that we children did not have information others might seek to extract from us – while we were growing up my parents spoke little of the hardships they suffered.

Dad had remained with the army only for as long as it took to complete his training in Kabul. Once action on the front line loomed, and with it the prospect of killing his countrymen or being killed himself, he had made a run for it. Now he had no option but to get out of the city as quickly as possible. My parents had heard chilling tales of 'recruits' and deserting conscripts being dragged from their beds in the middle of the night.

My father had escaped to Logar province, where he kept a low profile, moving from village to village as necessary, and then to Pakistan, where he would spend several months at a time trying to earn some money to support himself and the family. Here he led a nomadic existence, trading currency and buying and selling antiques and other ethnic bric-a-brac. He would travel around the North-West Frontier, whose villagers were happy to make a few rupees from traditional household items they'd had knocking about in their homes for years, and sell on his purchases at the antique market in Peshawar. He was a charismatic man, and had a good eye for what would appeal to the antique shop owners, and to visiting foreigners keen to take home a cultural memento of Pakistan.

I would not see my dad again for months. He was journeying back and forth between Logar and Pakistan via the routes used by the Mujahideen to bring in weapons. It was an arduous and dangerous commute. The trails were mostly impassable to vehicles and he travelled on foot, with the occasional assistance of a borrowed motorbike. Horses were a luxury that was generally unaffordable. He would return to Logar during the summer months, when the heat in Pakistan was severe, heading back across the border before the winter set in and the heavy snow in the mountainous regions left him stranded.

In Kabul, my mum dealt impressively with anyone who came asking about my dad. The army were known to send genial emissaries, sometimes in civilian dress, claiming to be friends of the man they were hunting. She trusted nobody. When she opened the door to find a soldier in uniform standing there she must have been very scared, but she didn't show it. Instead she went on the offensive. 'Why are you asking me? My husband is with the army. He left this house in his uniform and we haven't seen him since. Where is he? Nobody has told us. You need to find him!' It was a bravura performance.

Our little black-and-white television offered little beyond propaganda and glorification of the regime except, on a Friday, a Bollywood movie. The broadcasts of the military might of the Soviet and Afghan armies being paraded through the streets of our city made me fearful. So did the tanks and armed men I glimpsed when I peeped round our front door, or from the cover of the narrow alleyway leading to the main road, and the aircraft we heard at night, because I knew these were the same tanks, men and aircraft that were wreaking such havoc in Logar.

'Moor Jani, are they going to kill us?' I would ask on my occasional foray out on an essential errand with my mother, holding tightly on to her hand.

'No, don't worry. They are not interested in us. It is men they are looking for.'

Technically my mum was telling the truth when she said she didn't know where my dad was. She genuinely didn't. However, she was, of course, well aware that he wasn't with the army. We had no telephone, and any communication was dangerous. But from time to time, we would have other visitors: elderly cousins from Logar, in their country clothes and turbans, who had arrived on the bus to bring their crops to market and made a quiet detour to Shahre Naow. They came to deliver a simple message: 'Your husband is back.' No more would be said, but soon afterwards the family would make the trip to Logar.

In the spring of 1988, when I was five years old, we arrived to find Kotobkhil a hive of activity. After an emotional but unusually brief reunion with my dad, my mum and the older girls joined the women, who were busy baking what looked like enough bread to feed an army. Dad returned to another room, where he was drinking tea and talking to the village elders and some other men I didn't recognize.

When my father came outside again I showered him with questions.

'We are going on a journey, Waheed,' he told me. 'To a peaceful place where we can all be safe together.'

'Am I going, Jan Agha? Are you coming?'

He laughed. 'Of course. You, me, Mum and all your sisters.'

'Where is it?'

He put his arm around my shoulders and pointed to a distant peak. 'Do you see that mountain over there?'

I nodded.

'Just beyond that mountain.'

With life for my father, and for us, growing ever harder and more precarious, my parents had, like so many families, made the decision to seek sanctuary in Pakistan. During the Soviet war alone, some 5 million Afghans fled to Pakistan, or west to Iran, with a further 2 million being displaced internally.

By the time we departed, the Soviets had begun the slow process of withdrawing their troops from our country. Some like to see the retreat of the USSR as a military victory, but in truth nobody won. It was a stalemate. The political will of the Soviet Union to maintain the occupation had been slowly dwindling since the death of Leonid Brezhnev in 1982 and the current leader, Mikhail Gorbachev, known for his policy of *glasnost* (openness) and for overseeing the introduction of greater freedom and democracy in the USSR, took the view that perpetuating the combat was no longer worth the high price in casualties. In 1986 they had replaced Babrak Karmal, the president they had installed, with Dr Mohammad Najibullah, and they would continue to support his administration after the removal of their forces.

I have a memory of seeing a procession of tanks heading out of the city past our front door in Shahre Naow, and of the indentations left behind in the street outside by their tracks. It would be almost a year before all of the troops left. In the meantime, the Mujahideen carried on attacking the government forces. The Soviets were trying to impose some degree of stability as they retreated, training Afghan troops to protect vital installations and keep the rebels at bay, and so conscription into the Afghan army continued apace.

The border with Pakistan at Torkham is less than 230 kilometres from Kabul using the main highways. Given a clear run in unexceptional circumstances, you can drive it in four hours. The journey from Logar is a bit longer, but in either case it can be made comfortably within a day. However, these were, of course, far from unexceptional circumstances. The Khyber Pass and the Torkham border were controlled by the military and closed to departing civilians. And our party included at least twenty men, most of whom were probably evading military service.

We would be travelling at walking pace on foot and horseback, off the beaten track, following a circuitous route to the border, on the same narrow, rocky trails and winding paths through the mountains used by the Mujahideen. It was a difficult and perilous trek that would take us seven days and seven nights.

It is impossible now to retrace the precise course of our journey. The escape routes fluctuated constantly according to who was controlling which area, and where there were battles going on, and the border itself was both fluid and porous. Control of the Gardez–Khost section of the ancient southerly road connecting Afghanistan with the Indian subcontinent was fought over for much of that war and the town of Khost, the last before the border, was under siege one way or another for eleven years. The Soviets had retaken it from the Mujahideen that January. My father, who moved between the two countries many times, remembers that we travelled via Charkh, Kharwar and Khost province.

Our family of eight was to travel in a caravan of somewhere between fifteen and twenty other families and several guides. To try to reach Pakistan without guides would have been suicidal. These guys made their living moving back and forth, leading Afghan refugees to the border and making the return journey with Mujahideen bringing in weapons and supplies. Not only did they know the terrain, but in the course of their travels they gathered information from the locals about recent developments: where there had been fighting, which areas were currently the focus of aerial attacks. They knew, as far as it was possible to know, where the landmines were, and how the journey should be paced.

The guides plotted an itinerary between safe resting places where they paid villagers a few afghanis to provide basic accommodation. In certain areas there was shelter to be found in abandoned bomb-damaged houses. Some guides owned houses along the route where their customers could sleep. This was why we needed to travel as part of such a big group. These trips involved detailed planning and meticulous organization, and the guides undertook them only once they had enough people to make it worth their while.

To avoid being spotted by the military we had to move through the night and rest out of sight during daylight hours. Our departure, from a neighbouring village, was arranged for early the following evening. Arriving there late in the afternoon, we found horses being saddled and loaded with luggage beneath the chilgoza pines. We were going to be riding horses! I was thrilled. I instantly fell in love with a white packhorse, to my eyes a beautiful thoroughbred. I patted his strong, muscular flanks, stroked his velvety nose and pestered my dad until he asked the guide who owned the horse if I could ride on him. He agreed, though he made it clear I would have to share him with a couple of my sisters. I didn't mind. I named him Speen, the Pashto word for 'white'.

We set off at dusk, a procession of horses, and a few pack donkeys, tied together in teams. The women and children were perched on horseback between the woven saddlebags containing our luggage. The men were on foot. There were three or four kids, or one woman with a couple of smaller children, to each mount. We had not been allowed to bring anything with us but bare essentials. As well as the need to keep the weight down, the sight of giant bundles of all our worldly goods would have marked us out as refugees fleeing the country.

Provisions were minimal. We had *pateera* bread, baked with oil and sugar, which would keep for longer, and thin flatbreads piled into stacks that could be easily transported, thanks to the baking extravaganza of the grandmas and aunties. The children were given a piece of *pateera* to put in their pockets in case they got hungry during the night. Water could be readily replenished from the rivers and streams or safe village wells (there were rumours of some wells being poisoned).

My parents were wearing such valuables as we possessed. Afghans placed little trust in currency or banks and whenever my father was able to save a little money, he invested it in gold, using it to buy a bracelet or necklace. Our current savings were hidden beneath my mother's *firaq partug*, along with her bridal jewellery, and our cash in the secret pockets my mum sewed into the inside of my dad's clothes, so skilfully that it would pass notice if he were frisked or robbed.

The men wore *chappals*, handmade leather sandals with very hard soles. They had to be strong to cope with the conditions. Trainers would not have lasted the course. My father may still have owned the pair of sturdy boots he had been issued with as part of his army uniform, but nobody could wear anything that hinted at military involvement on either side. If we were spotted or challenged by anyone they needed to look as innocuously civilian as possible in their turbans or *pakol* hats, with waistcoats topping their *perahan tunban* to provide extra warmth and pockets.

A sizeable crowd of locals had gathered to wave us off. I was incredibly excited to be embarking on such an adventure. Among the adults, more attuned to the hardships and dangers that lay ahead, the excitement was more muted, but nevertheless everyone was in high spirits. The children who had mocked me for falling off a donkey were now pointing at me in awe as I clip-clopped past them on my majestic white stallion. Surveying the beautiful scenery all around me, the mountains glowing mauve and purple in the twilight, the farmers still working in the green fields, I felt like a prince in one of my dad's tales.

As darkness fell I chattered with Zari, sitting behind me, making up stories and, when my eyelids became heavy, I leaned against her, lulled by the rhythmic plodding of the horse. If sleep came, we would soon be jolted out of it as Speen kicked a rock or his foot caught a pothole.

With the dawn we stopped at a village to eat and rest. The horses were fed and watered out of sight and a reasonable distance away so that the whole party wouldn't be immediately discovered, or blown to smithereens along with them, if they aroused suspicion. A couple of the guides and one or two of the men remained with the horses. We slept in two rooms in an empty mud house, the men and boys in one room and the women, girls and small children in the other.

The rooms were bare but for some dusty rugs on the dirt floor. I remember the farmyard smell of those rugs, the legacy of being sat on by a succession of farmers, and the powdered-straw dust that tickled my nose and made me sneeze. Dad covered me with his *pedhu*, the versatile long scarf put to any number of uses by the nomadic Pashtuns: it doubles as a prayer mat, a cloak for extra warmth or a blanket. Tired out, I soon fell asleep.

As the afternoon waned we returned to the horses, and I was confused to see them being made ready for another trip. I had assumed that our long ride had already brought us to the peaceful place my dad had spoken of. In fact we were still in Logar, in the south of the province just beyond Charkh. My mum explained that it would be a few more days and nights before we reached our destination but, at five years old, the concept of any journey lasting a whole week was beyond my grasp.

'How far is the place we are going?' I asked my dad.

'Just after the next mountain,' he told me.

We travelled quietly through the chilly darkness of the next night, and the one after. I passed the time by 'racing' the other children's horses. Of course, we had no control over our progress, and the pace was sedate, to say the least, but when Speen took the lead I punched the air in delight. In my mind I was galloping him to victory.

It must have been on the third morning that we stopped in a glade amid a stand of trees while a guide, one of the other men and my dad went to investigate a nearby village for somewhere suitable to sleep. My dad took me with him.

As we approached the village we heard a sound in the air, a dull drone. My dad's grip on my hand tightened and he began to run, pulling me with him. He knew that sound only too well: a spy plane scouting the area. We were caught between the cover of the trees and the village. We had no time to go back. He scooped me up into his arms and ran for the village as fast as he could, his *chappals* flapping against his feet.

Dad banged on the first door we came to and tried to push it open but the house was locked up. By now we could hear the loud whine of a Su-25 assault jet overhead. He made a dash for the next house which, thankfully, seemed to have been long abandoned. The door gave easily. Inside he hurtled from room to room, searching frantically for something that would offer some protection.

With moments to spare he found what he was looking for: the clay bread oven, sunk into the floor like the one in the farmhouse in Kotobkhil. He bundled me inside, clambered in on top and crouched over me, wrapping his arms around me and shielding my head with his body. 'If anything bad happens to me, you must go back to Kabul, to your uncle, and stay there,' he whispered urgently. 'Do you understand?'

Whether the pilot had seen us or this was a random bombing he had no way of knowing. Had the rest of the family, hidden in the trees outside the village, been spotted? The government forces were known to actively target children in this region, on the assumption that they belonged to the Mujahideen.

And now it came: the screech of rockets, the sound of cracking stone and masonry cannoning into the walls of our hiding place; shells crashing from above. I couldn't hear my own howls of fear above the thunderous noise.

As the roar of the jet engine faded, Dad lay still. He knew that these bombardments could last for half an hour or more. The aircraft would circle a village, attack, then fly round and return for another go at it. And next a helicopter would appear and start shooting.

Now the helicopter gunships were tearing into what remained of the roof. Terrified, I tried to burrow deeper into the ungiving base of the oven. When the world finally stopped shuddering, Dad waited silently for maybe ten or fifteen minutes to make sure they had all gone. My ears singing from the deafening explosions, all I could hear was the thumping of my heart. I couldn't see or breathe. All the while Dad lay there motionless, pinning me beneath him. I didn't know whether he was hurt, or dead.

At last his voice floated through the white noise in my ears. It sounded as if it was coming from a long way away. 'Can you hear me, Waheed? Are you all right?' He pulled himself out of the oven and lifted me out. I still couldn't see. The air was thick with smoke and choking dust and the acrid smell of gunpowder. Amazingly, neither of us was injured. All around us, the house had been virtually destroyed. If Dad hadn't found the oven in time we would have been killed.

Now he picked me up and felt his way carefully through the rubble and out of the building. Thankfully, everyone else was unscathed, too. The two men who had been walking into the village with us had found shelter and the families hiding beneath the trees had escaped the attack. Not surprisingly, my mother and sisters were distraught, convinced that my father and I could not have survived. They couldn't believe it when they saw us limping through the swirling dust towards them.

As we all embraced each other, weeping with relief, a guy on horseback materialized, as if from nowhere. He wore a military jacket over his *perahan tunban* with a bandolier full of bullets and an American M16 assault rifle slung across his chest. He wasn't pleased to see us. 'What are you people doing here? Are you mad? This is the area where we are fighting!'

The men were furious and rounded on the guides. 'You knew this, and yet still you stopped here? It is your job to find a safe route. That is what we pay you for!'

With hindsight, it was clear the guides had known that this was a risky place to stop, but dawn had been breaking, we were tired and everyone needed to rest. Now they were wrong-footed. The day was well underway, the sun was blazing and we were exposed. We had to press on and the guides would have to deviate from their planned route and find us somewhere to eat, sleep and sit out the daylight hours as soon as possible. We could tell that they weren't sure where to go.

I was still shaky with shock as we spent a stressful and exhausting few hours locating another village. During the afternoon the guides had to work out how to get us back on track. Soon after setting off again at dusk, we found ourselves traversing a wide, open plain, a kind of mini-desert. The mountains we were heading for were visible in the distance but it was going to take us a long while to reach them. As darkness fell we could see pinpricks of light, far away, which kept disappearing and reappearing. The guides urged the horses and donkeys to speed up and told the kids to hold on tight. Even though I knew from Logar that lights usually meant tanks, I was excited, because it felt as if we were moving really fast now. I could feel the wind in my hair. It was probably no more than a gentle trot – the men were jogging alongside us – but this was the first time the horses had accelerated beyond a walking pace. We could see that the guides were very worried. Out here there was nowhere to hide. We were sitting ducks.

It seems impossible that the men in the tanks didn't see us. They would have been scanning the area with binoculars and it took us a good couple of hours to get to the safety of the mountains. And yet they did not fire.

When we finally reached the foothills of the mountains, with the grown-ups praying and thanking God under their breaths, we met a band of Mujahideen coming in the other direction. The most likely explanation for those tanks holding their fire now became clear to the adults. They were probably lying in wait for this platoon of guerrilla fighters and hadn't wanted to give away their presence by attacking us. Our guides warned the rebels not to attempt to cross the plain that night.

Those mountains just kept on going. They were higher than any we had crossed so far, the temperatures colder, the passes narrower, the trails more dangerous and the drops more terrifying. If you dared to look down into the moonlit shadows your stomach would lurch. I leaned back to gaze upward and tried to count the stars shining in the great black vault of the sky.

I was nodding off as Speen picked his way up a narrow, rocky mountainside track when he lost his footing, spraying out a shower of small stones. Jerked awake by a piercing scream, I suddenly found myself teetering at an alarming angle above an endless black abyss as my dad and the men walking with him grabbed the leather rein and the horse's neck, struggling desperately to prevent him plunging into the chasm and taking me with him.

If they hadn't succeeded, I wouldn't have been the only one to fall to my death. So would two of my sisters and others being carried by the horses tethered to Speen. Many people died on these gruelling journeys, in accidents like these as well as in military attacks. Since the first day, in the dim light of dawn or dusk, we had been coming across the bones of those who had been shot or shelled. My parents tried to tell us these were animal bones, and no doubt some of them were. But not those skeletons shaped like human beings, still wearing the remnants of their clothes with their possessions scattered nearby.

I was beginning to wonder if these high, jagged paths would ever lead anywhere. I'd lost count of how many mountains we had climbed. We were all exhausted, our food supplies were running low and what we had was becoming pretty stale. I would fall asleep sitting upright and every time I was jolted awake I shouted for my dad, so used to his frequent disappearances that I was afraid I would find him gone again. Occasionally, a little house or unoccupied shelter would unexpectedly appear where we could rest. It seemed incredible that anyone actually lived in these remote, inhospitable regions which, during the winter, must have been cut off from the world by deep snow for months at a time. But often someone would materialize from who knows where and open up a house for us.

We stopped before first light the next morning on a beautiful plateau carpeted with pine-nut shells. I remember collecting pine cones with the nuts inside them with my sisters and the other children as my dad washed his blistered feet, gasping in pain and calling for salt to disinfect them.

In an empty house beneath the trees, we fell into a fitful sleep, but it was not long before we were roused by the familiar, sinister sound of planes flying low overhead.

Everyone rushed outside, fearful of being trapped in a building when the bombs came. We stayed outside for the rest of the day, hiding in crevices or gutters or beneath bushes. No bombs fell in the end, or at least not on us. By now we would have been in Khost province, close to the border, where there were altercations over perceived invasion of airspace from time to time between the Pakistani and Afghan air forces. It is likely that we were caught up in one of these spats.

We pressed on and, at long last, in the early-morning light of yet another day, we started to catch glimpses of activity ahead of us through the pine trees. As we drew closer, we could see shops, stalls and people, some of them Pakistani soldiers, and hear the buzz of men talking and calling out to one another. The wonderful smell of cooking food reached our nostrils.

Our caravan came to a halt in the midst of this oasis. My father lifted me from Speen's back and the men and guides began to unload the horses and donkeys. I looked around me at shops selling kebabs and others hung with hand grenades, Kalashnikovs and rocket-launchers.

The atmosphere was cheerful and friendly. A policeman smiled at me and said hello. I was confused and wary. In my experience, men in uniforms were bad news, but this was a uniform I hadn't seen before and he spoke to me kindly, crouching down and holding out his hand to me. 'You are welcome!' he said. I took his hand and shook it solemnly.

The territories of Pakistan's North-West Frontier along the border with Afghanistan were semi-autonomous, formally designated as federally administered tribal areas. Their ethnic make-up was the same as that of Afghanistan, with Pashtuns forming a majority of the population. This was Tana Babrak, one of three checkpoints that were centres of cross-border operations and smuggling. With the authorities backing the rebel cause, they served as secure bases for Mujahideen travelling to and from Afghanistan and as stalking horses for the US supporters equipping them from Pakistan.

The guides would be leaving us now, taking the horses and donkeys back with them bearing a new cargo, which meant bidding a regretful farewell to Speen. Not long afterwards, news would reach my dad that both horse and owner had been killed by a rocket on one of those dangerous trails.

We were to rest here for twenty-four hours, Mum told us, to get our strength back. My sisters and I spent the day playing with the other kids while the grown-ups made arrangements for the last stage of our journey. This involved negotiating with a local driver to take us early the next morning to the town of Thal, the departure point for our final destination: Peshawar. We travelled there in style, squashed into a battered Datsun, the vehicle of choice in Afghanistan and the border territories, all sitting on top of one another.

From bustling Thal there were plenty of buses heading north-east on the main highway to Kohat and Peshawar. Here our travelling party began to disband and we had to say the first of our goodbyes to the children we had made friends with over the past week. There were more farewells along the way as people took other buses heading for Islamabad, or different districts of Peshawar, until just our family was left. Throughout my childhood, friendships were temporary. Families were constantly on the move and we had no phones or any other way of keeping in touch. A few of the children we befriended at various times would not survive. Our lives intersected with theirs for a short while, we said goodbye and we never saw them again.

Zari and I were delighted to be allowed to sit on the roof of our brightly painted bus, on top of the luggage. As the clear alpine vistas gave way to flatter, hazier farmland, this was the best seat on the bus: the temperature was rising and it was a relief to feel the slight quiver of movement in the shimmering air generated by the slow progress of the bus as it crawled along, rarely going faster than 30 or 45 kilometres an hour. There were frequent stops at police checkpoints and we had to change buses and walk some stretches of the road.

But there were no soldiers or tanks or bullets or bombed buildings blotting the landscape and people were out going about their business, looking relaxed and carefree, not creeping about fearfully or hiding away. In spite of the blistering heat and the increasing fog of pollution, the world seemed brighter: the foreign clothes, the shops, the newer, smarter cars. Everything, we hoped, was going to be all right now.

3

The Refugee

LATE THAT NIGHT, FLAGGING from the heat and bone-weary, we arrived at Babu refugee camp, an arid plain covered in white tents at the end of a long, rutted dirt track, 20 kilometres outside Peshawar.

Now my father, who had made advance arrangements for us to stay here, had to find the man who was due to register us, an Afghan working for one of the non-governmental organizations (NGOs) helping there. Dad knew roughly where he lived, but nevertheless it wasn't easy. He tried several dwellings before eventually rousing the man from his sleep as we waited in the hot darkness. This guy took us to a mud guest house where we could spend the night. As the adrenaline ebbed away it was starting to dawn on us how worn out we were. He smiled at us. 'You are safe now,' he said.

In the morning we were given some basic rations: bags of flour and rice, some ghee, cooking oil and sugar, and a tent. My father disappeared to put it up in the allocated spot among the row upon row of dusty white canvas, occupied by thousands upon thousands of people, that stretched in every direction as far as the eye could see.

In 1988 there were hundreds of camps like this in the North-West Frontier region, and in the coming years they would multiply and mushroom as the waves of refugees from across the border continued. Afghanistan's élite fled further afield, to the US or Canada; the well-off to more desirable homes in Peshawar or Islamabad, some directly, others after a brief stay in one of the camps.

Refugees who could afford it would upgrade to slightly better accommodation: little mud houses, for which you had to pay rent. Some of these were under construction in a field at the far side. The camps were tribal societies in exile, establishing their own systems and infrastructure, and had their own basic clinics, schools and mosques. Some of them had already been in existence for years, almost all overseen by the Mujahideen.

Babu camp, however, had only just been set up and had fewer facilities. It was unusual in that it would remain outside the control of any faction. Later it would be populated largely by Turkmens from northern Afghanistan, 50,000 people endeavouring to survive mainly by weaving and selling carpets. The downside of such self-sufficiency was that they received no government handouts or international aid.

Donors allowed the government in Islamabad to distribute humanitarian aid as they saw fit, and they funnelled it through the Mujahideen groups they chose to recognize. Much of it did not trickle down to the refugees in the camps in any case. Evidence of where it ended up could be seen in the beautiful houses in upmarket areas of Peshawar where the bosses of these organizations lived, the expensive cars they drove and the excellent private schools their children attended.

In 1988, Babu camp was just trying vainly to keep pace with the sheer number of arrivals. We ate hungrily from our rations as we tried to acclimatize to our surroundings. There was no direct water supply. Clean water was brought in tanks, from which we had to fill our buckets very carefully, making sure we didn't spill a drop. There was untreated water available for washing, but you couldn't drink that. Our bathroom was a latrine dug behind the tent, surrounded by a wall built of mud bricks and curtains of clothes hung from bamboo poles to provide a little privacy. We washed with buckets of water. Mum cooked outside, over a small fire. It was just as well we had virtually no possessions with us: perhaps a couple of cooking pots, a lantern, blankets, a few basic clothes. There wouldn't have been room to put anything else.

That night we slept, all eight of us, under the canvas roof we would share for the next couple of months. It was claustrophobic and far too hot to sleep covered. There were mosquitoes everywhere, keeping us awake and biting us. We could see them battering against the tiny tent window. Malaria is endemic to this part of Pakistan and, very quickly, we were all infected with it. Everyone had high temperatures, the shivers and vomiting. Then I developed a cough. As a toddler I'd had whooping cough, requiring months of treatment, but this was different. I became thinner and thinner, sicker and sicker. I could not walk far without becoming breathless. I started to cough up blood.

As my condition worsened, we went to the camp clinic. There was only one, for all these thousands of people; a two-roomed mud building with a small pharmacy at the front and a doctor working at the back. There was always a long queue outside of refugees sitting, standing or lying for hours on end in the broiling heat. The clinic stayed open until late at night but the queue never got any shorter.

In the clinic I was put on the scales. By this time I was so weak I was virtually a walking skeleton and when my parents and sisters saw the proof of how much weight I had lost, everyone was crying. The doctor, a local man working for an NGO, gave my dad medicine for me but told him that my condition was too serious to be treated in the camp. They just didn't have the resources. He would need to take me to a lung specialist in the city. If he didn't, it was unlikely I would survive.

Specialists were expensive. I don't know how my dad managed it – he must have sold something from his gold reserves – but he found a pulmonologist in Peshawar and took me there on the bus, carrying me in his arms. The doctor listened to my chest with his stethoscope and sent us off to get me an X-ray in the busy Khyber

Bazaar. When we came back, he gave me his stethoscope to play with while he examined the images. I was taken to sit outside the door because he wanted to talk to my father. I still caught some of the conversation, even if much of it went over my head.

As the doctor at the Babu camp must have realized, I had TB. Tuberculosis, like malaria, remains one of the biggest killers worldwide, and in the desperately unhealthy environment of the refugee camps this disease, and so many others, spread like wildfire. Pakistan had, and still has, one of the highest levels of TB globally. The specialist told my father he could treat me and talked him through the lengthy antibiotic courses I required, but he warned that treatment alone would not be enough. I needed proper nourishment and decent living conditions. Without them, there was only a 20 or 30 per cent chance I would survive. Even then, there were no guarantees.

My dad was in tears. 'I cannot give up on him! I will not let him die! I don't want to hear numbers. I just want you to tell me what I have to do to save him.'

The specialist said that I would have to be kept apart from the rest of the family. If my body was to build the strength to fight TB, I must have fruit, meat and milk. It was also important that I was made as comfortable and happy as possible and encouraged not to give in to despair.

'Jan Agha, what did the doctor say?' I asked my dad when we were back on the bus. Uncharacteristically, he didn't answer me. He just wept all the way home.

Like practically everyone else, we had extended family scattered around Peshawar. My mother's parents were there, and when they heard how ill I was they offered us the cheap, one-room mud house they were renting in the village of Badaber, 10 kilometres south of the city on the Kohat Road. As the camps became more permanent fixtures people were being allocated parcels of land within some of the organized settlements where they could build their own homes. My grandparents had been given one of these plots at one of the biggest camps and had been constructing a better mud house, into which they were about to move.

Badaber was the location of an old US air base that had been taken over by the Pakistan air force as the headquarters for their basic staff school. Throughout the Soviet occupation of Afghanistan, it was used to train Mujahideen fighters. There was also a jail there for prisoners of war, the scene of a famous armed uprising four years earlier.

I have little memory of this base: its operations would have been secret, and it would have been self-contained and out of bounds. If there were planes flying in and out of there, they wouldn't have particularly registered with me. In this frontier region we were used to seeing jets flying about. The village was not a designated refugee camp, and the NGOs and aid organizations were not operating there, although, by the time we left, tents were springing up on the other side of a dry river bed, on the perimeter of the air base. My grandparents knew all the neighbours, mainly local Pakistanis, and reassured us that it was a good place to live.

The little house was surrounded by a mud wall that enclosed a small yard where my mother cooked in the summer. Although it consisted of only one room, plus a kitchen and storage area, the yard was just big enough for our parents to put up the tent we brought with us from Babu camp to create a little more living space.

It may not have been a vast improvement on Babu camp, but when you have so little, even the smallest things can make a big difference. With everyone else sleeping in the tent while I was ill, technically it fulfilled the requirement for me to be isolated.

The sanitary facilities were the same as they'd been in the camp, but we had easier access to water. Our neighbours, the Khans, had a piped supply and let us use their tap. Before long there were two of us in the family isolation ward when my little sister, Gululai, also contracted TB. Now my dad had to take two of his children to the doctor in Peshawar.

I was very sick for a long time and the cough would not go for months. There was a fire in the room, set below a metal grille, for baking bread so it was always full of smoke. The heat at the height of summer was unbearable – the average summer temperature in this area is over 40 degrees. I lay there watching armies of insects crawling up and down the walls of the mud house, in so much pain that Mum or Nageenah had to hold my ribs whenever I coughed. The sight of the blood was frightening and there was always somebody crying, although they tried not to do it in front of me. They would quickly wipe away their tears and blame them on the heat. I did not know that they were crying because they were certain I was dying.

Dad was already trading currency in Chowk-Yadgar, near the Khyber Bazaar, buying bags of torn notes, which my mother helped him repair, and reselling them. He would sometimes disappear for several days to travel back towards the border checkpoints to trade the currency at Babrak Tanah or Miramshah, or around the North-West Frontier – Kohat, Bannu, Sada, Thal, the Swat Valley – in search of antiques he could sell on in Peshawar. We were no longer the beneficiaries of donated rations and somehow the money had to be found for extra food for me, luxuries like honey, little oranges, bananas and sugar cane, as well as for expensive medicine, doctor's bills and our rent.

Dad bought milk from a neighbouring farmhouse and every couple of weeks he would return with a mouth-watering lamb kebab to tempt me, and Gululai, when she was sick, to eat. Since there was no means of keeping milk cool, it was always heated up. I was made to drink hot milk so often that I started to hate it.

As well as piped water, the Khans next door had an electricity supply, which they let us plug into to warm the milk and to make tea on a little heater powered by a single bulb. We also used their electricity to run a fan in the summer months. That family were so kind to us. They had a small black-and-white TV, too, and sometimes they invited us to watch it. We would put up a ladder to view it through their window so as not to impose too much on their privacy.

At first my dad had to take me to see the pulmonologist every month. Poorly as I was, I looked forward to these visits. It was wonderful to escape the baking cauldron of that mud room. I would sit near an open window on the bus and stick out my hand to feel the breath of a breeze. The doctor would send us to get an X-ray, which he pinned up against a light and scrutinized. I was fascinated by these photographs of the inside of my body. I asked lots of questions and he answered them all patiently. As my condition began to improve I became more and more impressed by the knowledge that gave this man the power to heal me.

One day he asked me what I wanted to be when I grew up. 'I want to be a doctor, like you,' I told him.

When I started to put on weight, he praised me and gave me a present, an old stethoscope and an outdated medical textbook, as a reward for doing so well. It was a hefty book, written in English, full of pictures and diagrams of the human body. 'If you want to be a doctor, you'll need these,' he said.

Many of us can trace back the course our lives have taken to a pivotal moment, or to the influence of a person who has inspired us, often a teacher, a mentor in the early days of our careers, or simply someone who has kindled our enthusiasm for something they feel passionate about. The seed of my ambition to become a doctor was planted by that pulmonologist. I'm sure he would have been astonished if he could have foreseen how it would grow. Most of us will be unaware of the impact we may have on those whose lives brush ours. I always try to remember that this is one very good reason why we should all motivate and encourage, listen and show patience and kindness. Who knows where it may lead?

That seed may have taken a while to put down firm roots, and along the way it was nurtured by others, but from the time I had TB it was incubating within me. I saw so much suffering, in the refugee camps, and worse later, during the civil war in Afghanistan, that to me, acquiring the knowledge and skill to relieve and heal seemed to be the best aspiration anyone could have.

Dad would bring home notebooks and pens for me. Even though he could barely read and couldn't write in any language, it was he who taught me the English alphabet. In the course of his work he had picked up a vocabulary of basic phrases which he passed on to me, supporting these nuggets with a children's ABC book he'd found at the market.

I would also pore over the pictures in the medical tome the doctor had given me, and when Dad left in the morning he would say, 'I want you to copy out ten pages of the words in that book by the time I get back.' I'd start neatly copying out the text but after a while I'd get tired and end up just scribbling down any old thing. Of course, he couldn't tell the difference. It didn't matter. All he was concerned about was keeping me occupied, engaged and learning something, anything.

My sisters continued to try to teach me my letters and numbers, and when he returned in the evening Dad would take me to the mosque, or for a stroll around the village, carrying me in his arms when I was still too feeble to walk, pointing out the tractors, the people working in the fields and the kids playing cricket with sticks for stumps and a tennis ball wrapped in tape. It was the first time I'd ever seen cricket. My sisters and I played a village game with a ball made of rolled-up old clothes which we whacked around the house.

Later Dad would give me one of his inspirational stories, often a round-by-round account of how Muhammad Ali beat Joe Frazier in

New York, or in the 'Thriller in Manila'. He was driving it home to me – and probably reminding himself, too – that whatever punches life throws at us, we must never give up.

I carried on seeing the doctor for eighteen months altogether but once he had managed to get the infection down my follow-ups were less frequent. As I grew stronger I was able to really enjoy those trips to Peshawar. The Khyber Bazaar was exhilarating. A constant stream of vans, cars, motorbikes and motorcycle rickshaws wove in and out of each other, horns blasting, and loud, joyful music blared everywhere. After my appointment, there would be a treat, sometimes a kebab, eaten sitting down in a proper restaurant.

Outside the cinema, enormous colour posters advertised the films that were showing, and sometimes we would go and see one. It was always an action-packed American movie or imported television series, full of gunfights and car chases. My favourite was the TV show *Knight Rider*, whose hero drove an artificially intelligent car that talked: a customized 1982 Pontiac Firebird Trans-Am, equipped with high-tech crime-fighting equipment and impregnable to the rockets rained down on it by criminals. How I dreamed of owning a remote-controlled toy replica of that car.

Eventually I was well enough to start school. I must have been seven years old by then. My sisters did not go to school in Badaber. Living amid this diaspora of people of all manner of backgrounds and beliefs, many parents took the view that daughters needed to be kept close and protected. School fees for us all were probably unaffordable and, as the eldest son, I was the one in whom my parents' hopes were invested.

The village school was owned by the headmaster, not unusual in Pakistan, where around a third of schools are privately run and pupils are fee-paying. It was set behind a metal gate, three or four mud rooms built around a central courtyard, where we would all sit together, cross-legged on the ground, for communal activities like singing. In the classrooms we sat on rugs on the dirt floor with our wooden boards and chalk. The teacher and all the other pupils were Pakistani and I learned my times tables by chanting them in Urdu.

My dad brought more books from the bazaar. He had no idea what most of them were, but if he spotted any second-hand book in English going cheap and he had a few rupees in his pocket, he would snap it up. I was accumulating a mini-library of random books, which I carefully stored in a box in a corner of the house.

My mum, always conscious of my vulnerability, walked me right up to the school gate and was always there to meet me. I spent a lot of afternoons at the village pharmacy, where I had my TB jabs. My dad had persuaded the pharmacist to let me stay on for a while afterwards. 'My son can make himself useful,' he suggested. 'Sweep up, or fetch things for you. Anything you need. He is very interested in doctors and medicine.'

I would watch the pharmacist dress wounds and he explained the medicines to me – which ones were for infection, which for pain. I learned to identify common drugs like paracetamol, ibuprofen and penicillin by name, or from the colours of the bottles or packets. When a customer came in, he would call out to me, 'Waheed, can you bring me the penicillin?' It made me feel very important and helpful.

My dad used to boast to his friends that I knew all the medicines, which wasn't remotely true, of course. 'Look at him,' they would exclaim. 'So tiny, and already a doctor!'

My father patiently allowed me to practise my 'medical skills' by injecting him with boiled water using the family syringe, an old-fashioned model made of glass and metal, which he'd bought from the market. It was a lengthy ritual: first we had to heat the water over the fire outside to sterilize the syringe and the needle, then allow the rest of it to cool down for the injection. My poor dad: he calmly mopped up the blood that spurted forth and, once one arm was blue with bruises from my efforts, he would simply offer up the other. He would do anything to encourage me to learn.

We lived in that mud room and tent at Badaber for the best part of three years. The whole family was malnourished and I can still remember the physical pain caused by hunger. Although the sweltering heat of the summer months was by far the worst, the winters were not without their hardships. Winters in Peshawar are not considered particularly severe, but temperatures that could hover around freezing at night feel far from mild when you have inadequate shelter. All we had on the floor was plastic sheeting. The children had mattresses but our parents slept between us directly on the plastic, with just pillows for their heads.

This is not a monsoon area and rainfall is spread through the year, but there is more of it in winter. And occasionally the monsoon currents reach as far as Peshawar, bringing with them torrential downpours. The roof of the house was made of thin, ill-fitting bamboo matting and it leaked constantly in the colder months. There were often pools of water on the floor, and outside the ground would be a sea of slippery mud.

My sisters collected scraps of kindling wood to help feed the smoky fire, and followed carts carrying straw as they trundled by on the road to pick up what fell off them. After the harvest they gathered discarded dried stalks from the fields. On the far side of the dry river bed there was a mountain of rubbish. This was where everyone dumped their waste and, because nobody ever took it away, it just grew and grew. It was a serious health hazard, and yet you would see children poorer than we were clambering about in it, scavenging for things people had thrown away that they might be able to clean up and sell. Everybody was just doing what they had to do to survive.

The whole family suffered from a variety of illnesses directly caused by the conditions. My parents had malaria several times but I don't remember either of them ever lying down and saying they were too ill to move. They had the family to take care of, and so they simply soldiered on. My mother gave birth to two more children at Badaber: my brother Khalid in 1989 and another sister, Shabana, towards the end of our time there. There was no medical care available. Both were born in our mud house with the help of neighbouring women.

Life wasn't any easier for our relatives in other refugee camps. We had an uncle we would visit, my dad's step-brother, and there would always be a discussion about when it might be safe to go home. News would reach us of those who had left the country and others who had been killed in the fighting. We were so homesick. The Pakistanis were lovely people and our neighbours were helpful and welcoming, but they were from different backgrounds and spoke a different language.

Peshawar was a terrific city, a thriving hub of trade and culture, and the North-West Frontier region was beautiful. I saw some of that when my dad took me on one or two of his antiques-trading trips. I loved having the opportunity to practise my English when required. My dad would stand back and proudly allow me to talk to the customers in the market. The English books I had were so ancient that my conversation ('Good afternoon. How do you do?') must have seemed charmingly old-fashioned, which may have softened up a few hard-headed hagglers. And maybe it gave me an early understanding of the importance of negotiation and persuasion in making things happen.

It wasn't Pakistan itself, just the appalling conditions we had no means of escaping, the hardships, disease and the intolerable weather, that were so difficult to endure. When people have so few resources, simply fulfilling the basic imperative to keep body and soul together is incredibly time-consuming and exhausting. While many wealthier Afghans integrated, set up businesses, bought proper homes and stayed on in Pakistan permanently, we were never going to be able to lift ourselves far enough out of the daily grind of maintaining our own existence to afford anywhere we could live in comfort.

In Afghanistan, there was ongoing conflict between the PDPA, supported by the Soviets, and the resistance, still being backed by the West and several pro-Islamic nations. With the withdrawal of the USSR, the genuine Mujahideen, who had been fighting what they saw as a righteous war against foreign occupation of our country, had laid down their arms. But the leaders of the rebel groups in which the Mujahideen had served were now pursuing their own political agendas to further the causes of their particular ethnicities and gain power for themselves.

President Najibullah was trying to build universal acceptance of his government by moving away from socialism towards a united nationalism and portraying his regime as Islamic. His policies went just far enough to disgruntle PDPA hard-liners, but not far enough to please the leaders of the various ethnic factions. For the moment, though, a fragile peace was being maintained and the country was comparatively stable.

My dad kept up with developments on his radio, picking up the BBC World Service and Voice of America, broadcast in Urdu from Washington DC to Pakistan. From the time I started school he was talking to me about everything – politics, what the government was doing at home, how the refugee camps worked, family matters – and involving me in all his discussions and debates as we sat around the mud houses and tents of friends and relatives in the places they felt free to talk. He was always engaged, enquiring. He would throw out rapid-fire questions or ask me to read out things for him.

This was in keeping with his character and temperament, and perhaps partly due to a desire to educate me as best he could and prepare me for my role as head of the family if anything happened to him. The impermanency of life was a reality that stalked us on a daily basis. In Pakistan we were prey to fatal disease, at home to the ever-present threat of sudden, violent death. The average life expectancy of an Afghan male, even in the unusually peaceful year of 1990, was not quite fifty.

However, if a sense of his own mortality lay at the back of my father's mind, I don't think it was his prime motivation. His world view has always been relentlessly positive. He genuinely wanted to hear my opinions, and I will for ever be grateful for that. Not only did his inclusive attitude broaden my awareness of how the world worked, it stimulated my mind and gave me a grounding in how, rather than what, to think, and in making decisions and solving problems.

My father even consulted me when a young man living in one of the camps asked for Nageenah's hand in marriage. He was the son of a schoolteacher, and they had met through a low-key family introduction. An Afghan wedding, like any the world over, can create a great deal of anxiety and stress on both sides, and a wedding taking place in the straitened circumstances of a refugee camp is no exception.

Traditionally, the groom's family pays for and hosts the wedding ceremony while the bride's takes responsibility for equipping the marital home with rugs, houseware and so on. Some girls' fathers demand high bride prices but my dad asked only for enough to honour this tradition, as was expected of him. I suspect the figure he came up with was no more than he needed to cover his expenses.

My mum brought her matchless problem-solving skills to bear and, through a combination of economic sacrifices and clever improvisation, she managed everything, as she always did. Both bride and groom were resplendent in beautiful new clothes, relatives from other camps were in attendance and Nageenah left Badaber to set up home with her husband's family.

The government in Kabul was encouraging the return of refugees which, my dad reassured us, meant that going home would now be considerably easier than leaving had been. The rebel factions, on the other hand, frowned on people returning from exile. They saw it as implied acceptance of Najibullah's 'puppet regime'. And since almost all the refugee camps were overseen by one rebel faction or another, they were all full of government detractors. My dad knew more people among the resistance than he knew government supporters, and the tribal leaders within the camps were well aware that, while he remained non-aligned, he had helped the Mujahideen with food and shelter in Logar. So as long as he was careful to steer clear of involvement in camp politics, nobody bothered him.

Afghans are notoriously vague about birthdays and dates in general. In addition to the high level of illiteracy among our people, our lack of official documentation and the fact that we have a different calendar from Western countries, in the midst of the chaos imposed by war, suffering and displacement, dates are neither easy to keep track of nor uppermost in anybody's mind. But my dad's official age was recorded in black and white on his military ID. As the date registered as his fortieth birthday drew near, we began preparing to go home.

We would be leaving one family member behind. Nageenah remained in Pakistan with her husband and in-laws right through the civil war and beyond. It was not until well after the Americans arrived in 2001 that they returned to Afghanistan.

Even as we set off in the early spring of 1991, Dad wasn't 100 per cent certain that he would be deemed exempt from national service. It had been the subject of much discussion but nobody seemed to know where the cut-off point was, or how it might be interpreted by the border guards. Was it when you turned forty? Or were you still eligible until you were forty-one? But we were desperate to leave before the dreaded hot weather set in, and perhaps he calculated that, if he hadn't already passed the correct milestone, he was so close to it that nobody would consider it worth the trouble to quibble. Whatever the case, he was a bag of nerves all the way to the border at Torkham, praying over and over again, 'Please God, save us. Please God, save us.' It was not until we were safely on home soil, checked and waved through by the guards, that we were able to stop holding our breath and celebrate.

This time we were able to take the normal route through the Khyber Pass, and make the whole journey by bus, along with many others doing the same thing. There was no shelling, no fear, and everyone was light-hearted and happy. We paused for the night halfway at Jalalabad, where a government hostel had been set up specifically to accommodate returning refugees, and were given a decent place to sleep and a good meal.

The weather in Jalalabad was still quite warm but as the bus climbed towards the hills of home we could feel it becoming blissfully cooler with every kilometre. When we reached the Surobi Dam, and knew we were almost there, the mix of elation and relief was immense. It felt as though we had been let out of jail.

4

A Glimpse of Hell

OUR ORDINARY HOUSE AT Shahre Naow, so familiar and comfortable, felt like a palace after the way we'd been living for so long. The contrast with our old Kabul life was hard to believe: my dad was no longer hiding away and we could go out, play with our cousins and friends, go to the park. It was a freedom I had never known before and the possibilities it offered seemed limitless.

We walked around outside, saying hello to the shopkeepers and marvelling at how their children had grown. My dad acquired a Chinese-made bicycle and sat me on it, riding around to visit various friends and relatives and re-introducing me to them. He also bought me a real ball, the first one I'd ever owned, and some cheap, mismatched Western clothes, shirt, biker-style jacket and shorts, from the selection spread out on the ground at the central market. We appreciated every little thing about Kabul. Much as I had loved the high-octane, chaotic buzz of Peshawar, our calmer streets, agreeable weather and the backdrop of the zigzagging, snow-tipped mountains made my heart sing again.

Dad quickly returned to work at the Sarai Shahzada financial and trading market and Nazifa, Perveen, Zari, Gululai and I were all enrolled in school, the girls at the Zarghona School and me at Amani High School. My school was beautiful, a solid building constructed in 1924 by the Germans who, historically, have had strong relations with Afghanistan. Until 1985, it had received direct support from Germany, latterly from the communist German Democratic Republic, including the provision of qualified staff, and it still had a reputation as one of Kabul's élite schools. It boasted the first gymnasium I had ever seen and proper desks and chairs in the classrooms.

I looked forward every day to the walk to school, which was about fifteen minutes away from our house through elegant streets lined with government buildings and embassies. I would stride purposefully along in the morning sunshine, dressed in my uniform of Western shirt and trousers, my school bag slung over my shoulder, not a care in the world.

I was almost eight years old and placed in the class deemed appropriate to my age. As I'd completed only half of Grade 1 in Pakistan, this meant I had skipped several grades and our textbooks were more advanced than any I'd ever seen. But it wasn't wise to make a big deal about having been in Pakistan, as that could be interpreted as some family allegiance to one or other of the warlords. Not surprisingly, I struggled, particularly with language. Lessons were in Afghanistan's two main native tongues, Pashto and Dari (Farsi). Both use the Arabic alphabet, with a few variations, and most people grow up bilingual to some extent as families merge through intermarriage, especially in the more cosmopolitan urban areas.

Of course, my only formal lessons to date had been in Urdu, and my classmates laughed at my pronunciation of the letters of the alphabet. 'Go on, now do your times tables,' they would urge, highly entertained by this strange boy who multiplied his numbers in what sounded to them like gibberish.

When I heard that the UN Development Programme was running a course in English, I went to their office to enquire about enrolling. I was told that it was for adult government employees only, not for children. 'But one day I will be a government employee,' I reasoned, 'and I will need to speak English.' The man was not to be persuaded. I begged him to allow me to see the head of the programme, just for five minutes, and in the end he gave in.

My dad came with me to pay my visit to Soraya Hakim, the woman in charge. 'How can I help?' she asked kindly. When I explained what I wanted she reiterated that the course was for grown-ups who worked for the government. 'Perhaps when you are older,' she suggested. In a bid to impress her, I trotted out a few of the English phrases I knew. My dad, suppressing a smile, left me to it.

'So you can already speak a little English?' she said, surprised.

'Yes, but I need to learn more. When I grow up and work for the government, what use will I be if I can't speak English properly?'

She laughed at my youthfully transparent attempt to convince her that by agreeing to let me join the course she'd be doing the government a favour.

'You are not a boy who takes no for an answer, are you?'

She called in the Englishman who ran the course, mainly for his amusement, I think, but they then got involved in a debate about the accessibility of the lessons. 'We need to think about this,' she said. 'Come back in a week.'

When I returned I was enrolled on the course and became the only child to take English lessons among all the adults.

Soraya Hakim invited me to her home to meet her son, who was about my age. She was an influential woman in Kabul and I had never before laid eyes on such a grand house. It had a big, smart dining room, with a beautiful tall table surrounded by dining chairs. Everyone I knew ate from a low table, sitting on cushions or low sofas, or from a cloth spread on the floor. And the Hakims' son, Mustafa, had a bedroom all to himself. I couldn't believe how many toys and gadgets he owned – table tennis, video games and, best of all, a Scalextric toy car track. To a boy who had only recently acquired his first proper ball, it was an Aladdin's cave. Mustafa was as nice as his mother. We quickly became good friends.

Soraya Hakim told me that not only was I the first student outside the government to be enrolled in the UNDP English course but that my persistence had led to the rules being changed to make the lessons available to a wider range of candidates. 'We hadn't realized so many people would be interested,' she admitted. 'But you showed us that they were.' I was very proud to be seen as such a trailblazer.

That landmark year gave me my first taste of what childhood should be like: going to school, kicking a ball around in the park with other kids without the worries of the world on my shoulders and soaking up all the education I could, just so happy to be learning. In addition to my UNDP English lessons, I also did a typing course, and I took up Taekwondo, which was a big thing in Afghanistan in the 1990s, earning my white, then yellow belt. I had my first best mate in Mustafa Hakim, made more friends at school and began to take it for granted that they would still be there the next day.

After school, and in winter, when the schools were closed, Dad took me with him to the money exchange. The entrance to the market was crowded with currency dealers brandishing a calculator in one hand and a bundle of afghanis, Iranian rials and Pakistani rupees in the other. In the big business of the Sarai Shahzada the dollar was king, but the ebb and flow of migrants saw a brisk trade in smaller quantities of local currencies. By 1989, about a fifth of Kabul's population had fled abroad, but now many citizens were, like us, coming back. Inside the Sarai Shahzada were all the shops run by bankers, goldsmiths and gem traders. Dad couldn't stretch to a shop, but he had his own little stall against the parapet of the Kabul River, warmed in wintertime by an oil stove, where he taught me how it all worked. It was a great way of learning maths and economics.

At home, we acquired a better TV and a video-player. In addition to Bollywood movie night, still a family fixture, there was a bit more on offer from the state broadcaster, which, after years of being pretty much restricted to government propaganda, was now rifling through its archives in search of old programmes to show. People ran video rental businesses from their homes, or the back rooms of shops, and we swapped films with friends and neighbours. Enthused by my new passion for Taekwondo, I devoured martial arts movies – Jackie Chan, Bruce Lee, Jean-Claude van Damme. Films were all in their original languages, but I had some Hindi and Urdu now, as well as English. As a family we tended to go for action movies or physical comedies (Charlie Chaplin was a great favourite with Afghans), something without too much dialogue going over people's heads, which everyone could sit down and enjoy together.

If the occasional crash of a rocket falling on a building or the sight of the odd tank on the street was a reminder of the vulnerability of this relatively tranquil existence, it did not happen often enough to cause serious alarm. But on 25 April 1992, all hell broke loose.

To many political commentators, the only surprise was that Najibullah's government lasted as long as it did. The last straw was perhaps the dissolution of the Soviet Union at the end of 1991, which left his administration without foreign aid or support. There were serious food shortages in the army, and the Afghan air force, vital to maintaining stability, could no longer fly their aircraft because they had run out of fuel. The desertion rate in the military was running at 60 per cent.

The resistance movement had always been uncoordinated, an ad hoc collection of factions that remained divided along ethnic, tribal, political and religious lines. The rebels operated out of something like 4,000 different bases, generally in units consisting of one commander and around a hundred men. During the Soviet war, the seven predominant groups, which had originated in Pakistan, had formed an alliance known as the 'Peshawar Seven', supported by two or three home-grown organizations representing ethnic minorities. In 1989, they had met in Peshawar with the aim of setting up a government in exile, but that plan bit the dust when they failed to gain control of Jalalabad, where they had intended to base themselves. The fact that two of the warlords disagreed with the Jalalabad operation – one of them even claimed he knew nothing of the attempted invasion of the city until he heard about it on the BBC news – is just one illustration of the disjointed nature of the resistance.

Even while battling the Soviet troops some of the groups had fought each other as well. Into the vacuum created by Najibullah's weakened administration poured this mass of revolutionaries with their foreign backing, assorted objectives and hunger for power. In March Najibullah agreed to step aside to make way for a neutral interim government and lost what control he had left. Already riven by internal strife, his party split into factions which quickly re-aligned themselves.

General Abdul Rashid Dostom, whose 40,000-strong militia, drawn from the Uzbek minority, had supported the government, switched sides. Alongside Ahmad Shah Massoud's Jamiat-e Islami forces, Dostum took control of Bagram Air Base to the north. While most parties had agreed to the peace and power-sharing agreement, Gulbuddin Hekmatyar's Hezb-e Islami had not, and his men were creeping up from the south.

With Kabul surrounded, we monitored the news on the radio. Some of the rebels, it seemed, were not prepared to wait for the ordered transition brokered by the UN. When Hekmatyar tried to take the city on 25 April, his rivals standing by to the north stormed in to prevent him from seizing power. Suddenly, and with extreme violence, war came to the heart of Kabul. In the administrative quarter of Shahre Naow, we found ourselves at its epicentre. The rival forces were attacking each other ferociously, heedless of civilian lives.

Very soon after the invasion began, we fled to Logar. My dad had no idea where in Kabul, if anywhere, we might be safe. We hurried in the dark through the grounds of the Presidential Palace, making for Balahissar and the main highway out of the city, in a little procession with Dad at the front and Mum bringing up the rear to keep all the kids together. There were tanks shelling each other, bullets whistling over our heads. In the darkening sky you could actually see them flying towards you through the air.

We fell into the gutters, or threw ourselves into them in response to our parents yelling at us to get down, and we would all be crawling, commando-style, through the mud. Mum and Dad dragged us this way and that, dodging from street to street as the forces of the competing warlords battled for control of them, urging us on past dead bodies, lying where they had fallen, soldiers, civilian men, women and children, and people with their limbs blown off, crying out in agony, who would soon be dead too. Scenes of unimaginable horror that I simply could not absorb or process but which would return as nightmares and flashbacks in the months and years to come.

Beyond the city the highway was an apocalyptic vision of destruction, blazing buildings, rubble, artillery lighting up the night. The road was strewn with burning military vehicles and the ash-grey carcasses of civilian cars. We found a bus to take us some of the way, though we were terrified that it would be hit – many were – or that we would be hauled off and kidnapped or killed. We ended up walking most of it.

With the fighting centralized in Kabul, Logar was peaceful, but with no means of earning a living there, we could not impose on our relatives indefinitely. Whether our return to Kabul was timed to coincide with some perceived lull my father had heard about on the BBC World Service, I don't know, but throughout the civil war the armed conflict in Kabul was almost constant and completely unpredictable. Nageenah was safe in Pakistan; Nazifa, now married, had fled Kabul for Logar with her husband's family. The rest of us would spend three long years bouncing between boltholes in every corner of the city, Khair Khana, Kote-Sangi to the west, Karte Naow, with respite in Logar every so often.

As the rebels who had found common cause against the Soviets turned on each other, this quickly became a war between ethnicities. With the groups continually making and breaking alliances, nobody ever knew who was leading whom, who was fighting whom, who was controlling what, or where the violence would flare up next. If one day a Pashtun unit killed Hazara guerrillas or civilians, the next the Hazaras would mount a revenge attack.

A city that had remained relatively intact throughout the decade-long Soviet conflict was now being utterly destroyed, day by day and street by street, and with it went all of its infrastructure, services and any semblance of law and order. The massive arsenal of weaponry left behind by the Red Army and the retreating government troops was now in the hands of various warlords: the tanks, the rocket-launchers positioned on TV Mountain and Safi Mountain, with their huge, heavy missiles, the jets and helicopters which, once the combatants obtained fuel from their foreign supporters, they deployed against each other. On one journey to Logar, we found that a section of the main highway had been taken over to serve as a makeshift runway, forcing cars and trucks into lengthy detours across rocky tracks.

The territorial battles in Kabul, conducted with complete disregard for their effects on the civilian population, were ultimately pointless. In the end they were all fighting over rubble. Entire blocks of houses and shops were obliterated, offices, bus stations, schools, markets, hospitals. Power lines were knocked out and there were both indiscriminate and intentional attacks on people's homes. Large-scale looting was routine. You would see guys coming out of damaged or abandoned buildings carrying fridges on their backs, or hauling air-conditioners, carpets, roof beams, electricity cables – anything and everything. Some of the foot soldiers received no wages from their warlords and viewed such spoils as payment in kind.

In the first year of the conflict, between April 1992 and March 1993 – the terrible year of 1371 in the Afghan calendar – tens of thousands of civilians were killed and thousands more abducted and never seen again. By the summer, half a million people had fled Kabul and the streets were empty of everyone but armed soldiers. International humanitarian laws were violated daily. All of the rebel groups had blood on their hands. None escaped blame for the countless atrocities that were committed as they pursued a scorched-earth policy of ethnic cleansing.

They would stop buses and cars looking for specific ethnicities. It was said that some of the people kidnapped were kept in containers that were deliberately set on fire, or else simply hit by rockets. If fighting broke out and the captors didn't know what to do with their prisoners, they just shot them. Civilians were tortured merely for speaking the wrong language, children killed, and women and young girls gang-raped. We will never know how many suffered, or the true extent of the lifelong impact of such brutality on those who survived it.

Depending on when and where the fighting erupted, we would take refuge in other families' homes and, in turn, share our roof. Neighbours helped each other, regardless of ethnicity. Nobody knew where their relatives were or whether they were alive or dead. Many were killed by the bombs, or while fleeing them. Often you wouldn't hear what had happened to them for a long time. There could be no funerals, no mourning. Families often struggled to bury even those loved ones who had died right in front of them. Bodies would have to be left lying in the street, in the midst of crashing rockets and flying bullets, until night fell and their families could sneak out to retrieve them and bury them in the dark.

Sleep came only with sheer exhaustion. The little ones would drop off sitting bolt upright, their heads drooping and their mouths hanging open. When the shelling got close it would wake us with a start. We could trace the whole journey of a rocket by the tone and volume of the noise. All of the children would be wailing. 'Mum, it's coming! It's coming!' I would scream. Then all we could do was hold on tightly to each other.

The next day we would go outside and somebody's house would have been vaporized. There is no other word for it. Some of the missiles were enormous, metres long. They would destroy two or three houses at a time, but there would be nothing at all left of the one that had taken the full force, or of anyone unfortunate enough to have been inside. The bomb fragments travelled a long way, and others would be mortally wounded by shrapnel. People would be desperately trying to tie tourniquets round the limbs of friends and strangers alike but many injuries were too severe to be survivable.

Early on in the war, our home in Shahre Naow was struck by a rocket. We were there at the time, in the room next door to the one that took the hit, and everyone was injured to some extent by falling masonry, mostly cuts and lacerations. It was a miracle none of us was killed. I remember the UN coming to our street and taking photographs of us standing, bewildered, amid the wreckage.

I had several near misses. I was once out on an errand on my dad's bike when a rocket fell, blasting me into the gutter. I wasn't badly injured but the bike was bent and the wheel damaged, and I couldn't ride it home. I limped back, covered in dirt. My parents were beside themselves, certain I'd been killed.

In Karte Naow we had the use of a house that belonged to Nazifa's parents-in-law. I remember staying there in wintertime. There was no water or electricity, it was bitterly cold and we all slept in one room to keep each other warm. An icy draught blew through the broken windows until my dad managed to buy some plastic, which he fixed up as a kind of improvised double glazing. My sisters and I had to climb a steep hill in freezing weather to fetch water from a military centre and we scavenged for wood to keep the fire going. Window frames from bombed-out houses made good firewood but pulling them out was dangerous because of the possibility of unexploded artillery.

The empty house next door in Karte Naow happened to belong to a cousin of ours, and this became a sort of social club for my father and the neighbours. I would go round there with my dad, the neighbours would bring their kids, and the men would play cards in one corner and discuss the latest developments in the war while in another corner we children played our own games. We brewed tea and generally made ourselves at home.

We treated the place respectfully and, if nothing else, our presence perhaps prevented it from being looted. Even when people were lucky enough to find the home they had abandoned still standing when they returned, often it would have been stripped of every single fixture and fitting. Even worse, someone might have moved in and taken over your house. If they had, there was nothing you could do about it.

My dad bought a house in Kolula-Pushta, in the hope that this more suburban district would be safer than the city centre. Property was of little value (who would want a des res in war-torn Kabul which might be blown up at any moment?) and it didn't cost much. It was a single-storey, four-room home, built around a courtyard for cooking and washing clothes, in a row of similar houses, each with a little garden at the front. Its main selling point as far as my dad was concerned was a crawl space beneath its concrete veranda, which he thought would make a good bomb shelter.

Kolula-Pushta was quieter for a while, but as the fighting spread it was not really any safer than anywhere else. The crawl space did provide a bit of extra protection but it was tiny. When the bombing started we'd all be squashed together on a rug under the veranda. The walls were so rough you couldn't lean against them for very long before your back began to get sore. I'd be rocking one of the younger ones, feeling the little heart banging fiercely against my chest, and

Dad and I would be trying to reassure everyone that actually, that rocket must have come down a long way away from us.

Sometimes we'd be stuck under there for as long as twenty-four hours with no food or water, desperately thirsty and hungry, but we didn't dare come out until the shelling stopped. And when we did, we had no idea which group would have won the battle and taken over or what that might mean. My dad would turn to the radio for news of who was hitting whom and who was making an agreement with whom. 'We have to get out – it's not over. Which direction do you think that was coming from?' he'd ask my mum. 'Shall we go to your cousin's in Khair Khana?'

Moving around anywhere in the city was fraught with dangers and horrible sights. If the fighting kicked off again we'd be crouching in the gutters, howling in terror. We saw bloated bodies lying in ditches, and when anyone had to take cover in a derelict house it was quite possible they'd come across decomposing human remains, soldiers killed in a firefight or civilians murdered in their own homes, still clutching their Quran to their chests. Sometimes guerrillas would barge in and set up military positions in people's houses, and if the residents they found inside were the 'wrong' ethnicity, they would simply shoot them and leave them to rot.

You had to be careful what language you spoke where. I was walking along the street in Shahre Naow one day, chatting with my cousin, when a guerrilla attacked me, for no other reason than because he could. He stuck his gun in my face. 'Why are you speaking Pashto? Speak Dari! I'll teach you some Pashto!' He knocked me to the ground, beat me with his stick and kicked me ferociously with his military boots. I was ten years old. I went home in tears. It was the random, bullying nature of the attack, the sense of powerlessness it induced, that hurt as much as anything else. It brought home to me how the mere possession of a weapon had the capacity to instil in these undisciplined soldiers a sense that they were entitled to do anything they liked.

There were terrible food shortages because the trucks bringing imports and aid were prevented from entering the city, and the queues grew. We ate what the farmers were able to bring in, or supplies that were permitted entry from Pakistan, which meant there was little variety to our diet. It was mainly rice and vegetables. There was no clean water, no healthcare, no education, and no human rights monitors were able to get into the country.

We did our best to cling on to some of the threads of normal life. For my mum and sisters, the drudgery was constant, whatever was going on outside our front door. Often we'd have a houseful of guests, friends, neighbours or relatives escaping or left homeless by the bombing, or simply visiting. Hospitality, and showing courtesy to all visitors, irrespective of their race, religion or place in society, is a cornerstone of Afghan culture, in bad times and good. My mum, the general, would be issuing the orders to her lieutenants, and they would all be cooking and cleaning morning, noon and night, with dozens of little ones running around, trying to keep everyone fed and as comfortable as possible.

My dad would be reassuring us all that better times were just around the corner. 'Good news!' he'd say, perceiving some ray of light in the unremittingly bad reports on the radio. 'These people can't hold out much longer. By next month they'll have been taken down.' As usual, Mum kept her own counsel, but you could see from the look in her eyes that she was not convinced.

Whenever he could, my father went to trade at the money exchange at Sarai Shahzada which, incredibly, continued throughout, if mostly on the streets rather than at shops or stalls. With warlords and forgers simply printing their own currency to fund their activities, it must have been chaos. By the time the war was over, the afghani would be declared worthless.

I tried to go back to school, only to find that it had been used by tanks to launch attacks and part of the building had been destroyed by rockets. The teacher came in, probably because otherwise he wouldn't have got paid, but perhaps also to try to support us and instil some sense that life does continue, even in the direst circumstances. There was no attempt to give lessons. We just sat and talked about the war and what had happened to whom. Our books had been looted and many of my classmates were missing. It was heartbreaking to have made friends and now to find that so many of them had gone. Some had fled abroad; others had been killed, one or two of them along with their entire families. Those of us who turned up did so really only to comfort each other and to register our attendance so that we would pass our grade.

At home I kept up with my school work as much as I could. I bought textbooks, science books and books in English which had found their way to market stalls after being looted or stolen from school cupboards. Once my father had heard enough news for one day, I would borrow his radio and listen to the BBC World Service to broaden my English. When we had to take cover in our 'bomb shelter' I'd bring a book and a lamp with me and try to read.

The war put paid to my Taekwondo lessons, but I practised at home, shutting myself in a room and putting all our mattresses and pillows at one end to cushion my falls as I threw myself around in imitation of Jackie Chan. We were still able to watch television and videos sometimes, if we had electricity. The supply would come and go: one warlord would destroy a power station another had commandeered and we'd be cut off. Then we'd have to buy wood to cook on a fire in the courtyard and use oil lamps. TV programmes appeared intermittently, depending on who was controlling the state broadcaster.

One chilly night we very nearly managed to kill ourselves by carbon monoxide poisoning as we slept around the *sandeli*. In the early hours I became foggily aware of the sounds of shelling coming closer and my parents, whose voices seemed very far away, telling each other they had to get up. But nobody moved and I drifted off again. Eventually, they managed to drag themselves to their feet and rouse us, but when we stood up we found that none of us could walk properly. We staggered groggily outside and collapsed into the snow. The older kids were trying to pull the little ones up but we'd make it only a few more metres before our legs would go again and we'd have to sit down. 'Put the children's heads in the snow to bring them round,' I heard my mother say. My parents finally manoeuvred everyone underneath the concrete veranda as the bombs rained down worryingly close by.

They recounted later how they'd found themselves completely unable to wake. My dad was always a sound sleeper. My mum was the one who was sensitive to the sound of a pin dropping, day or night, and it was she, not my dad, who slept with the big stick at her side in case of intruders. Luckily, neither of them had sunk so deeply into unconsciousness that the alarm bells in their heads had stopped ringing altogether, and through some superhuman effort they had succeeded in getting us all out of the house. It was twenty-four hours before any of us started to feel right again.

We laughed about it afterwards and the story of how we nearly poisoned ourselves with the *sandeli* went down in family history. But it was a reminder of how, amid the carnage of war, ordinary life and death continue as usual: accidents and injuries, minor ailments, cancer, heart attacks, strokes, childbirth and deaths from natural causes. With the healthcare system non-existent, people with regular illnesses just fell by the wayside. The only hope for anyone who had something serious wrong with them was to get to Pakistan for treatment.

We had to manage our own healthcare as best we could. People understood that the water was not clean and had to be well boiled before it was used for anything. Everyone kept a supply of boiled water, and disinfectant, at the ready for emergencies. The pharmacies only had the drugs and medical supplies that had been in their stock-rooms before the war began and there were no functioning doctors' surgeries. If you needed a doctor, you had to go to his house in the hope that it was still standing and he was still in residence.

Because I always had my nose in a science book – and because, since our return from Pakistan, my dad was always bigging up the skills I had learned at the pharmacy in Badaber – I was designated the neighbourhood medical specialist. My sisters used to tease me by calling me Dr Waheed. Although my dad's claims were obviously exaggerated, I did at least know the names of painkillers and anti-biotics and would be sent to the pharmacies to see which of these they might have in their stockrooms. I remembered, when I'd been ill in Pakistan, being given Neurobion, which was widely distributed among the refugees, and the idea that this simple vitamin supple-ment cured all ills was firmly lodged in my mind. In truth, it would not have done much to address any of the problems I was recom-mending it for now, but on the plus side, it wouldn't have done anyone any harm, either.

My mother always seemed to know what to do, and whether a problem could be dealt with or hospital treatment was required. During the civil war, going to hospital was rarely an option. Kabul's hospitals all came under fire at one time or another, taking hits to children's wards and operating theatres. When they were able to function, they were overwhelmed. There would be wounded people everywhere, on the floors and in the corridors; doctors skidding across surfaces slick with blood, kids being rushed through the front doors in wheelbarrows by distraught families. Rockets and heavy artillery rip chunks out of the body, and many died where they lay before any clinician could reach them. When the fighting was bad it was sometimes impossible to get in and out of the building, and the bodies would have to remain there for days, sometimes weeks.

My mother had two more children, Javid and Mahvash, during

the civil war and, amazingly, managed to get to the maternity hospital to give birth. Even so, it was not in any sense an organized process. There was little antenatal or postnatal care at the best of times. It was just a matter of turning up at the hospital, if it was open, when your contractions started and finding a doctor to help you.

After an attack, I would assist with cleaning and bandaging the less severe injuries, having seen it done in the back of the pharmacy in Badaber. My mum and sisters would bring me clean old clothes or cotton pillowcases to use as bandages. I found being able to help immensely rewarding. War robs you of any control over your own life and it felt good to be able to take some positive action, to do some small thing to ease somebody's suffering.

Less visible was the damage to mental health, which has always been under-resourced and insufficiently understood the world over, even in regions with far greater resources at their disposal. In countries like Afghanistan, mental health services were, and remain, virtually non-existent. For those with populations traumatized by conflict, violence and mass displacement, a prevalence rate for post-traumatic stress (PTSD) of anywhere between 17 and 50 per cent has been reported, compared with 5 per cent globally. And in the post-COVID-19 world, those figures will only increase.

Depression is another big problem. As a child I had some personal experience of this in 1994, while we were staying in Logar. At eleven years old, I had reached an age where I was trying to make sense of the world for myself, rather than simply accepting my parents' reassurances at face value. And the world I saw around me made no sense at all.

I lost my appetite, slept badly at night and would wake well before dawn. And during the day I was lethargic. I was questioning the meaning of life and what any of us were actually here for. Having had no real childhood, I was in many respects a miniature adult, and I felt weighed down by my responsibilities as the eldest son.

What was I going to do if anything happened to Dad? How would I manage to educate myself and take care of the family?

I would cycle to the end of the village on a borrowed bike and gaze up at the sky, looking for answers. I couldn't find any. Resilience is something we all need to develop to equip us to deal with what life throws at us. But being resilient doesn't mean we can always hold everything together. Sometimes things seem impossible because they are. I know now that, at these times, it helps to identify and acknowledge our grief and trauma, to hold on to the belief that they will pass, even if it doesn't feel as if they ever will, and find a way to navigate round or through what we cannot change.

It was hard for me in 1994 to envisage that these times would ever pass, because they had been the backdrop to my entire existence, with the exception of that one bright spot before the civil war broke out. In some ways, during these dark days, to have been given that brief glimpse of what life ought to be like, only to have it snatched away, felt crueller than never having known it at all.

I just couldn't see what the end of all this was going to look like, and my dad's reasoned analysis and irrepressible optimism no longer seemed to have the power to give me hope. Keeping a flicker of hope alive is fundamental to carrying us all through whatever periods of trouble and despair we encounter in our lives and I had lost sight of mine. I didn't talk about this to anyone in my family, but I visited a local doctor, who gave me medication. It was a sedative of some description and all it achieved was to make me drowsy and spaced out all day. I took the tablets for a week and then threw them away. They weren't helping and, with the constant need to be on alert and on the move, I couldn't afford to be half-conscious.

I coped by imagining a future for myself that was ordered and normal, a place to which I could retreat where I felt positive and happy, conjured from notions of the West picked up from BBC radio programmes and my battered English books. While the other kids played games with marbles or walnuts, I would sit on my own outside our house at Kolula-Pushta, either buried in the pages of a book or dreaming of this alternative life. I had my daily routine all planned out. I'd get up in the morning in my nice flat, furnished with an office desk where I could study and shelves full of pristine new books. I'd do some exercises, have a good breakfast and then head off to school or work on the bus, or perhaps even on my motorbike or in my car.

The setting for this idyll was undefined and variable. Sometimes, when we'd heard news of someone we knew making a good life for themselves in the UK, US or Germany, it would resemble my concept of one of these foreign lands. Other times it was a peaceful, regenerated Kabul, where I pictured myself attending the medical school. At my lowest ebb, when I couldn't connect with any glimmer of hope in the present world, I kindled it in this imaginary one, until such time as I could feel this dream, or something like it, within my reach.

5

Separation

BY THE END OF 1994, a new political movement was bidding to overturn the chaotic rule of the warlords. The Taliban were founded by Mullah Omar, a Pashtun scholar at a madrassa in Pakistan, and his followers, religious students (or *talib*) mainly from the south and east of Afghanistan, and established in Mullah Omar's home town of Kandahar in the far south.

Their objective was to end the reign of terror, corruption and crime of the warring factions and to restore law and order by installing an Islamic government to rule the country according to a strict interpretation of Sharia law. Within months their ranks had been swelled by thousands of students, many of them Afghan refugees, from religious schools in Pakistan, ready to sign up for military training to fight for the Taliban cause.

That November the Taliban overtook the city of Kandahar, and by January 1995 they were in control of twelve provinces and moving towards Kabul. In March they tried to invade the city, but were repelled by Ahmad Shah Massoud's forces. As they retreated, Taliban fighters shelled Kabul, killing yet more civilians.

We were still leading a nomadic existence between various Kabul boltholes and Logar. Trying to cling on to our lives day after day, month after month, in the thick of this endless strife was becoming so impossible that my parents felt we had no option but to flee once again to Pakistan and sit it out as refugees for as long as we could bear it. It was decided that I would be sent on ahead to the camp where my grandmother lived. I took with me, in addition to a long list of instructions from my dad, my brother Khalid.

I was eleven years old and Khalid would have been no more than five. It might sound shocking for us to be undertaking such an expedition on our own in the midst of a raging war but in truth our lives were in more danger from the bombs in Kabul than they were on the road. Looking back, although my father would not have alarmed me by saying so, I have a sense that he saw this plan as a kind of insurance policy. With the family's two eldest sons safe in Pakistan, there would be someone to take care of the family if he did not make it out alive.

Neither the anti-government militias nor the Taliban were interested in comings and goings between Afghanistan and Pakistan, and there was not much chance of us losing our way: legions of refugees were pouring out of the country every day and all we had to do was follow the crowd. The North-West Frontier was familiar territory and I had a good head on my young shoulders. Which is not to say, of course, that the journey wasn't hazardous.

We left very early one morning on a bus setting off in the direction of the border at Torkham. We didn't get far before the driver spotted a roadblock up ahead and everyone had to get off. The highway was littered with such barricades, all controlled by different rebel groups who were still attacking and seizing land from each other, as well as trying to keep the Taliban at bay. As the wooden barriers marked the front line of the fighting, it would have been foolhardy for the bus to continue. These 'checkpoints' were notorious for robberies and hostage-taking. Some of them were run like personal fiefdoms by sadistic highwaymen for their own enrichment. The passengers now had to make a detour on foot, or hitch a cross-country lift in a passing car or pick-up, until it was safe to rejoin the main road and wait for another bus to appear.

Aware that we were vulnerable to kidnapping for ransom, I took the precaution of latching on to other families during our journey, approaching fathers on the road with wives and children and requesting politely, 'Uncle, is it OK if we come with you? If anyone asks, will you say we are your sons?' Our fellow travellers were sympathetic and protective and looked out for us.

With these frequent interruptions, it was a long haul across the dry, dusty landscape – walk, bus, walk, bus – and I was on high alert throughout. At last we just strolled across the border at Torkham, from where I navigated us by bus to Peshawar. It felt safer to keep going. We could nap on the bus. In Peshawar I got my bearings and asked about buses to Shamshatoo camp, about 25 kilometres southeast of the city. I had been here a few times before and I knew the name of the bus stop where we needed to get off.

Khalid and I were exhausted. We arrived very late at night and it took me a little while to find my grandmother's mud house in the dark, but I had directions from my dad, and neighbours were able to point it out to me. My uncle, who lived with her, was quite well known in their part of the camp because he taught at one of the schools. I had to rouse them from their sleep. They had no idea we were coming, but among Afghans it is considered perfectly normal for relatives to turn up unannounced, especially in these long years of continual displacement.

We were made a great fuss of, given bread, *quroot* and tea, and then we crashed out. The next morning I left Khalid with my grandmother and went with my uncle in search of some accommodation for the family before the rest of them arrived.

Set in barren, rocky hills in an area previously inhabited by tortoises (*shamshatoo* is Pashto for tortoise), the camp resembled an ancient metropolis, an unbroken reddish-brown landscape formed from the clay mined nearby and the rows upon rows of mud houses. One of the largest and best-known of Peshawar's refugee camps, it had been in existence since the beginning of the Soviet war.

Gulbuddin Hekmatyar had leased the land from the government and local owners and it was managed by his Hezb-e Islami group, which, as the faction then most favoured by Islamabad, received most foreign funding and arms. It was a regular port of call for anyone coming to Pakistan to see the refugee situation for themselves, from journalists and television crews, leaders of aid organizations and international politicians, to UN Secretary-General Kofi Annan.

Shamshatoo had by this time evolved into a small city with its own administrative departments, rules and laws, schools, a 'university', quite a few clinics and pharmacies, a bazaar, shops, stalls and little restaurants, a big main mosque and many smaller ones. People built their own mud houses, much like the one we'd lived in at Badaber, except that, with many refugees having been here for a long while, some were bigger and had been made a bit more comfortable, with extra rooms added over time. Piped water and electricity were available in some areas of the camp, which had numbered sections and named streets.

This was where my mother's parents had moved when we took over their old home six years earlier. My grandmother was now widowed, my grandfather, who had been working here for an aid organization, having died of a heart attack at the beginning of the civil war.

Like all the camps, Shamshatoo saw the continual ebb and flow of a huge tide of migrants as people escaped Afghanistan and then returned, according to the situation in their own region or their personal circumstances. My uncle and I walked up and down the dirt streets, looking out for homes that had been left by departing families or notices pinned to poles advertising houses for rent. My father had given me details of the type of place that would suffice, and how much rent we could afford to pay for it. We finally found a mud house that ticked the essential boxes. It had two rooms, plus a latrine and washing area, a reasonable-sized, walled yard and some basic cooking facilities. There was access to water and electricity and the rent was within our budget.

My obligations discharged, I started to become very worried about whether my family would make it here in one piece. My dad had said they would be at Shamshatoo within a week. What if they didn't come? I counted off the days in a state of high anxiety, passing hours out on the roadside watching for them, with Khalid sitting quietly beside me, playing in the dust.

Late one evening, after we had returned disconsolately to my grandmother's house, there was a knock on the door.

'Jan Agha, Moor Jani, is that you?'

'Yes, it's us. Open the door!'

And there they were. Tears of joy and relief flowed. Everyone was safe. And there was one more of them than expected. When I had left with Khalid the week before my mother had been pregnant. She had gone into labour on the bus en route to Pakistan. The driver had stopped for her to seek help at a house by a river where, with the assistance of some fellow travellers and local women, she had given birth to my brother Farid. In the morning, my father recounted admiringly, she just got up, dressed herself, picked up the baby and boarded a bus to continue their journey.

All eleven of us moved into our two mud rooms, where we adjusted to the familiar battle with the conditions. We were perpetually covered in a film of sandy dust and pestered by the sandflies that darted constantly around the camp. As the heat of the summer set in, they were joined by mosquitoes. I became feverish, veering between burning up and shivering with cold, begging for more blankets, my whole body aching. Unable to eat or drink without vomiting, I became weaker and sicker. Several of my brothers and sisters were in the same state.

The clinic took blood samples and announced, 'You've got malaria,' which didn't come as any great surprise. Most of us had had malaria more than once during our last stint as refugees. Good hygiene is unachievable when you are surrounded by open ditches and there is not enough clean water. Even the fruit and vegetables in the camp shops, brought back from the market in Peshawar by the shopkeepers in their trucks or beaten-up old cars, were crawling with mosquitoes.

We had no mosquito nets, no insecticide – nothing but a fly-swatter. And of course, usually you don't see a mosquito coming for you until it's too late. You just hear that high-pitched whine, feel the sting and that's it. Basic medication was sometimes given, rather randomly, but none of the expensive anti-malarial drugs were available. If somebody was rushed into the clinic with a dangerously high fever it was quite standard for primary treatment to consist of dousing them in water and pointing a fan at them. The clinic doled out paracetamol and administered a drip if you needed one, or just gave you the drip and a bag of meds to take back to your mud house, with the instruction to drink plenty of fluids and keep hydrated. Even that elementary requirement is not easy to maintain in refugee-camp conditions.

I spent a lot of time at the clinic, trying to address these recurrent bouts of malaria, and other illnesses, in the family. Gastro-intestinal problems were also rife. I was fascinated by the on-site blood-testing. Nothing was sent out to a lab, of course, as it might be elsewhere – any analysis was done right there in the clinic or the pharmacy by a man sitting in a tiny mud room out the back. I'd watch him spin the blood samples in his centrifuge or carefully transfer a smear of fluid on to a slide, add a few drops of an agent from a pipette and study it under his microscope.

I interrogated the doctors and the pharmacists on the different types of malaria and questioned them closely about medicines. Why were they prescribing this one? What was that one for? I wanted to make sure we had the right drugs for the right complaint and that the medication was actually capable of alleviating the symptoms. It wasn't unusual to be fobbed off by a shopkeeper with something ineffective or inappropriate for the problem in question and we didn't have the funds to waste on non-essential meds.

The doctors here were refugees themselves. One or two of them were properly qualified: Afghan medical degrees were not recognized in Pakistan and clinicians fleeing for their lives would arrive to find they had no marketable skills on this side of the border. Many others, however, had only basic training because their education had been abruptly halted by the war.

Shamshatoo had its own micro-economy. At its peak, it had about 800 shops, which were rented out to refugee businesses offering car repairs, carpentry, electrical work or labour for hire, and traders selling bread, fruit and vegetables, cooking oil, household goods and medicines. What you could not buy were films, music or cigarettes, which were banned. We could not watch television anywhere, either, except for cricket. Hezb-e Islami were also strict about religion and how people dressed.

The camp was pretty safe and secure. You could wander around comfortably even quite late at night. Crimes such as robberies, rapes and assaults were very rare. The downside was the undercurrent of pressure to 'join' Hezb-e Islami and a culture of discrimination against those who declined. Hezb adherents supervised the distribution of humanitarian aid, policed their rules and imposed their ideology on the community. Infringements of the regulations sometimes resulted in harsh punishment. I once saw a woman in full burqa being beaten because the robe was not considered long enough and showed her ankles as she walked.

My father found a regular job with a currency trader who had his own shop in the Chowk-Yadgar market. With eleven mouths to be fed, it was decided that my mother and sisters would take up weaving carpets at home, as a lot of families in the camps were doing.

Carpet-weaving was prominent among the businesses of Shamshatoo, many of which employed child labour. Young, small fingers are more efficient at teasing out the hundreds of strands that hang down from the top of the frame and the intricate work of interweaving them, one strand at a time. It took about a month to complete a metre of carpet.

My mother's younger sister, known to us as Khala Jan, was also living at Shamshatoo. Her husband, an engineer, helped us to acquire the equipment, loom, yarn, dye and so on, and my father made contact with a carpet dealer. It was hard and pressurized labour, because the rugs were commissioned in advance and had to be produced to a deadline dictated by the dealer.

I took steps to pick up the threads of my education, which had unravelled in Kabul early in Grade 6, although, having done my best to keep learning on my own at home, the idea of starting again where I'd left off felt like going backwards. Who knew how long we were likely to be staying here and I wanted to cut to the chase by focusing while I could on the subjects I would need in my quest to become a doctor.

I had my sights set on the course in medicine on offer at the Islamic University at Shamshatoo, housed in a modern, concrete building which had been constructed only about two or three years previously in the corner of a field at the entrance to the camp. This was not a university as defined by the outside world. Its primary function was to teach the skills for which there was a need in the camps. As it was so new, nobody had yet graduated, but its certificates were not likely to be recognized in Pakistan. All of the camps had their own education systems so there wasn't any consistency of standards.

That said, the Islamic University was a real force for good. It gave refugees from Shamshatoo and other surrounding camps the chance of a worthwhile education and training in medicine, engineering or law. The six-year courses broadly followed recognized syllabuses and gave their graduates a foundation in their chosen discipline on which they could build in the future. If I could earn a place here to study medicine it would set me on the right road.

To be eligible I had to pass the *kankor*, the Afghan baccalaureate, the exam designed to demonstrate that you have reached the educational standard required for university. Schools and other institutions all had their own versions of the *kankor*, but they conformed to the same pattern and contained similar questions. I got hold of some old papers. I was only twelve, but as I worked through the questions I thought to myself, I could pass this.

My youth wasn't any great barrier. Given that trying to establish the precise ages of many refugee students would have been an impossible task, age probably wasn't considered a particularly relevant criterion. However, to be able to take the *kankor*, I needed my Grade 12 school leaving certificate.

I went to a school in central Peshawar, run by Afghan refugees, to ask if I could sit their leaving exam. I told the teacher I had completed the curriculum up to Grade 12 in Kabul but just hadn't yet been able to take the exam to acquire the certificate. He peered at me suspiciously. 'Are you sure? You seem very young.'

There were only about two months left of the semester and I knew that the class would be using this time to prepare for the leaving certificate. It was a modest school, set up in a rented house, with everyone sitting on the floor, no chairs, desks or other scholastic luxuries. But I couldn't afford to attend for longer than that. In addition to the fees, there were other expenses, like the bus fares in and out of Peshawar, to be considered. The leaving certificate required a fairly basic level of competence in subjects like maths, science, history and religious studies, and I was confident that I could pass it with a couple of months' coaching.

Whether I was right to pursue this short cut is, with hindsight, highly debatable, but I was a boy in a hurry. The precariousness of my life had taught me that I had to seize whatever opportunities were available to me in the here and now. In the midst of war and displacement, you don't have your future mapped out in carefully planned stages. What I did have, though, was an end goal. And so, as I have done often in my life, I looked at where I wanted to be and then I worked backwards to figure out what I needed to do at this particular moment to get there.

I managed to persuade the teacher to let me enrol at the school for the remaining couple of months of the term and to sit their leaving certificate. Schools like this were driven by economics. They struggled to maintain enough pupils to survive and were not inclined to ask too many searching questions about your credentials. I went to class every day and, with my finger on the pulse of the topics and the kind of questions that would come up in the exam paper, I was able to study furiously at home as well. Theoretically, at least, I needed to haul myself up six grades.

I passed the school's test – in truth it wasn't very hard and they passed almost everyone – and handed over my 50 rupees for my grandly named 'baccalaureate'.

The next hurdle was the *kankor*. Medicine was the most popular university course and, with the applicants who scored the highest marks in the exam given first choice, therefore the most difficult to get into. But what I lacked in years I more than made up for in sheer commitment and determination.

My parents found the money for me to do a couple of outside courses, in maths and science, at a place on Arbab Road in the city. Otherwise I prepared myself. My classmates on the courses were a mixture of refugees, trying, like me, to further their education, or to plug holes in it, and locals. I made friends on my maths course with an older boy named Hakim, who lived just down the road with his family. He would sometimes invite me to his home, where we'd do our course work together, I'd eat with the family and Hakim would give me a lift back to the bus station on his motorbike. His family came from the Panjshir Valley, a gem-mining area just north-east of Kabul, and were quite affluent. Hakim's father, a gem trader, had a shop in Peshawar where he sold precious and semi-precious stones.

At home in the evenings, I applied my maths to real-life matters as I sat with my father discussing the political situation and the exchange rate. When should he sell? When should he buy? If the war took this turn, what would be the impact on the currency? What if something different happened instead? These were complicated problems involving lots of calculations and variables and I considered them carefully. If I got the answers wrong it might well have a detrimental effect on our family income.

As ready as I could be, I sat the *kankor* and, when I received the news that I had passed and was being offered a place at the Islamic University to study medicine, I was ecstatic. But before long my joy would be clouded by a difficult choice.

My family desperately wanted to go home. I don't remember what glimmer of hope prompted them to leave precisely when they did. When your options are limited to hardship, disease and insufferable heat in a foreign land or bombs and guns at home, it is not always a question of being able to choose a better quality of life, just the least bad one at that moment.

Our stay at Shamshatoo had only ever been intended to be a temporary measure and it therefore hadn't seemed worth going to the time and expense of trying to upgrade our mud house. We'd already had to move once after a Hezb worker reported my father for not attending the mosque. In vain he tried to explain that, as he had a full-time job in the city, he left very early in the morning and did not get back until late at night. This man made our lives such a misery that we had to relocate to another area of the camp.

My dad would have been worried about leaving the houses at Shahre Naow and Kolula-Pushta for too long. They represented everything the family owned. If we lost our property, we would be destitute. But my parents' decision to leave left me in a quandary. With the Islamic University my only hope of getting an education, unlike everyone else, I desperately wanted to stay.

I persuaded my parents that I was grown up enough to remain behind in Pakistan and continue my studies. Khala Jan had a guest room in her house and it was agreed that I could live there. My dad gave me some money he had saved and I said goodbye to my parents and all of my brothers and sisters, promising them that I would be fine. I was putting on a brave face. I had never before been completely separated from my entire immediate family, and inside I was anxious and scared. I tried to focus my thoughts on the exciting prospect of going to medical school.

The university had classrooms, playing fields, dormitories and its own mosque. The syllabus for the foundation year was a grounding in physics, chemistry and biology, or PCB. We also had lessons in maths, English and religious studies. I'd say, looking back, that the PCB year and the first year proper were pitched at about the equivalent of GCSE level in the UK. There was one class for our intake and we were all taught together, in Farsi and Pashto, about ninety, a hundred of us.

We were a disparate crowd, a mix of ages and backgrounds, but a majority of the students had probably grown up and attended school in Pakistan. Others might have missed out on some of their education but I doubt anyone else was as young or had as little schooling as I had: maybe a year and a half in total.

The committed tutors did their best with limited resources. One retired professor who was not even on the payroll came in regularly from the city, at his own expense, to teach us. The foundation year was perfect for me because it started all the science subjects from the very beginning ('What exactly is a cell?'), helpfully going over the basics covered at school level.

The outgoing chancellor was Dr Faizullah Kakar, who would later become Afghanistan's deputy minister for public health. An epidemiologist by profession, Dr Kakar was a kindly man of liberal outlook. He had studied and taught at the University of Washington in Seattle and was married to an American. He was about to move to Islamabad, where he would be appointed medical officer for the World Health Organization. I remember, in my early days at the university, being one of a group of students taken to his house in a lovely part of Peshawar to be interviewed by the UN or an NGO about our education in the camp.

We had desks, chairs and a blackboard and a basic science lab with a few pieces of essential equipment – cheap microscopes, test tubes and Bunsen burners. There were no computers or books. Some of the teachers would write everything on the board in each lecture for us to copy out; others would prepare their notes in advance for the whole semester, all handwritten, with hand-drawn diagrams, and a couple of students would take them to the photocopier in the market and get them copied for everyone else. Otherwise we had to bring with us whatever books, stationery or materials we needed.

That first year I bought the most important set text. I couldn't afford any of the others. I had to pay for my photocopies of the teachers' notes as well. Every couple of weeks I would go to a bookstore in Peshawar and casually leaf through one of the texts, trying to look as if I was planning on buying the book, and scan a couple of chapters at a time, taking surreptitious notes.

In the city I used to see the students from the proper medical school, the Khyber, attached to the Lady Reading Hospital in Peshawar, which is one of the most important postgraduate medical institutes in Pakistan. They carried bags bulging with shiny new books. Laughing and confident in their clean, white lab coats, their stethoscopes slung artlessly around their necks, they were oblivious of the refugee kid in his old, patched clothes and little white hat. The hat wasn't strictly compulsory, but I wore it to ensure I blended in. It was generally frowned upon to go around the camp bareheaded and people would look at you askance.

To support myself, I found a job teaching science to the young children of a family who lived in a large house on the road to Peshawar. They ran a car sales business and were very well-off. I was pretty much teaching these kids what I had just learned myself. In the evenings I would return to my rug, pillow and blanket in the mud room at Khala Jan's house, my bag of clothes at one end of the carpet and my box of books at the other, and read by lamplight long into the night.

When there were guests, they were in there with me, not just to sleep but often during the day as well, which meant it wasn't always easy to concentrate. I spent a lot of time reading outside, sitting under a tree, or going to the mosque to work.

Once I'd settled in at the Islamic University, I decided to move into one of the dormitories there, which I hoped would be quieter. I shared with seven other students, all much older than I was. These were grown-up men, big, bearded country types whose families came from provincial Afghanistan but who had been brought up in refugee camps. I was a thirteen-year-old boy pretending to be an adult, a city boy at that, and I didn't belong with them. I didn't understand their topics of conversation or get their jokes. They were Hezb-e Islami and it didn't feel right to talk openly to them about the kinds of things I was used to discussing with my dad. They were always perfectly pleasant, but not much interested in me and it seemed best to keep myself to myself.

The atmosphere around the camp in general was not conducive to open chat or carefree banter. It was a hotbed of politics and you had to be aware of who belonged to which group. You would get respect if your father was on the front line fighting for Hezb; if your relatives had been in the Afghan army or supported Najibullah, everyone looked down on you for it.

At the university a higher level of adherence to Hezb-e Islami's rules was expected of us. We had to stop classes at fixed times to go to the mosque and make sure we always wore our hats. The controlling environment instilled a sense that we were not free in either mind or body. I considered myself to be a good Muslim. My faith was strong and I didn't feel I needed to be told how to be a good Muslim. People did break the rules, but only on the quiet. Some of my room-mates had little radios or cassette-players on which they listened to music clandestinely in the dorm.

We slept, eight to a room, in bunk beds. Your bed was the only private space you had. Mine was a bottom bunk. I had a curtain which I hung around it at night so that I could lie there and read with the illusion of privacy. I was embarrassed to be seen putting up my curtain, worried that my room-mates might see me as scared or standoffish. I would wait until everyone else had left for evening prayers at the mosque and do it before catching them up.

We were given two meals a day, usually bread and tea in the morning and rice and beans in the evening. We took it in turns to go with our communal bowl to the kitchen, where the 'chef' doled out the food for our dorm to be shared out among our room-mates, and to use the 'shower' (bring your own bucket), where we also washed our clothes.

I was very lonely. With no life outside the classroom, I focused totally on my work, spending practically every waking moment reading and studying. The academic year was divided into two semesters, with a long break in the baking summer months, and I did go back to Kabul in between, but I missed my parents and my sisters and brothers terribly. However, there was more than the pain of separation to my sense of isolation, something darker, on the edge of fear. Without the protective structure of my family, I felt exposed and hyper-aware of my vulnerability. I was quite capable of handling the practicalities of taking care of myself. Yet, while I might not have thought of myself as a child, I was now much more conscious that this was how others saw me. And I was a child living alone among adult male strangers.

Slightly built and fair-skinned, I attracted stares and sometimes jeers. My tormentors may just have been the kind of people who found it amusing to intimidate younger kids but, given the undercurrents at Shamshatoo, I couldn't be sure. What if someone tried to harm me or kidnap me? Who would step in to help? Men were a potential threat and women were powerless to act against them. I did what I could to make myself look like everyone else. I tried to shave before I had anything to shave, because I'd heard that would encourage my beard to grow. When that didn't work, I attempted to make myself invisible by going about with a scarf wrapped around my face.

Anxious and constantly alert, I was often uncomfortable in large groups of people. I'd tense up, feel my palms starting to sweat and my voice would quaver if I tried to speak. I would, much later, come to recognize this as a manifestation of PTSD. I was experiencing other symptoms, too. It wasn't the first time I'd had nightmares, dreams of rockets falling and my parents being killed in front of me, of finding myself on the wrong end of a Kalashnikov, or daytime flashbacks. They had begun, as far as I can recollect, during the civil war, when they were often indistinguishable from the real thing. Here, on my own and out of range of the bombs, the effects were more pronounced.

I developed a do-it-yourself form of cognitive behavioural therapy. I would go to the desert area outside the camp and sit there quietly by myself. I prayed, and tried to acknowledge my feelings and concentrate on the positive aspects of my life, to count my blessings: I was safe from the shells and rockets; I was doing well with my studies; I had been given the opportunity to learn medicine, which was what I'd always wanted. I practised Taekwondo and followed an exercise regime. Exercise calmed me down and restored some perspective.

I sent letters home to my parents, full of upbeat reassurances about how well I was doing and how well I was coping, which Perveen, Zari or Gululai would read out to them, and they dictated their replies for one of my sisters to write back. They were now living through a new chapter of Kabul's bloody history. In September 1996, just as I was starting at the Islamic University, the Taliban had succeeded in moving into the city. At Shamshatoo everyone had been keeping tabs on what was going on, of course, and the gruesome newspaper images of the mutilated body of our ex-president, Mohammad Najibullah, did the rounds of the camp.

Ever since his resignation and the outbreak of civil war, Najibullah had been holed up in the sanctuary of the UN headquarters in Kabul while the UN fruitlessly attempted to negotiate safe passage for him to India. On the day the Taliban took over, their soldiers had come for Najibullah, tortured him to death, castrated him and dragged his body behind a truck through the streets before suspending it from a traffic light outside the Presidential Palace. There could have been no clearer or more savage notification that Afghanistan was under new management.

This act of barbarism was condemned around the globe. The Taliban's defiant response was to pronounce death sentences on General Dostum, Ahmad Shah Massoud and Burhanuddin Rabbani, who had been the president of the interim government.

Yet while the perception of the outside world was one of horror, in the eyes of a sizeable part of the Afghan population the arrival of the Taliban was – early on, at least – not entirely unwelcome. It was probably difficult for anyone who had not lived through the previous seventeen years of unrelenting war and brutality to appreciate what it meant to ordinary people to experience the order and structure this draconian regime was able to introduce and maintain. Everyone was so weary of the lawlessness and excesses of the feuding warlords that many accepted the Taliban with a measure of guarded relief.

The word from Kabul was that the street-by-street fighting had all but ceased. One or two of the factions had joined forces with the Taliban and taken up arms against the others, but now that the Taliban had control of the government, most of the unrest was out in the provinces, where they had a huge presence. In Kabul, corruption was being stamped out and crime had plummeted. Murders, rapes, kidnaps and robberies had stopped almost overnight. The severe penalties were a very effective deterrent. People were cautiously reassured by this dramatic restoration of law and order. Yes, they said, the regime was repressive, but as long as you obeyed the rules, you could live your life in peace.

6

Escape Plan

MY FIRST ENCOUNTER WITH the Taliban came in 1997, travelling home in my PCB year to spend the summer with my family. At the Torkham border I was stopped by a man with a long beard and a big turban.

'Where is your beard?'

'I don't have a beard.'

'Have you shaved it off?'

'No, I'm too young to shave,' I explained.

'Where is your hat?'

'I'm sorry. I forgot it.'

I was marched off to an office at the checkpoint, where I was asked by another man with a long beard and big turban where I had come from, where I was going and questioned again about my absent beard and hat. It looked as if the hat was going to become a sticking point. If it was decided that I had committed an offence, it was quite likely that I would be whipped.

I pointed out that wearing a cap was *sunna* – good practice, under Islamic law – as opposed to 100 per cent compulsory, or *farz*.

'Ah, so you know your Islamic law!' The man seemed pleasantly surprised.

'I know that wearing a hat is *sunna*, not *farz*.'

Debating this matter with a *talib* was not sensible. They had the power and the guns and standing your ground was dangerous. But I felt I had to defend myself, to try to convince him of the unfairness of whatever penalty he might be thinking of imposing. I held my breath.

The man's face broke into a smile. 'I admire the fire in you! You speak your mind.'

'I am just speaking the truth,' I replied, in a tone I hoped sounded conciliatory.

I had escaped punishment this time, but I realized I was going to have to be more careful.

I got off the bus in Kabul to find the same ravaged city, except that the atmosphere was muted and it was eerily quiet. The people looked different. The men all had beards and turbans and the women . . . well, there weren't any women. Women were not allowed outside the house unless accompanied by a male relative. Those who did venture on to the streets occasionally with their escort were covered from head to toe in burqas.

In Kolula-Pushta, my father had bought an old car and was working as a taxi driver. He could no longer earn a living from currency trading because the market at Sarai Shahzada had been closed down. The shops at the front of the house at Shahre Naow had long been abandoned and had brought in no rent for years. Money was tight and food and other commodities scarce, with roadblocks between Kabul and other provinces preventing imports and aid from getting through.

The whole of the rest of the family were carrying on with the carpet-weaving business they had set up at Shamshatoo. Everyone was involved, even Javid and little Mahvash. She wanted to help and was good at it, with her tiny, dextrous hands, but so vulnerable. Her hands would be raw and bleeding and she was often in tears from the pain.

My dad warned me that there were guys patrolling the streets in their Datsuns, their weapons in the back ready to enforce Sharia law on the spot. 'It's prayer time. What is your shop doing open?' For this transgression a trader could expect several lashes. An over-charging butcher might suddenly find his finger being sliced off by a *talib* right there in his shop. Petty thieves had their faces smeared with charcoal, a sign hung round their necks reading: 'This is what will happen to you if you steal' and were made to walk the streets beating a drum. The penalty for stealing on a bigger scale was to have your hands chopped off. Fornicators were whipped and adulterers stoned.

The sense of oppression hung in the air but everybody knew where they stood. During the civil war, the rebels would have killed you just for speaking in a dialect they didn't like.

I had been nurturing the hope that at some point I might be able to transfer to Kabul University and continue my studies there. While I was home for the break I went to enquire about their medicine degree and whether my grades at the Islamic University at Shamshatoo would be transferable. The answer to my question was no, but I was invited, as part of a group of interested students, to visit the university and meet the new minister for higher education, who would show us round and talk to us about what it had to offer.

This tour was farcical. We assembled in an upstairs room and, before the minister had said anything beyond welcoming us, we were interrupted by a call to prayer. We trooped downstairs to pray, came back up and then the minister clapped his hands and said: 'Let's play sport!' We all went downstairs again and outside, where there were some Taliban soldiers playing volleyball. There were not enough of them for a proper game so we were asked to join them to make up two teams. Unbelievably, we had to play a game of volleyball before any of us got to hear about any of the things we wanted to know.

I don't remember the visit producing any real information. Its primary purpose was evidently to recruit young men to the Taliban. 'Burying your nose in books is all well and good,' the minister responded to one question about a degree course, 'but the greatest calling is to work hard in the way of God. Join us and we can teach you to become the best guerrilla fighters. We can teach you how to eat a snake!'

When I told my parents what had happened they were horrified. But the visit had merely served to confirm my fears. Everyone had been telling me that the university was finished and it was clear from what my brothers were being taught that the school curriculum had completely changed. Everything was driven and enforced by religious principles. Small boys were being indoctrinated at those primary schools that were still open. Many had to close due to a lack of teachers, since a majority of primary-level teachers were women and they were not allowed to do their jobs.

With all traces of secularity censored, the science teaching was no longer scientific. In fact, most medical professionals had left the country in the early days of the civil war and there had been no real government-run medical training programmes since then. The impact on our people would be disastrous. We had no international relations and our own rulers were not interested. All of our ministers were mullahs. The minister for higher education, who should have been a teacher, was a mullah. So was the minister for health, who should have been a doctor.

With more and more Afghans fleeing abroad, the healthcare system had been virtually non-existent for years. We had no facilities, equipment, drugs, and anyone seriously ill with the means to make the trip went to Pakistan. Where were our young doctors going to come from and what kind of training could they hope to have? Medicine was the only field in which women were allowed to work, because the Taliban had decreed that women and girls could not be medically attended by men. At the same time they forbade education for girls. How was that going to work out?

In those days I wouldn't have been conscious of Afghanistan's dire position in the global league tables, but our infant mortality rate was the worst in the world, far outstripping that of other low-resource countries. A quarter of children were dying before the age of five.

Some people said to me, 'What's the point in hanging on to this dream of becoming a doctor? Even if you manage it, you're not going to get paid much. Better to forget about it and set yourself up as a shopkeeper.' It never occurred to me to think like that. I had my gaze fixed on what I wanted to do, it was just a question of how I could achieve it.

I returned to Shamshatoo for the new semester with a heavy heart and threw myself into my work. My relentless studying produced exceptional results. We learned in a traditional way, absorbing the lessons and set texts and regurgitating them in the exams, and because I committed everything to memory so obsessively, I knew it all forwards, backwards and sideways. At the end of that foundation year, I came second or third in my class of almost a hundred students.

The curriculum for the second year, the first year proper of 'medical school', was anatomy, biochemistry and physiology. I loved being able to put the pieces of each subject together and to start to make sense of them. It felt as if the door to the workings of medicine and the human body was beginning to creak ajar. But how far could it open for me here?

I knew now that the course could only ever be a stepping stone towards a medical career. The crumbling of the medical school in Kabul was a big blow. It would be another four and a half years before I graduated from the Islamic University, and then what? My qualifications would not, it seemed, be recognized in Afghanistan any more than they would be in Pakistan. They probably wouldn't even be officially accepted by the NGOs working with the refugees in Peshawar.

Outside the classroom, I withdrew even deeper into myself and the dreams, flashbacks and anxiety were escalating. I was sleeping a lot, a classic sign that I was suffering once again from depression; I had no appetite and, as a result, I was losing weight. My thoughts turned increasingly often to that alternative life I had constructed in my head – the room of my own with my desk and my books; the daily routine at work or college in an ordered universe. The image began to solidify in my mind as a potential solution in the real world rather than a mere pipe dream. Was the answer to try to seek asylum in the West and train as a doctor there?

There had been family conversations over the years about escaping abroad, usually after we had news of emigrants who were making good lives for themselves. These had been no more than comforting fantasies, really, although, during the civil war, my dad had briefly seriously considered trying to move the whole family to America or the UK. He soon acknowledged to himself that the notion of selling up and leaving our home for ever, effectively erasing our whole history and culture to start again in a strange land, was just too radical for him to countenance, in spite of everything. But I could do it. And I could secure the future of the family in the process.

The only problem was, I didn't have the first clue how to go about it. The red tape was doubtless complicated and it would unquestionably be expensive, but others had managed it. Why not me? I knew there were a lot of scams that exploited refugees. To find a legitimate route out would take a lot of effort and research that I couldn't accomplish while I was studying full-time. I concluded that to give myself the breathing space to explore it properly and, if the plan proved impossible, to take stock of my situation and decide where I went from here, I would need to put my education on hold.

I asked my teachers if I could defer the next semester, citing family issues. That way I wasn't shutting the door on the Islamic University altogether if I came up against a brick wall. They agreed. In the meantime, I doubled down on my college work until the end of the term. After the exams, the physiology teacher asked in class, 'Who is Waheed?' I raised my hand tentatively.

'Congratulations, Waheed. You have full marks.'

I had done so well in physiology, I later learned, that the teacher suspected I might have cheated. Apparently, the other teachers had reassured him, 'No, Waheed is an excellent student, quite capable of getting full marks. He was in the top three last year in everything.' But he was concerned because I had reproduced his notes almost word for word. Unbeknownst to me, they'd had invigilators monitoring me closely in the rest of the exams to make sure I wasn't somehow copying my answers.

The invigilators confirmed that I wasn't and the physiology teacher apologized to me afterwards. 'You have obviously revised very hard and you are just blessed with a good memory.'

I left the Islamic University that semester top of the whole class. It was, though, an illustration not only of how fanatically I was studying but of the way I was studying, which I would need to learn to adjust significantly further down the line. Still, I was pleased, and hopeful that my results would count for something, whatever the future held.

I now needed to find somewhere to stay. I had seen an advert pinned up in a bus stop for a very cheap room in the Tehkal district of Peshawar, and went to take a look. I walked for what seemed like ages after getting off the bus, eventually coming to a river laden with sewage and, just beyond it, an area of small mud houses where the city's workers rented rooms. In short, a slum. The building was a basement. That was literally all it was, as the rest of the house was still under construction: ten, maybe fifteen underground rooms, which the landlord was already renting out in his haste to make money from them, sharing one toilet and washroom area.

I viewed the tiny, dark, subterranean cell. The stench from the river was awful. 'I'll take it,' I said.

I stayed in that slum for two or three months, surviving on what I earned from the family who paid me to teach their children. It was a terrible place but I was happy. At fourteen years old, living there in peace on my own, for the first time in my life, I felt free.

Needless to say, I only used my room for sleeping. Quite apart from the revolting smell, there was a constant hammering overhead from the builders all day. In the morning I fetched my own water and queued up with my neighbours to use the facilities and then I would go out for the day. If I had nowhere special to be, I would head for the mosque or the park. The mosque was a great sanctuary, clean and cool, and an excellent place to think and pray for help and guidance. I would browse in the air-conditioned bookstore for as long as I could.

I heard that Hakim, my friend from my maths course, had gone to London, where he was working as a taxi driver. I went to his father's shop to get his phone number. When I rang Hakim he was surprised and pleased to hear from me. 'Yeah, it's OK here, Waheed,' he told me. 'I'm doing fine. It's not hard to find work. And if you want to study, the government helps.'

Next I consulted my physiology teacher from the Islamic University. Concerned for my welfare, he had stayed in touch and was a good friend to me. He gave me a tape-player to keep me company in my muddy cell and pressed a few rupees into my hand to help me out with my rent from time to time. Although he was supportive of my plan, he could not give me much practical guidance. Then I had a stroke of luck. The children I taught had two uncles I often used to chat to at their house. I hadn't seen one of them in a while, and when I asked after him his brother, Samad, told me he had moved to the UK. This seemed like a good opportunity to gather some more information, and the next time I saw Samad I asked his advice. He knew the travel agency that had made the arrangements for his brother and obligingly came into town with me to point it out to me.

The agency was in a side street off the Khyber Bazaar between a shop selling rugs and a restaurant. A few days later I called in. The man I spoke to asked me quite a few questions and then disappeared into a back office. A few moments later, he returned and invited me through the door. In the air-conditioned back office, the boss sat in a big chair. He was an overweight man in his forties, sporting a ring with a diamond in it and a gold Rado watch, the brand of choice in our part of the world for those who have made it and want to make sure everyone knows it. He invited me to take a seat on an expensive-looking sofa.

Western governments, he told me, were very aware of the desperate situation in Afghanistan and welcomed refugees. I emphasized that I would need to obtain the appropriate permissions and visas. 'As well as arranging your flights, we can offer a superior service which includes processing your passport and refugee visa for the US, UK or Germany,' he said. 'But there are complicated and sensitive political issues involved. The good news is that we can deal with all the paperwork for you. But if you want us to arrange your travel you will need to leave it all in my hands.' He then quoted me an astronomical price. I thanked him politely and said that my plans were at an early stage, but I'd think it over.

I visited several other travel agencies. I soon realized that some subtlety was required. I would ask about a flight to Dubai or a Haj trip, and then enquire, as if as an afterthought, about London or Canada, and whether they arranged visas. Some agents said curtly that they didn't do that kind of business. Others would have a word with their bosses who, behind closed doors, offered me similar packages and quotes as the first travel agent. I'd suspected that he had been trying to fleece me, but it seemed this was the going rate. How on earth was I going to raise $10,000?

My physiology teacher introduced me to some friends of his who had spent time in the UK.

'There are great opportunities for talented people to study there,' they told me. 'If you can raise the money to get out, you will be able to pay it back. Afghanistan is screwed. You only have to look at what the Taliban are doing in the provinces. You have no future there.

'Refugees are always talking about the West. Don't be another one who just talks about it: go, go, go!'

I looked at other options and travel schemes, spoke to anyone I thought might have any useful light to shed and made endless lists of positives and negatives. I came to the conclusion that the first travel agent I had visited was the best choice. If I were able to find this money, which was a big 'if', it was unthinkable that I should put it at risk, so I had to be sure that everything was in order and my refugee status was watertight. You heard stories of people being sent back and at least this agent had a verifiable track record in that he had successfully arranged Samad's brother's journey to the UK.

I had now convinced myself that, whatever it took to make it possible, and however long, a new life abroad was my only chance. I was now going to have to convince my parents. They had no idea I had left the Islamic University or that I had been living alone in Tehkal. My father trusted me to look after myself and pretty much left me to it; my mother would only have worried. I'd needed space to decide what I wanted to do before talking to them about it. Now that I had, it was time to go home.

By the summer of 1998, the Taliban were in control of about 80 per cent of Afghanistan and their iron grip on society was tightening. The only real remaining opposition was the Northern Alliance, a united military force established by Ahmad Shah Massoud and Barhanuddin Rabbani. Both General Dostum and Gulbuddin Hekmatyar had fled the country. Within the territory he controlled, Massoud set up democratic institutions and signed a declaration of women's rights. Half a million to a million Afghans fled to these areas.

In the ruins of Kabul, there was still no infrastructure, no running water, intermittent electricity and few working telephones, and the economy was through the floor. Although it was largely quiet and safe, the occasional bomb or rocket still shattered the ghostly city, courtesy of the rebel groups.

Afghanistan was now cut off from the rest of the world. At its peak, the Taliban regime was recognized by only three other foreign powers: Pakistan, Saudi Arabia and the United Arab Emirates. International sanctions led to the airport being closed. The Taliban seldom communicated directly with non-Muslim outsiders and they were mistrustful of the international aid organizations and NGOs whose help had been vital to the survival of the people of Kabul through the civil war. As a result, these organizations were already finding it increasingly difficult to deliver aid. The UN accused the Taliban of starving people to further their military agenda and of using humanitarian aid as a weapon of war.

As well as causing alarm in the West, the Taliban were antagonizing the Americans by giving shelter to Osama bin Laden, the stateless Saudi Arabian leader of Al-Qaeda, a transnational network of extremists that had put itself on the map in August by bombing the US embassies in Nairobi and Dar-es Salaam, killing more than 200 people. Bin Laden, who had founded Al-Qaeda in the late 1980s while supporting the Mujahideen during the Soviet war, had in recent years forged close links with Mullah Omar and had been living in Afghanistan since 1996.

That summer, the UN and NGO offices in Kabul were shut down, exacerbating the shortages and resulting in a huge hike in food prices. Before long the economic situation would become so bad that it would take my father six months to earn enough money to buy a sack of rice.

At home, I told my parents about my sabbatical from the Islamic University and began to broach the subject, lightly at first, of going abroad to study and work to help support the family. Neither of them said very much.

My dad taught me to drive so that I could take his taxi out sometimes. The streets were pretty empty and all of the passengers were Taliban. Nobody else could afford to hire a cab. But it gave him a break and me the opportunity to earn some money. I insisted that I was going to save up to pay for my journey to the West, although we all knew that was never going to be achievable.

In Kolula-Pushta I helped with the logistics of the carpet-weaving operation, collecting equipment and yarn and dealing with the carpet traders. The deadlines were pitiless. My mum and sisters would have to start work ahead of early-morning prayers, before it was even light. It was complicated and labour-intensive. The yarn was all one colour, for example, and had to be dyed before it was woven. My mum handled this process, and the other preparations for weaving, ran the household, took care of little Farid and rushed around putting cream on raw hands. Everyone else worked all day at the loom, under the watchful eye of Zari and Gululai, the bosses. Only Khalid and Javid had time out to attend school. As boys, they were the only ones permitted to go.

Television was banned, films were banned, music was banned. Even kite-flying was banned. It is a common belief that all sport was banned as well, but this is not strictly true, except in the cases of those sports deemed unIslamic. Women could not participate, of course, and men had to be appropriately dressed, which meant footballers, for example, playing in long-sleeved shirts, long shorts and long socks. But I was able to join a Taekwondo club, and cricket, volleyball and boxing flourished under the regime, especially as other leisure activities were so limited.

There was a twelve-team soccer league operating at the Ghazi Stadium throughout the time the venue was being used for the beatings, executions, mutilations and stonings for which it was more notorious. My dad remembers that these would be announced on the radio, a tactic used to strike fear into the hearts of the public to remind them of the consequences of disobedience.

The radio was our only connection with the outside world. I listened to the BBC World Service assiduously, trying to stay abreast of what was happening but mainly to keep learning and polishing my English. We still had our video-player, kept out of sight in a cupboard, and there were videotapes in secret circulation, smuggled in from Pakistan. We swapped them around with other families, and we all knew the shops that rented them out illicitly under the counter. Videos were easy enough to hide beneath a roomy *perahan tunban*.

I had a cassette-player and some tapes of Afghan and Bollywood music which I hid under my seat when I was out driving. I could play them while I was on my own in the cab as long as I kept the windows wound up. I also had a tape of Islamic chanted songs, *nasheeds*, which were allowed. If I was stopped, I produced this for the scrutiny of the Taliban enforcers. I was stopped often and usually asked for my licence. I would explain politely and apologetically that I didn't have it with me. Then I would mention, as if in passing, that I had just brought some Taliban soldiers into town, drop some made-up names into the conversation and they would invariably let me go. In the end I applied for and was granted a licence (the minimum age of eighteen wasn't in force then). The examination didn't involve any actual driving, just answering some questions about road signs.

My Taliban passengers usually spent their journeys trying to recruit me to their cause. 'Listening to *nasheeds*, eh? A fine, devout boy like you would do well to join us in the holy war.' They would tell me inspirational stories, talk of how by fighting for them I would be fighting for God and eulogize the spiritual rewards that could be mine. The angle was always religious, never military or political. In Islam there are many kinds of *jihad*, or struggle, including the greater *jihads*, the struggles against our own base instincts. None of them describes or permits terrorism. It was grooming, plain and simple. I tried to keep my responses neutral. By the time they got out my heart would be thumping and my palms clammy.

My parents were increasingly worried about my vulnerability to the Taliban. Boys with no prospects were joining them all the time. If I stayed in Kabul, with no glimpse of a future and every day just a scrabble to survive, how long would it take for me to be worn down by their blandishments? Might I conclude that the only way I could ensure a decent life for myself and my family was to give in to their hollow promises of riches and rewards in this world and the next?

Young men were not being forced into their ranks but there was every fear that it might only be a matter of time before fighting for the Taliban became unavoidable. Years of my dad's life had been blighted by the threat of conscription and he didn't want the same for me.

Barely a day went by without me making the case for studying abroad and my parents knew I was not going to let it go. I talked about the travel agent and made it sound as if the arrangements would be straightforward. I reasoned that I had proved I could stand on my own two feet by living independently in Pakistan; that I could send money home to ensure the survival of the family.

My parents had always supported me unwaveringly and taken the long view of education. They never looked at it simply in terms of short-term financial gain, understanding that ultimately it would lead to a better life for us all. I could tell that my father, the risk-taker and optimist, was coming round to the idea of sending me away. My mother, though, was silent. She knew people whose sons had moved to the West and lost touch with their families for ever. All she would say was, 'I don't know. I don't know. I can't let go of my son.'

Although they were concerned that something bad could happen to me in a distant land, they were well aware that nowhere in the world was my life more at risk than in Afghanistan. We had seen terrible times before but, with the political situation in constant flux, there had always been a chance that the next development would pave the way for improvement. Now the Taliban were only growing stronger and, by the spring of 1999, with no hint on the horizon of any opposition capable of toppling them, it felt as if we had reached the end of the road. Even my dad's reservoir of hope had been drained dry.

The final straw was the night our neighbour's house took the full force of a rocket fired by rebels who had been aiming at a military presence on a distant hillside. We were lurched awake by the screech of a missile that seemed to be heading straight for us. Somehow it missed us and instead destroyed another family. Their house was flattened and they were all killed, little children I'd seen playing marbles out on the street only that day. We were devastated. This tragedy underlined the hard truth that the threat of warfare was never far from our door. Somebody had to get out and secure the future of our family from a place of safety, and that somebody had to be me.

7

The Weight of the World

I SET OFF FOR Peshawar the very next morning. My father would join me once he had raised the funds for my escape, but my heart was breaking with the knowledge that this would be the last time I'd see my mum for a long time. Perhaps for ever. A couple of my sisters performed a traditional parting ritual, holding the Quran above my head as I passed through the door and following behind me, splashing water on the ground where I had walked.

My mother clung to me and kissed me fiercely, sobbing uncontrollably. I set my jaw and suppressed my tears. I was the big man, going off to save my family. It was my duty to stay strong. But when I got into the taxi taking me to the bus station, the dam burst and I cried my eyes out the whole way.

In Peshawar I asked Samad to come with me to the travel agency as I was not old enough to enter into a contract without adult representation. I shook hands on the deal on my father's behalf. There was no turning back now: I had committed Dad to honouring it.

There followed an anxious two or three weeks while I waited for him to come with the funds, which were to be held by a third party until I reached my destination. I still did not know for certain where that would be: it depended, apparently, on the availability of 'refugee visas'. Eventually he arrived and placed the money safely with a cashier he knew in the Chowk-Yadgar exchanges. I was alarmed to learn that to provide it he had sold the family house at Kolula-Pushta.

'Don't worry about us,' he said firmly. 'We will be OK.' I promised I would pay back every last dollar as soon as I could.

Now it was all systems go. Dad joined me in Khala Jan's guest room for another week while I took the bus in and out of the city in response to messages from the travel agent.

He was difficult to pin down, all smiles one minute and curt orders the next. He would not discuss anything on the phone and drip-fed me information. I would be summoned into the office and told only what the next step would be. And he didn't appreciate questions. I must travel with two bags. One would be checked in and should contain only Western clothes. I need not concern myself with that: they would sort it out for me. I could take a small bag in the aircraft cabin for whatever I needed on the flight, but I shouldn't bring anything from home.

The next time I saw him, he was in expansive mood. 'Congratulations!' he beamed. From a drawer in his desk, he produced a burgundy-coloured passport stamped with gold insignia and handed it to me. 'European Union,' I read. 'United Kingdom of Great Britain and Northern Ireland.' I was going to London.

I was thrilled. London was where I most wanted to be. I leafed through the precious passport. My face, in the photograph taken here in the office, stared back at me but my name wasn't quite right and neither was my date of birth. When I pointed this out, he dismissed my concerns with a wave of his hand. 'This is just for your travel. Once you arrive, you can change it.'

He motioned to me to give him back the passport and put it away in his drawer for safekeeping.

Now he was talking again about the international sensitivities of the situation. Provided I followed his instructions to the letter, all would be well. At Heathrow Airport, to avoid bureaucratic entanglements, I must dispose of my passport in the lavatories before going through border control. This was very important. Once I was out of the airport I would be fine. I opened my mouth to speak but he raised his hand to silence me. Everything was almost ready, he said. I should now buy some Western clothes in the Khyber Bazaar for my journey and get myself a haircut.

I was uneasy about the anomalies in the passport. But it was too late to back out now and I did not want to alarm my dad. He was gambling almost everything we had on this one chance and I could not afford to jeopardize it by looking for problems. I had no choice but to trust the agent.

A couple of days later we received the message that I would be leaving on a flight the following morning. I must present myself at the agency at 6am sharp. There my dad and I found two other boys who would be travelling with me. Nadir was about my age and Ahmed a bit older, about nineteen or twenty. We were all nervous and excited, but shy of one another. I felt self-conscious in the jeans I'd bought in the market. I'd never worn jeans before and they were stiff and uncomfortable.

The agent handed out our passports and papers and gave us each $120 for the journey. 'Everybody loves the dollar, eh? Now, remember everything I have told you.' He said a prayer and, with that, we were hustled out.

I had so little time to say goodbye to my dad. We were both crying. He kissed me on each eye. 'Be strong,' he said. 'God be with you.'

'Jan Agha, don't worry,' I told him, choking back the tears. It was only now hitting me that it was possible I might never see any of my family again. 'I don't know when, but I will find a way to get in touch.'

One of the staff drove us to Peshawar Airport. Although I had passed it many times on the bus, I had never set foot inside the terminal. Everyone seemed to be in a mad rush, pushing and shoving in the melting heat. 'Don't lose sight of me,' called the man from the travel agency. He chivvied us at the desk where we had to check in our luggage and herded us towards passport control. 'If anyone asks,' he said, 'say that you live in the UK and have been home on a visit.'

When I questioned why we couldn't just tell the truth, he said the officials 'wouldn't understand'.

The border officer took an age checking my passport. 'What was the purpose of your visit to Pakistan?' he asked.

'I am a student. I have been visiting my family.'

Time seemed to stand still. Then I saw an exchange of glances between the officer and the travel agent. My heart lurched. The agent nodded almost imperceptibly and the officer stamped the passport with a flourish and waved me through impatiently.

I had watched plenty of military planes taking off and landing but I had never heard the engine of such a huge aircraft close up, or seen inside one. It was majestic. Outside the June heat was ferocious, but the air in the cabin was deliciously cool. The space was bigger and more comfortable than I'd expected. Delighted to find I had a window seat, I sat down and tried to figure out the seat belt.

When the engines revved for take-off I experienced no nerves: my excitement and wonder at the power and pull of the plane as the wheels left the ground outweighed any sense of fear. The pain and panic came from the realization that I was leaving the only kind of life I'd ever known. I felt the tears streaming down my cheeks and turned my face to the window. Looking down at the houses encircling the airport, I was astonished at how green the land around them seemed. As we soared high above the slums of Tehkal I held on to the image I had constructed of myself as the saviour of my family, and gradually the heartache gave way to glorious visions of what my new life would have in store.

I met up with Ahmed and Nadir when we landed that afternoon in Dubai for a scheduled stopover. My heart thumped violently every time I had to show my passport, but we moved smoothly through the controls and reported to a designated reception desk as instructed. We had reservations at a hotel and a car was sent to pick us up from the airport and take us there.

Dubai was still under construction and as we drove through the hot, humid landscape in our air-conditioned taxi, we gazed out of the windows at the tall, futuristic buildings springing up, all smooth concrete and glass. I had never stayed at a proper hotel before. And we had a room each, on the fourth and fifth floors. We were so impressed to find them equipped with telephones that we couldn't resist calling each other on the slightest pretext. We arranged to take a nap and meet later for something to eat. I couldn't sleep. I prayed, and looked out of my huge window at the city and the people walking around below. This world seemed totally unreal and none of it was sinking in.

We had vouchers for the hotel restaurant but the menu was incomprehensible to us. Then we noticed, to our relief, a more casual dining area where kebabs were being served. My fellow travellers were far more laid-back and happy-go-lucky than I was. We didn't speak much of what we had left behind or the futures we hoped for. We were just living in the moment.

After we ate Ahmed wanted to go out and have a look around. 'We have to see a bit of Dubai,' he reasoned. Although more inclined to stay safely in the hotel, I agreed. I took care to make sure we didn't get lost. We avoided the smart malls and browsed in a smaller souvenir shop. I tried on a pair of sunglasses with an eye-watering $20 price tag and looked in the mirror at an unfamiliar, sophisticated Waheed. They felt like something a Londoner would wear. I splashed out, wondering what my mum would have had to say if she knew how much they cost.

In the morning a car came to take us to the airport and we checked in our bags and boarded another plane, already accustomed to the routine. It was only after collecting our boarding passes that we discovered we would be making another stop, in Amsterdam, before reaching London. None of us knew where Amsterdam was.

On the long flight, between spells of reading and dozing, my worries began to gnaw away at my mind. One thing I was certain of was that I fulfilled all the criteria for asylum in the UK. I had checked that for myself. And I had been told by several armchair experts that once I set foot on UK soil I couldn't be sent back. But I was troubled by the inaccuracies in my passport and about the ways in which the instructions we had been given did not stack up. It hadn't helped that the agent had been so secretive. We had been given no advice on how to respond if things did not go according to plan. Ever since I'd first been shown my passport, I had been composing answers to the type of questions I thought I might be asked on my arrival and now I rehearsed my script in my head.

When we landed in Amsterdam we were told we would just be changing planes and needed to wait airside for our connecting flight. It was a relief not to have my passport checked again but I was becoming more and more anxious. At last we boarded our flight to Heathrow. We had no concept of how far we had left to go.

On this last flight Ahmed and Nadir were seated quite near me. It was Ahmed who came up with the idea of burning our passports in the plane lavatory. He had a lighter, he said. I was dubious. It was not what we had been instructed to do. He went off to the toilet. When he returned to his seat, Nadir took the lighter and followed suit. Now I was the only one left in possession of a passport I had been told to destroy before going through border control. I would have to burn mine as well.

It was probably going last that led to my downfall. There was already an acrid smell emanating from the lavatory as I tried unsuccessfully to set fire to my passport. It wouldn't burn. I put it in the loo but it wouldn't flush. By now someone was banging on the door. 'You are not allowed to smoke in the lavatory. Open up!' In a panic,

I fished the soggy, half-burned passport out of the toilet, wrapped it in paper and put it in the bin. But I had taken too long. The cabin crew were forcing the door.

One steward pulled me out while another retrieved the remains of the passport from the bin. Other passengers were pointing out Ahmed and Nadir. The crew moved all three of us to seats nearer the front of the plane where they could keep an eye on us and one of the stewards called ahead to Heathrow asking for the flight to be met by police.

The bottom fell out of my world. I was convinced that the plane was going to circle, turn round and fly us back. But when the wheels bumped on to the tarmac, I felt a flutter of hope in spite of myself. A mantra was drumming through my head: 'Remember, once you have set foot on British soil, they can't send you back.' But surely we would be sent back, if not on this plane, then on another. As we taxied towards the terminal I could see police cars parked down on the ground, lights flashing, six or seven of them.

The airbridge clunked on to the plane, the doors opened and the other passengers disembarked. We were kept back, guarded by a steward. Then three or four police officers boarded. They handcuffed me. I was only metres away from the country I fully believed was waiting to welcome me. 'This is a mistake,' I told them. 'This is not correct. I haven't done anything wrong. I have been accepted by the UK as a refugee.'

'Where's your passport?'

I had no simple answer to that. I saw that Ahmed and Nadir were also being cuffed. I had no idea what to do. As they led us out of the door and on to the airbridge, instinct kicked in. I broke free of the grip of one of the policemen. Another officer grabbed me. Terrified and desperate, I pushed him away. A third officer seized hold of me roughly and held me down, hard. There was a boot pinning my face to the floor of the airbridge and one of the policemen was sitting on my back. They cuffed my hands tightly, behind my back this time, and led me down a set of steps on to the tarmac and into a waiting van.

The tarmac! For a few moments, my feet had touched British soil. I had a fleeting, grim sense of achievement. Perhaps it was true that they couldn't send me back now. I caught a glimpse of a cloudy evening sky and felt the gentle, cool air on my face before I was bundled into the back with Ahmed and Nadir. 'This is your fault,' said Ahmed angrily. 'It's because of you we were caught!' He cursed me furiously in Dari.

I was taken on my own to a cell in the terminal. There was a bench and a tiny spot of grey light from a window in the ceiling. Plane engines roared overhead. After what felt like a long time there was a knock and someone opened a hatch in the door to talk to me from the other side. He said he was my solicitor. I was going to be charged with possession of a false passport and assaulting a police officer. I didn't even know what 'assault' meant.

I could just about see him through the hatch. He was Asian and he wore a suit and tie. He was speaking to me very fast in English, as if he was reciting something he knew off by heart.

I needed to explain. My English was rudimentary and my words gushed out in what must have been an unintelligible torrent. I had escaped from Afghanistan, where my life was at risk. I had been accepted by the British government as a refugee.

'No, you haven't.'

'What?'

'You haven't been accepted as a refugee. You are in this country illegally.'

I could not comprehend this. 'What is going to happen to me?'

'Well, you will go to prison.'

'How long for?'

'Probably a year and a half. And then you will be sent back home.'

I was distraught. I didn't understand these charges. The solicitor didn't even explain to me what the next step would be. He closed the hatch and went away, leaving me sobbing and trying to get my head round this new, harsh reality. I had completely messed up. I was going to prison and my family would be destitute. How could I possibly bear that?

I was exhausted and in shock. I'd been travelling for nearly two days and my eyelids kept closing in spite of my agitation. I alternated between napping on the bench and pacing my cell, trying to calm down and think rationally. By the time the cell door opened again I was resolved. I'd fought for everything I had achieved in my life and I was going to fight for this, too. The UK had given others a chance. Why not me?

A security guard arrived and took me to a room where two policemen were waiting to interview me, with the help of an interpreter. They switched on a tape-recorder and read me my rights. I answered all their questions truthfully and told them exactly who I was and where I was from. I gave them my correct name and date of birth, not those on the half-burned passport they now produced in a plastic bag. Half of my face was still visible in the photograph.

Again I tried to explain that I had been accepted as a refugee but they didn't seem interested in where I was from or how many people were dying there. They were much more concerned about the passport, which they said was a forgery, and where I had got it from. I had broken the law and that was all that mattered. My claim for asylum was not the issue here.

When the interview was over I asked what was going to happen to me next. The police told me I would be going to prison and then would go to court to answer the charges against me. With that, I was returned to my cell. I still didn't know what the word 'assault' meant.

It was an uncomfortable night. Although I had reported that I had pain in my wrists from the cuffs, and in my face, neck and back,

I was never given a medical examination. I wouldn't have realized I was entitled to one. The next morning, I was reunited with Ahmed and Nadir in the back of a van. It was a bright, sunny day, which made me feel a bit better, although I had nothing to feel better about. It was just a relief to be out of that airport cell with the planes screaming overhead. The van driver, a jolly man, had his radio tuned to a station playing upbeat music. We didn't speak much, each of us lost in our own worries.

We couldn't see a lot out of the van, just sunlight and shadows, and most of the short journey was on busy, noisy dual carriageways, but once we turned off on to a smaller road I had a hazy view of streets and people walking about. When the van stopped I was taken out. I was now a guest of Her Majesty at Feltham Young Offenders Institution.

I was detained at Feltham for two weeks. Initially I was just attempting to process the extraordinary events of the previous few days. But as nothing continued to happen, I knew I should try to make contact with somebody. I asked if I could make a phone call. I rang the only person I knew in London: Hakim. I had memorized his number.

'*Waheed?* Where are you?'

'In a prison in London. It's called Feltham.'

'Feltham! What the hell are you doing there?'

He couldn't believe how stupid I'd been. 'You *burned* your passport? What did you do that for? Why didn't you just bin it? Listen, never mind about that now. We need to try to get you out of there.'

Hakim got permission to visit me at short notice and came as soon as he could. I was called from my cell and taken to a large room where other boys were sitting at scarred tables talking to their relatives. Hakim was waving from one of them.

'I have to go to court,' I told him. 'This will be my chance to explain and tell them my story.'

'No, no, you need a solicitor to do that for you.' He unfolded a piece of paper he'd brought with him. 'I will find you a solicitor, don't worry. Just sign this. I need your permission to act on your behalf.'

I signed the document and returned to my cell, to my push-ups and prayers and the preparation of my defence. 'Why are you bothering with that?' asked Ryan. 'That's what your brief is for.'

I was given only a day's notice of my appearance in court. I worked feverishly on my defence statement that night. At the magistrates' court at Uxbridge, I was escorted from another van into the back of another building, catching no more than a tantalizing glimpse of everyday life going on in the streets of London.

There I ran into Ahmed. He had calmed down since I'd last seen him and while we waited to be processed we chatted about what we would do when we got out. If we got out. He seemed much more clued up about the UK than I was. He had a cousin here he would be living with and plans to take a computer course. IT, he said, paid well.

The solicitor engaged for me by Hakim arrived. He was Asian, too.

'Today we are here for a bail hearing.'

'What is bail?'

'To get you out of prison. Today. You can stay with your friend Hakim, which means you have an address, so that is good.'

'Am I a refugee?'

'No, you are not a refugee.'

'Can I speak to the judge?'

'No.'

'Just for five minutes? Just to explain.'

He seemed irritated by my questions. All the time we were talking, he was jiggling his leg impatiently under the table.

'Don't worry! We will get to all that. Today is just to get you bail.'

'I am not guilty!'

'You have admitted that you pushed that police officer.'

'But I didn't mean to hurt him. I was trying to protect myself.'

I felt it was likely that I had come off worst in any case. My wrists were still marked and painful two weeks after my arrest.

I was not reassured by the prospect of this bail. Placing my fate in the hands of others hadn't worked out too well for me so far and I was clueless about the system I had been thrown into. I went into the courtroom fully expecting to be sent back to jail and came out bewildered and delighted to have been released into the care of a social worker, on condition that I stayed with Hakim. I would have to come back to court at a later date to answer the charges against me.

I was allowed to phone Hakim from an office.

'Wait there. I'll be there in an hour.'

Ahmed also got bail. What happened to Nadir I never knew. I don't remember him being present at that hearing. I think his parents were in the UK so his case may have been handled differently. I trust he was safely reunited with them one way or another.

Hakim offered Ahmed a lift to Paddington Station, where he could catch a train to wherever it was his cousin lived. As we left the court a policeman called out my name. I froze. I knew it. There had been a mistake. I was going back to Feltham.

He was waving to me. 'You forgot your luggage, son!'

And there was my case and the small bag I'd had with me on the plane – and the possessions I'd handed over at Feltham: my watch, my new sunglasses and my remaining $100. I'd forgotten all about them. I put on the sunglasses, the symbol of my new life, and stepped into Hakim's car.

At last I was able to see something of the huge city I would be calling home. The sun was setting and it was a beautiful evening. There was a lot of traffic but the drivers were so calm and polite and everywhere there was a sense of order, clear air, cleanliness. All the roads were smooth, even the little side roads. In Kabul they were full of rocket holes. Even in Peshawar, the most sophisticated city I knew, the streets were dirty and chaotic, and although the main routes were paved, the moment you turned off them they tapered off into muddy, rutted tracks.

We said goodbye to Ahmed at Paddington. Was he able to stay in England and get his high-earning job in computers? I don't know. It was the last time I ever saw him.

Hakim told me that his flat was not far now, somewhere called Portobello Road. The streets along the way were lined with elegant white houses, their doorways framed by tall columns. It started to rain gently. I could see the drops landing on the street and on the windscreen, smoothed away by the wipers. I felt brand new.

Part Two

8

Finding My Feet

HAKIM'S FLAT, WHICH HE shared with a couple of other guys, was on the second floor above a shop, a short walk from Ladbroke Grove Station. Two more friends, Sharif and his brother Rafi, lived in the flat below on the first floor. I would be sleeping on Hakim's living-room sofa.

I was so excited to be in London, and to be free. I kept forgetting I was only out on bail. I just wanted to enjoy this time. I was fascinated by everything. The streets, though teeming with men, women, kids and traffic, held no fear. Their unbroken rows of buildings stood firm and in good repair, with no bullets in the walls. In the sky there was nothing but the white vapour trails left by the airliners gliding soundlessly high above us. The people living and working in Portobello Road appeared to come from all over the world. I couldn't get over how many nationalities I came across, some of which I'd never heard of.

The first thing I needed to do was to get in touch with my parents. It had been over two weeks since I'd said goodbye to my dad in Peshawar. I found them still in Kolula-Pushta, where they had to be fetched by a neighbour I was able to reach by phone. My mum was in floods of tears. Unfortunately, news of my imprisonment had travelled fast. My dad had been informed by the agent – or, as I should more accurately describe him, people-smuggler – when he handed over the money. Once I had arrived in the UK, this man's job was done. He must have had some way of checking I'd made it, perhaps someone working at the airport who reported back to him. What happened to me after that wasn't his problem.

My mother, whose knowledge of prisons was confined to what went on in Afghan jails, was overjoyed that I was even still alive. 'Did they beat you up?' she asked. I played down the situation, assuring her that it had just been a temporary measure while my refugee status was being verified.

My next task was to find a job. I was desperate to start paying my father back as soon as possible and I could hardly expect Hakim to support me. I was in such a hurry to show willing that, within a couple of days, I was hawking semi-precious stones for Hakim on Portobello Market. He had some lapis lazuli brought from home that he would sell to regular contacts from time to time to top up his finances. While he was at work, I decided I'd give him a helping hand. I enjoyed interacting with the passers-by, channelling my dad's affability and sales techniques. I made £100 for Hakim, to his surprise and my satisfaction.

I was not, my social worker had told me, allowed to work. And I would not be entitled to housing benefit until my sixteenth birthday on 5 August. I don't remember school being mentioned but it wouldn't have been worth him starting that process. The summer term was almost over and, after my birthday, only a few weeks away, the state was no longer obliged to educate me.

'Where do I start looking for a job?' I asked my new flatmates. They suggested I tried the nearby Edgware Road, a cosmopolitan area where the workforce tended to come and go and employers were willing to pay cash in hand. 'Look for grocery shops or chicken shops,' they advised.

One of them dropped me off in his taxi at Edgware Road the next morning. I enquired at several places, without success, before a notice in a shop window caught my eye: 'Staff needed'. It was neither a chicken shop nor a grocery store but a place that sold gifts, perfume mainly, and bits and pieces for travellers and exiles – phone cards, watches, gadgets.

A guy behind the till sent me downstairs to the basement, where an enormous man sat at his desk. 'I've come about the job,' I said.

'Take a seat. I'm Patrick. Well, what can you do?'

He had an unfamiliar accent that I would later learn was Irish.

'You have an amazing shop. I can sell things for you.'

'Have you got any experience of selling things?'

I explained that I was a refugee and how, back in Afghanistan, I had helped my dad to sell antiques. 'I was very good,' I assured him.

'A refugee, eh? How old are you?'

'Fifteen – but I will be sixteen next month.'

'Do you have a work permit?'

'No. But I must work. I have a large family at home to support. I love working and I am a very, very hard worker.'

Patrick didn't reply. If I didn't say something else quickly to convince him that I would be a valuable employee, the next words out of his mouth were going to be 'I'm sorry'.

I'd heard some customers in the shop speaking Arabic. 'I can speak Arabic,' I added. 'And Farsi. And Hindi and Urdu.'

'Oh?' He mulled this over for a moment. 'When can you start?'

'Now, if you want me to.'

'OK. I'll give you a chance. I will need to pay you in cash because you don't have a work permit. Just don't be telling anybody.'

I was delighted. In less than a week I had somehow, through a combination of tugging on heart strings and demonstrating my keenness, persuaded someone to give me a break. Looking back, I can see how vulnerable I was to all manner of exploitation, but I was lucky. Patrick was firm and demanding but he was very fair. And my wages were better than I'd been led to expect. He was paying me the same as his other staff, even though he could have got away with less. He had a soft spot for me and would often take me to one side to ask if I was doing OK and whether I was eating properly.

That morning I went back upstairs and set to work. The two guys chilling behind the counter looked on, eyebrows raised, as I dashed around, straightening things on shelves, asking endless questions and greeting customers with charm and enthusiasm. They must have loved me. After a couple of days, one of them finally said, 'Waheed, please, just take it easy, OK?'

The shop was open from 8am until 12am and we worked in two shifts, one supervisor and two staff on each. I was put on the evening shift, from 4pm to midnight. When I received my first brown wage packet I bought a jacket for £5 from Portobello Market. I had little more than the clothes I stood up in. The case packed for me in Peshawar had been crammed with random, ropey old stuff.

Later I added a pair of green trousers with a nice sheen to them that had caught my eye. Afghans like shiny things. Suffice it to say I was not into Western fashion then and it took me a long time to find my own style. I wore the same pair of trainers, purchased in the Khyber Bazaar, for two years. My only other investment was a mobile phone, without which I'd have been unable to function. I was determined that every last penny would go home to my parents. As I didn't start work in the shop until 4pm, I immediately searched for an additional job and found one as a cleaner at a block of flats in the Edgware Road.

I was not able to stay at Hakim's flat for much longer than a week and had to come and go surreptitiously while I was there because the landlady did not allow guests. She made a good profit from renting to people on housing benefit. It meant she was being paid per person, rather than per room or flat, because the housing benefit for each tenant came to her directly from the Department of Social Security. She didn't care how many people were packed into her properties like sardines as long as she was getting paid for all of them. She would secretly let herself into the flats when everyone was at work to make sure nobody else was staying there and getting a free ride.

In case of emergencies, my parents had given me the phone number of a distant relative living in London. I had met him perhaps twice, as a young boy, but I gave him a call and he took me in. He was a taxi driver and shared a flat in Hounslow, in the western outskirts of London, with about four or five other Afghan taxi drivers. By the time I finished work at the shop the Tube had stopped running, which meant a long, slow journey home by night bus. I didn't get back there until about two or three in the morning and then I had to be up again to go back to my cleaning job.

The flat was already bursting at the seams so I slept on the living-room floor. The men worked round the clock and there were people coming in and going out all day and all night, stepping over me to get to their beds or the front door. It was not ideal, but it was only for a few weeks, and I was very grateful: I could have found myself sleeping on the streets.

While staying at Hounslow I had to go back to court to face those charges. I took the Tube out to Uxbridge full of dread that my new life would be over before it had even begun. What would I do if I was sent back to prison?

I was not optimistic when I saw that the officer I was accused of assaulting had come to the courtroom with his arm in a sling. But I was blessed in the choice of barrister the solicitors had made for my case. I did not meet Russell Steadman until I arrived at Uxbridge Magistrates' Court.

'Can I speak to the judge this time?' I had my defence all ready.

Mr Steadman told me that the case would be heard by a magistrate, not a judge. I began to gabble so fast in my haste to tell him everything that I was tripping over myself. He was very kind. He sat me down and went to buy me a coffee. 'Have you eaten?' He returned with a sandwich as well. Then he took me clearly and calmly through what was going to happen.

The question of whether I would be allowed to stay in the UK would be dealt with separately. Everyone understood my situation, but this case was about the criminal charges, which related to possessing a false passport and assault. I would be entering pleas of not guilty on both counts and the charges would need to be defended on a legal basis. He had the knowledge and experience of the law to do this, and therefore he needed to speak for me. He did an expert job.

I was unaware of how blessed I was, too, in the timing of my arrival in the UK. The matter of the false passport was, I later learned, a serious one. If the authorities had chosen to throw the book at me, they could have charged me with possession of false documents with intent, punishable by up to ten years in prison. Even the lesser charge of simple possession carried a maximum sentence of two years. The passport provided for me was unquestionably false, of course. It was somebody else's with my photograph carefully superimposed on it, a type of forgery that could be got away with in the days before biometrics. And there was no such thing as a 'refugee visa'.

However, this issue was the subject of some controversy. The UK had an obligation to honour Article 31 of the UN Convention relating to the status of refugees, which stipulates that asylum-seekers with false documents should not be penalized, provided they 'present themselves without delay' to the authorities and 'show good cause for their illegal entry or presence'. Inevitably, many people fleeing war and oppression do not have legitimate immigration papers, or any way of obtaining them, and therefore have no other means of accessing a 'friendly shore'.

The interpretation of this article in the UK had been inconsistent, leading in the previous few years to a large number of refugees being routinely convicted and sentenced – a high proportion of them, according to campaigners, asylum-seekers of good character who had pleaded guilty on the advice of duty solicitors, some of them detained while in transit to another destination. Having such a conviction on their records prejudiced their asylum claims in the UK and often barred them from entering other countries.

At the end of July a case was due to be heard in the divisional court, which would ultimately result in legal clarification of this point. Russell Steadman secured a deferral of the charges against me in the meantime. When we returned to court a couple of weeks or so later, the magistrate was not in a position to pursue the false passport charge and had clearly decided that it wasn't in the public interest to take the assault matter any further. The charges were dropped. I was free to go.

It was a long while before I pieced together some of the likely reasons for what had happened to me and began to realize just how dangerous unwittingly putting my life in the hands of people-traffickers could have proved. There are those who think nothing of pocketing the money they are paid to smuggle refugees and simply killing them. I might have disappeared without a trace: that taxi to Peshawar airport could have been taking me anywhere.

But all that mattered to me back in the summer of 1999 was walking away from that courtroom with the threat of prison lifted. Russell Steadman wished me good luck, gave me his business card and invited me to contact him if I needed anything. He knew, he later told me, that although I was now in a much better position I still had a difficult road ahead of me. He was right. Establishing my residency would prove a slow process – that was not resolved until 2002 – and until then I couldn't feel fully secure and was not officially allowed to have a job. In the meantime, the Home Office simply renewed my temporary residency every couple of months or so.

The social worker remained assigned to me until my sixteenth birthday. After that I was entitled to housing benefit and able to return to Portobello Road. Hakim suggested I shared downstairs with Sharif, with whom I got on well. As long as the landlady was being paid for me to be there, she was happy. She would be doubling her money on Sharif's flat. The place was in a horrible condition. The toilet was broken, there was hardly any furniture and one of the beds had holes in it. Sharif and I took it in turns to sleep on the floor.

You could apply to the Home Office for permission to work, but if it was granted, you would lose your housing benefit. The sky-high rents in London were well beyond the reach of people in low-skilled jobs, creating a poverty trap into which many fell and one that was routinely exploited by landlords like ours.

I was rarely in the flat except to sleep. Always on the look-out for extra work, I moved on from the cleaning job to a greengrocer's in Portobello Road. I'd been walking down the road one night on my way back from my shift in the shop when I'd seen the greengrocer's on fire. There seemed to be nobody around so I phoned 999. The next morning I went over to check that everything was OK. The place was open and the greengrocer was clearing up some of the mess left by the firefighters' water hoses. When I explained that I was the one who'd raised the alarm, he thanked me effusively for my intervention. Apparently, it had resulted in the fire brigade arriving quickly enough to contain the fire before it took hold. Seeing a window of opportunity, I asked if there was any possibility of some work in his shop.

He looked me up and down briefly and then said, 'You can start tomorrow if you like.'

The next morning somebody threw me a belt with a money bag attached to it and said, 'There you go, mate.' Within five minutes I was standing there calling out, 'Lovely plums! Two pounds for a quid!' like a local.

I didn't know what half of the fruit and vegetables were. Those I did recognize, I didn't know the names for in English and I mispronounced the ones I read from the greengrocer's handwritten signs. I was constantly asking my workmates for translations ('What is a "geezer"?'). They were a cheery bunch who didn't take life too seriously. They laughed when I pronounced 'courgette' with a hard 'g' and amused themselves by teaching me Cockney rhyming slang and swear words.

After that I got a regular morning job at a busy café in Great Portland Street. The boss, an Egyptian, worked extremely hard, setting a fast pace and handling a rapid turnover of customers. My role was to prep the lunches, finishing at 3pm. From there I would get the Tube to Edgware Road for my evening shift.

Breakfast was a Mars bar or Snickers on the way to work; at night I ate whatever my housemates had left in the kitchen. I spent as little as I could on food. The guy who ran Salwa, an Asian takeaway on the Edgware Road with three or four sit-in tables, would give me a plate of rice and meat for £2 – cheaper than a McDonald's. Sometimes he refused to take any money at all. Those meals were a life-saver.

I was relieved that my temporary residency did not seem to bar me from pursuing educational opportunities, but it was clear that I would have to put that plan on hold for a while. I needed to find my feet first. My immediate priorities were the welfare of my family and working on acquiring permanent residency. The huge sum of money my parents had spent on getting me to London preyed on my mind. So did the image of little Mahvash toiling at the loom, her tiny fingers bleeding.

Within a month of my departure the US had imposed sanctions on Afghanistan, followed in October by the UN Security Council. The ordinary people of Kabul were struggling to survive and I needed to earn as much as I could as quickly as I could to help keep my family fed. With my future in the UK by no means assured, I felt I might be sent home at any moment. The periodic renewal of my temporary admission reminded me that I remained 'liable to be detained'.

In the meantime I had a lot of growing up to do. I was a sixteen-year-old boy going through adolescence alone, outside the social and cultural framework I was used to. Because I was almost always working I couldn't often get to Friday prayers at the local mosque. Instead I brought my prayer mat with me to the shop. Patrick didn't bat an eyelid when he heard me coming down to the basement to pray. The staff were a diverse bunch. My supervisor was Spanish and my co-workers were from all over the place – Bengali, Arab, Sudanese, Egyptian.

The predominance of the clubbing and drinking culture in London surprised me. I wasn't judgemental about it. It was just that, to someone brought up in a Muslim country where it wasn't a feature of social gatherings, the central role alcohol played in so many aspects of British life seemed strange. So did the kaleidoscope of different clothes and styles passing by me every day. Men, women and kids with brightly coloured hair, gel spikes or dreadlocks; guys in sharp suits and ties, or black Goth outfits, or hip-hop gear; women and girls in elegant dresses, jackets and heels or tiny skirts, tops and leggings; ripped jeans and tights.

I had no road map for how I should conduct myself with women and girls. When an attractive customer came into the shop I became tongue-tied and the others teased me: 'Hey, Waheed, the ladies like you!' My Bengali workmate tried to teach me his chat-up lines.

I was shocked at the lack of respect shown to women and older people in London. I would politely hold open doors and give up my seat on the Tube to elderly travellers, while others, it seemed, not only saw nothing wrong with completely ignoring them but sometimes even rushed to beat them to a free seat.

This didn't at all resemble the world of the well-thumbed teach-yourself-English books of my childhood, but it was intriguing, all the same, and the contrasts and surprises were emblematic of the wonderful freedom of the country.

My English was quickly becoming more fluent, but here, too, there was a lot to learn beyond the scope of textbooks. I remember my housemates once sending me out to the Moroccan shop nearby for French bread. I had no idea what that was. I enquired in the shop for 'bread from France', the word 'French' having escaped me, and returned, to howls of complaint, with a loaf of Mother's Pride. Often I would know what a word looked like written down but my attempts to pronounce it were so eccentric that my workmates would have to ask me several times to tell them again what the hell it was I'd just said.

Working every hour I could, I had little time for leisure activities. I was at the shop seven days a week, with extra shifts when I could fit them in, and had to be told that I must take a day off occasionally. There was concern for my health and welfare, certainly, but my wages may also have been unbalancing Patrick's books. Because of all the hours I put in, I was earning more than the supervisor.

After that I'd take perhaps one day off a month, when I might play pool with Sharif in a games arcade at Piccadilly Circus or we'd go to the cinema. Other times I walked, familiarizing myself with the streets and attractions of London. With my body always tired and my mind stimulated continuously by the newness of everything, I could shut out everything else, bury the sorrow of separation from my family and the horrors of the first fifteen years of my life. But those emotions and memories still seeped, unbidden, into my consciousness in the quiet small hours.

I would wake in the night, hit by a sudden wave of sorrow that seemed to come from nowhere, missing my family and crying for my mum, or startled by nightmares in which I was being shot or shelled.

I was disturbed when I began to experience daytime flashbacks. I was waiting one day on a Tube station platform, thinking about nothing in particular, when the roaring wind created by the train rushing through the tunnel towards me catapulted me back into the civil war. Scenes I thought I had banished from my mind played out in front of my eyes like a film.

The sound of the train had evoked the whooshing of a rocket, but any powerful, unexpected noise could do it: a police siren, or a loud bang or crash, and there would be a tank coming towards me. I'd break into a sweat and my whole body would become rigid. 'Loosen up, Waheed,' the guys in the shop would say. 'Look at your hands. You're clenching them so hard, your knuckles are white!'

I was confused by why this was happening to me here, in London, thousands of miles and several years distant from the bombs of

Kabul. But that, of course, is the nature of PTSD. The cause of the trauma may have been removed but the response remains, waiting to be reactivated by some echo of the original trigger, a sight, smell or sound. You get a feeling in the pit of your stomach that something is wrong, that something terrible is about to happen, and your body's automatic fear reflexes are screaming at you to run and take cover.

I dealt with these debilitating episodes using my tried-and-tested coping strategies: prayer, exercise and, late at night before I slept, taking a few moments to reflect on everything I had to be thankful for, everything I had achieved and what I wanted to achieve next. And the nightmares and flashbacks would pass, although I never knew when they might surface again.

I had a great deal to be thankful for. I was safe, I was working hard to help my family and I was living in an amazing city. It was wonderful to sit out on a bench in one of the local squares, just leaning back, watching the birds and the silent aircraft in the sky, enjoying the peace and the clean air and letting go. My favourite part of the day was coming home from work in the early hours when the streets were quiet, but not asleep, their lights still twinkling. I loved the walk back to Portobello Road or riding the bus through beautiful Notting Hill, up front on the top deck, looking out as the tree branches tapped the window, so happy to be in a place where I was free. Here I could see the opportunities all around me. In Afghanistan I couldn't see them anywhere: I'd had to imagine them.

I have always been a night owl. Whether it is my natural body clock or a result of the wakefulness induced by my wartime childhood I can't say. Perhaps a combination of both. Either way, it is ingrained in me now and I still walk, or go for a run, in the peaceful night hours. This is the time when I do my creative thinking and problem-solving. And still, sometimes, the crying for my mum.

9

An Education

AS I GRADUALLY ACCLIMATIZED to my new surroundings, my thoughts turned to how I could connect with the education system. For months I had poured all my energies into work but I was determined to find a way to do both. I had to.

I knew the openings were out there but I had no idea how to access them or how to map out a route to medical school. I asked my housemates: 'How do I become a doctor?' They laughed at me, though not unkindly. 'Oh, come on. You are in London! You have every opportunity to earn money for yourself and your family. Just find a job in a chicken shop. Then, when you're old enough, you can get your driving licence, run a minicab and save up for your own chicken shop. That's how it works for people like us.'

It would be impossible, they told me, to become a doctor here. 'That's only for those with a British education,' said Hakim. 'Not for refugees. We don't have the right schooling and none of our qualifications are the same as theirs. Forget it. Just concentrate on earning some money.'

I didn't forget it. On my walks around the city, I enquired at colleges and checked out GCSE and A-level textbooks and university prospectuses on the internet at the library. There is nothing wrong with aspiring to own a chicken shop if that is your ambition. But it wasn't mine.

I wrestled with the logistics. To study medicine I had to get to university, and for university I needed A-levels. From my research in the library, I tried to compare the British educational yardsticks with the standard I had reached. It gave me cause to be very grateful for that year and a half at the Islamic University at Shamshatoo. Thanks to what I had learned there, I calculated that A-level courses, which consisted of AS-level exams after one year and A-levels after two, should be within my grasp. The syllabuses for GSCEs, the previous level, seemed to cover stuff I mostly already knew.

Because I was receiving government assistance, college fees would be waived. I would have to give up my daytime job in the café to attend classes but I could still do my gift shop shift every day and try to supplement that with some more flexible work.

I'd been given a pay rise at the shop when, a year into the job, the boss had made me supervisor. I had quickly proved to be his best salesman. We had to keep a record of our individual sales and mine were nearly always twice as high as anyone else's, which wasn't surprising as I was probably twice as enthusiastic and worked twice as hard. To me, it seems strange not to want to do your job to the best of your ability, whatever it is. Whether you are sweeping the streets or running a multinational company, what sense of satisfaction is there to be gained from all the time you spend doing it otherwise? Besides, the boss had taken a chance on me and it was my duty to repay his faith.

My obsessive work ethic might not have made me too popular in some workplaces but at Edgware Road my laid-back colleagues just rolled their eyes good-naturedly and left me to get on with it. Increasingly, Patrick treated me as his right-hand man. He would ask me to cash up at night or to help him with the stocktaking, and he began to consult me about plans he had for expanding the shop or introducing new lines. It is a pretty bizarre state of affairs when the employee you rely on the most is the one you are not allowed to put on your payroll.

I decided to apply to the City of Westminster College, a further education college, initially to do two AS-levels, in biology and physics. It was sensible to test the water. I needed to make sure I had gauged the standard correctly and that I could fit study round work. It would be a waste of time and effort to discover that I had aimed too high and end up with nothing to show for it.

With no way of assessing my previous education or qualifications, the college asked me to sit a test to establish that I was capable of handling the courses. To prepare for that, I hunted for textbooks at the library. I passed the test, but only just. While the science all made sense, I realized that my English was not good enough. I was going to have to start improving that very quickly to keep up. I began the courses in the autumn of 2000 and embraced my lessons wholeheartedly, obsessively memorizing chunks of my textbooks. It was such a joy to be learning again.

I was encouraged to find that the work itself was within my comfort zone but having to perform the additional task of translating everything into Farsi in my head to absorb it, and then back into English again when I wrote it down, slowed me up considerably. I soon discovered that this was going to place me at a particular disadvantage in exams, when time was of the essence.

I kept a low profile in class and I doubt I made much of an impression on any of the teachers. The profound unease I had experienced before amid large groups of people reared its head again. My hands would tighten, my palms would begin to sweat and I found it extremely difficult to make eye contact with either teachers or students. I don't think I raised my hand to answer a question in the whole of that year. Just the thought of it would have my heart thumping in my rib cage. It felt as though I would be sticking my head above a parapet right into the sightline of a sniper. Certainly I didn't stand out academically. In one of my biology mocks I got a D. That came as a shock. I knew that I needed to be getting As to make it to medical school and I was going to have to pull up my socks before the final exams.

I probably cut a pretty scruffy figure, too. Partly this was because I didn't want to draw attention to myself, partly simple practicality. After getting home so late every night, I was always in too much of a rush to pay much attention to my appearance in the mornings. Since arriving in the UK I had retained my little beard so there was no need to shave. I would roll out of bed and jump on to the Tube, always reading, whether sitting or strap-hanging. In my lunch break I headed straight for the library. At the end of the day I read my way to my shift at Edgware Road and the books came out again on the bus back to Portobello Road at night.

Early in the term I had taken on another job, on a self-employed basis, which I'd heard about through an Afghan guy I'd met in the college canteen. There were two or three Afghans at City of Westminster. They were on different courses, but I'd stop to say hello if I saw them. One of them worked for an energy company and recruited me as a customer adviser – those salesmen who used to knock on doors offering people deals to change supplier. I could do as many or as few hours as I liked, so I was able to co-ordinate the work with college and my shop job in term-time and ramp it up in the holidays.

There was no opportunity to make friends on my course, but this was to some extent a deliberate policy. I couldn't afford any distractions. If I started spending my lunch breaks in the canteen, or tagging along with the students who hung out on Paddington Recreation Ground on sunny days, I would fall behind. They all seemed very immature to me anyway. I don't mean that as a criticism: those of us taking AS-levels were all sixteen, seventeen years old and it was natural for them to behave like kids sometimes. We *were* kids. Most of them had probably come to the college straight from school and still lived at home with their families. I was the one who was out of step.

Sharif was the only person I spent time with outside work or college. He had given up school and worked in one of the shops owned by our landlady, who was no more sympathetic as an employer than she was as a landlady. 'There are so many options here to study,' I told him. 'You're only nineteen. Don't waste your life.' Most young refugees in London had struggled to attain their safety and freedom and it was upsetting to see some of them drifting when the opportunities to build a better life, whether by learning or earning, were right there within their reach.

Sometimes people just need a little support and encouragement to raise their gaze from the daily grind and see what it is they want to do with their lives. We only get one, after all. Sharif did go back to his studies and eventually he went on to become a pharmacist. I'd like to think I played a part in that.

In January 2001, I received a phone call from a police officer at Heathrow Airport. My heart lurched. Surely I couldn't still be in trouble with them?

'We have a person here who says he is your brother,' he was telling me.

For a moment I was confused. Although the possibility of flying Khalid out to the UK had been discussed, I'd had no idea he was actually coming. Yet this person was unquestionably Khalid. It seemed that my parents, recognizing that his future in Kabul was as bleak as mine had been, and encouraged by my rose-tinted reports from London, had decided to act without involving me, for fear that prior knowledge of his escape might get me into trouble.

As I dashed off to rescue Khalid, I was not looking forward to revisiting the memories of my own incarceration in the bowels of Heathrow. I had never come clean to my parents about exactly what had happened to me. Had they unwittingly sent my brother into the same trap?

Khalid, it turned out, had not used the services of the same 'travel agent' who'd dispatched me to the UK, although the process had been similar. There was no other way of getting out of Afghanistan. Thankfully, he seemed to have been given better advice. At any rate, by luck or design, he had followed procedure, presenting himself to the immigration authorities without delay.

With that procedure requiring Khalid to make a claim for asylum 'as soon as practicable after arrival', there followed a good deal of bureaucracy and the involvement of various agencies, including social services, but the upshot was that he was granted temporary admission to the UK within days. In the meantime, he was allowed to come home with me on condition that he remained in my care at Portobello Road.

When I called my parents my poor mum was inconsolable, overcome by the twin emotions of relief that Khalid was safe and the heartache of now having two sons in a faraway land. 'Make sure you're mother and father to him,' she said. I did the best I could.

Our accommodation was already stretched to the limit and, sooner or later, the landlady was going to find Khalid in residence and go berserk. I had to get us somewhere else to live as a matter of urgency. Sharif and his brother Rafi decided to leave with Khalid and me, and the following month we all moved into a flat in Ravensworth Road in Kensal Green. This one we acquired via a letting agency and it made a pleasant change to be able to come home without discovering that your landlady had been prowling around your rooms.

I got Khalid enrolled at a comprehensive school in Willesden. I gave him money for his basic needs, liaised with the school, attended his parents' evenings, took care of his asylum paperwork and fought his corner on his application for permanent residency. And I was, of course, always on the other end of a phone in case of emergencies. But beyond that, I simply had no time to give him. I was either at work, at college or studying and he had to fend for himself. The best function I could fulfil for him was to be a good role model.

He was only twelve, and I felt for him. He, too, had suffered but, like me, he had been brought up to understand that hard work, dedication and sacrifice were the only way to a better life. So he accepted the situation, never complained and never got into trouble. He worked hard at school and was, on the surface, at least, calm and self-sufficient. I am a hopeless cook – I don't have the patience for it – but Khalid revealed a flair with food and soon became head chef at Ravensworth Road. He liked experimenting and would test out his recipes on Sharif and me.

As my AS-level exams approached I became increasingly stressed and anxious. My nightmares and flashbacks worsened. I closed myself off from everyone and revised around the clock at every possible opportunity. This was a pattern that would continue throughout college and university. Studying at home was not easy. The room I shared with Khalid was furnished with a single bed, sofa, small table and chair. We had no separate living room and the kitchen was tiny. I had the bed and he slept on the sofa. I had to creep in when I got back from work at night, trying not to disturb him. He had school in the morning and needed his sleep.

Mostly I tried to use the college library. At the shop, when Patrick wasn't there, I would have a book open under the counter. If it wasn't raining, I often went over to the park near our flat and sat working on the banks of the Grand Union Canal. In the run-up to my exams I studied late into the night sitting on the floor of our room, keeping the lamp low down so that it wouldn't wake Khalid. I lived on caffeinated high-energy drinks.

I got straight As in my AS-levels. I was both delighted and relieved. For the first time I felt I had my foot firmly on the ladder.

I rang Russell Steadman, the barrister who had defended me two years earlier, and told him about my results. I had nobody else to tell, or at any rate not anyone who fully appreciated what they meant. And I wanted him to know that I was not squandering the freedom he had won for me; that the frightened Afghan boy described in my file was not who I was.

Russell asked me to meet him at a coffee shop in Waterloo Station and to bring my certificates with me. Evidently he wanted to see the results for himself. 'Thank you for helping,' I said. He seemed pleased and touched. And when he heard that I was now supporting my brother, he invited us both out to dinner to celebrate.

The following year was going to be more complicated. What I wanted to do next would double my workload. Before specializing at A-level, I had to ensure that my language skills were keeping pace with the work and raise my game across all the science subjects and in maths. GSCE English was in any case a basic requirement for medical school. I decided to go one better and take it at AS-level. To be able to access all the appropriate courses under one roof, and keep my job, I had to move to another college. I was accepted on AS-level courses in chemistry, maths, psychology and English at Westminster Kingsway College at King's Cross, and started there in the autumn of 2001.

Before the new term got underway, the world was rocked by the 9/11 attacks on the United States, in which nearly 3,000 people were killed after four passenger airliners were hijacked by Al-Qaeda terrorists. Like everyone else, I looked on in horror as two of the planes were flown into the Twin Towers of the World Trade Center in New York, another into the Pentagon in Virginia and the fourth, missing its target of Washington DC thanks to the actions of its passengers, crashed in a field.

Suddenly, Afghanistan, where Osama bin Laden, the architect of the atrocity, was in hiding, was in the spotlight. The Taliban refused to hand him over to be tried by the Americans without 'convincing evidence' of his involvement in the attack and ignored the demand from President George W. Bush that they expel Al-Qaeda from our country. Within a month the US had invaded Afghanistan. Their objective was to dismantle Al-Qaeda and uproot the regime that was harbouring them. With the help of their allies, including the UK and the Afghan Northern Alliance, led by General Dostum – Ahmad Shah Massoud had been assassinated in a suicide bombing by two Arab men two days before 9/11 – and support from nations such as France, Germany and Canada, the US drove the Taliban from power.

Of course, I was very worried about my family and monitored the news with my heart in my mouth. There were airstrikes on Taliban installations in Kabul, but in the end, on the November afternoon when the allies arrived in the capital, they found that the Taliban had crept away in the night. Although there had been bloodshed en route, in the city itself the Northern Alliance fought a gun battle lasting no more than a quarter of an hour with a few guerrillas hiding in the park, and that was it: Kabul was liberated. On the phone my father was jubilant and looking forward to the better times he was sure would come.

The complexities of world politics, culture and religion give rise to a great deal of misunderstanding and some exiles from our region, and indeed Muslims from anywhere, found it an uncomfortable time to be living in the West, even though Muslims were suffering along with people of all nationalities and creeds and many lost their lives on 9/11. In Afghanistan we continued to suffer attacks by Al-Qaeda and, to this day, we suffer from atrocities perpetrated by ISIS or pockets of the Taliban. Throughout history, crimes have been committed in the name of many religions, not just Islam. The misappropriation by radical extremists of a warped interpretation of religion as a justification for committing terrorist acts in pursuit of their own agendas is something no good Muslim condones. Islam is a religion of peace, love and unity, and terrorism has no place in it.

In London, I was fortunate enough never to have encountered

any discrimination or hostility on the basis of my race or religion – or none I was aware of, anyway – and I didn't now. Yet, in the wake of 9/11, and after the bombings in London in July 2005, I did get a feeling occasionally that, once someone discovered I was from Afghanistan, a faint chill would descend or they would slightly distance themselves from me. It was nothing overt, but preconceptions about my origins, combined with my very different life experiences, might have contributed to the gulf between me and my fellow students which I found it so hard to bridge. And that only became more true when I went on to university. In so many ways, I was 'other'.

During my year at Westminster Kingsway, my presence probably went as unnoticed as it had at City of Westminster. I just swapped one group of young, more carefree fellow students for another. Any extra-curricular activities or openings for making friends were out of the question now that I had a lot more classes and less time than ever. My attendance and punctuality left a lot to be desired. I needed to leave college at 3.30pm to get to my job. When that clashed with a lesson I would have to sneak out early. Occasionally I skipped a lesson altogether. Even so, I was often late for work. Squeezed on all sides, I spent every day running from one place to the next.

Developing my martial arts skills helped me to stay physically energized and mentally positive. I joined the Single Arm Kung Fu Club in Harlesden, run by the famous Afghan kung fu master Ehsan Shafiq, who had once taught in the refugee camps, and I trained there, whenever I could manage it, for quite a few years.

My asylum application, along with Khalid's, finally came up for review by the Home Office. I was upset and angry to discover that the solicitors, the same firm that had been handling my case since the start, had submitted paperwork without the detailed notes and written and photographic evidence I had obtained from Afghanistan, as requested, to support my claim, which were gathering dust in a file in their office. My whole future, and my brother's, depended on the cases presented to the Home Office.

With not much time to spare, I changed solicitors to make sure that the paperwork was done properly. I wrote out a list of bullet points for my new solicitor. She took a dim view of what had been done, or rather not done, to represent me and spent time going through everything with me, sifting what we needed from what we didn't and explaining the difference.

No system is failsafe. The information you provide is open to interpretation and can work against you as well as for you. So much depends on understanding what it is important for the authority in question to know and what must be emphasized. When this involves refugees and the Home Office, these can be life-and-death decisions. And yet there were, I was told, certain law firms that had cornered the market in processing asylum claims. It was a huge business and some of them did the absolute minimum required to collect their fees.

I have met a lot of good people who have been denied asylum in the UK despite suffering untold traumas in their home countries. Others are left in limbo for many years before finally being granted indefinite leave to remain, unable to work legally or to use certain services. I always wonder, was their case given proper consideration? In all areas of our lives we have rights, but sometimes things don't fall into our laps. We have to fight, to ask questions and make sure omissions or mistakes are not being made. That was a lesson I had absorbed early, but it would take me much longer to learn to trust others whose support might have made it easier for me to navigate my new life.

At college and, later, at university, I spoke to no one about my history or my current circumstances until some problem or other arose. I wasn't deliberately trying to hide anything. I just didn't know how to talk about it. I didn't want people to feel sorry for me and I shrank from revisiting my past in any detail. Life still didn't feel quite real and my emotions were all over the place: a confusion of excitement about going to college and being able to earn, loneliness at being so far away from my family, sheer exhaustion and the spectre of the nightmares and flashbacks.

In February 2002, nearly three years after I arrived in the UK, both Khalid and I were granted indefinite leave to remain as refugees. We were free to stay permanently, to take jobs and to access health services. At last the ground beneath my feet felt a little more solid.

That summer, I passed all my AS-Levels with A grades, apart from English, in which I got a C. I was over the moon. I had permanent residency, top marks in the subjects I wanted to take at A-level and just one more year to go before medical school was within my reach.

It was inevitable that I was going to be at a particular disadvantage in my English AS-level. It was an exam designed for native English speakers and, while I could learn the vocabulary, grammar and structure of the language, I had no touchstones for the history or culture that underpinned them. The linguistic nuances, legends, writers and poets I had grown up with were completely different. I had never heard of Shakespeare until I started college.

In addition to my chosen A-level subjects – biology, chemistry and psychology – I also decided, to be on the safe side, to take English at GCSE, a lower stage than the AS-level I'd just passed. I thought perhaps a good grade at GSCE would make a better impression than an inferior pass mark at AS-level.

But there was a snag. I was now told by Westminster Kingsway that I would be exceeding the number of hours' free tuition I was allowed. Why this hadn't come to light with my AS-levels, I don't know. Oddly, there appeared to be no barrier to applying to a different college and being eligible for the same number of hours' tuition there. I was going to have to split the courses between two further education colleges and attempt to fit them round a job.

For the second year running, I would be leaving just when the teachers were sitting up and taking notice of me. The top grades in my final exams probably came as something of a surprise to them because of the uneven way I was working: ticking over through the year as best I could and then putting my foot down hard on the accelerator at exam time. I left with the advice that working through past A-level papers was the best thing I could do to help myself, wherever I attended my classes. You could buy these from the exam boards and in the summer holidays I ordered reams of them, about five or six years' worth for every paper in every subject, and system- atically ploughed through the massive pile stacked in the corner of my room.

In order to be able to work during the day I needed to try to do as many of my courses as I could at evening classes. Hammersmith and West London College at Barons Court offered what I needed but when I turned up there on registration day I practically had to beg them to take me. Young students of my age were expected to do their A-levels full-time at school, or at sixth-form or FE colleges operating during normal working hours. Because evening classes were aimed at mature students who had jobs or other daytime com- mitments, they were restricted to applicants over twenty-one. It was the head of chemistry, Richard Willmer, who kindly stretched the rules for me. He recognized that, in all respects except for my age, I belonged to the demographic the evening classes were there to serve, and made an exception for me.

By the start of the new term I was enrolled at Hammersmith and West London for my chemistry and psychology A-levels and returned to City of Westminster in Maida Vale for biology. I studied for my English GCSE independently.

I had calculated that leaving the shop and increasing my hours with the energy company would earn me more, as well as giving me the freedom to work when it suited me. And so I said goodbye to Patrick and my co-workers at Edgware Road. That was quite a wrench. The shop had been the one permanent feature of my three years in the UK and it was like stepping out into the unknown all over again.

Now all I had to do was to make my convoluted schedule work. I can't pretend it wasn't a struggle. Although I could choose my own hours with my customer adviser job, to earn decent money I had to make sure I didn't miss out on the most productive areas or routes, and sometimes that meant skipping classes and, occasionally, a full day of college.

After a while I changed energy suppliers myself, and moved to British Gas, whose area sales team was led by an Afghan named Nasir. I'd developed my own low-key approach with customers. If it was obvious that someone was in a rush, or there was a baby screaming in the background, it was both impolite and counter-productive to blunder on regardless. I asked everyone if they had the time to talk to me for a few moments, only delivered my pitch if they showed an interest and never hurried them. And I always told the truth. My sales figures – I was in the top ten for the region – proved to me that people respond better when they are not being badgered.

When the London market seemed to have been saturated we travelled further afield, to towns accessible from King's Cross or Marylebone. High Wycombe, I remember, and once I went as far as Oxford. It was an adventure: in the days before smartphone maps and directions we had to find our way with paper town maps and, in London, with our trusty A–Zs. This was the first time I'd seen anything of the England beyond London's borders and I loved those days, looking out of the train windows at fields of green and yellow, woods and neat housing estates, and appreciating the luxury of a free hour or so to catch up with my college work.

The culture at Hammersmith and West London College suited

me. As mature students, we were left to get on with more of the work in our own time. Although there was no real opportunity for me to make friends here, either, it was the same for many of the others. Most of the students were about thirty, forty years old, most of them British and many also had jobs or family responsibilities outside college. I felt less of a duck out of water among these students than I did with the younger people at Maida Vale.

The only continuity in my three years of further education was represented by one of my biology teachers at City of Westminster, Malcolm Evans, who'd taught me to AS-level two years earlier. Familiar with my hurried exits from the classroom, but also with my A-grade pass and capacity to catch up, he went easy on me in my A-level year. 'Take the time off when you have to, and don't worry about it,' he told me. 'I know the effort you put into making up the written work, and you're doing well. Just make sure you're here for all the practicals.'

It is perhaps one of life's ironies that the idea of aiming for Cambridge University was planted in my mind not by any of my teachers but by a friend of Nasir's, a Pakistani guy who was at Cambridge doing a business degree. 'You have great AS-level results,' he said to me. 'Why don't you think about applying to read medicine at Cambridge?'

Cambridge? I told him I didn't have the right education behind me. I didn't think such an elevated institution was going to look at an Afghan refugee with such inadequate schooling.

'Why not? If you get top grades in your A-levels, you stand as much chance as anybody else. You should look into it. If you like you can come and see me up there. I'll show you round.'

I did a bit of research on Cambridge and took up this invitation. What did I have to lose? I made the decision just in time: arriving in Cambridge by train, I found my host packing up to leave. He introduced me to some of his friends, mostly international mature students doing masters and PhDs, and took me round the town and some of the colleges.

Cambridge took my breath away: the beautiful old buildings steeped in history, the narrow cobbled lanes and passages and bridges, the river on which people were gliding on flat boats pushed along by poles. The town centre, free of the roar of traffic, buzzed with activity, pedestrians and cyclists weaving between troops of foreign tourists and language students all talking at the tops of their voices. But step off the street through a heavy wooden door and the noise seemed to evaporate; suddenly you were in another world, an oasis of quiet courtyards where so many eminent academics and scientists, writers and thinkers had walked, surrounded on all sides by ancient college buildings that had barely changed in maybe 800 years.

Back in London, I applied to attend open days at a couple of Cambridge colleges. At Trinity Hall, one of the university's oldest colleges, set by the riverside behind the larger Trinity College, we prospective students were given a tour. Dr John Bradley, the director of medicine (now Professor Bradley), talked to us in his room, which was where, he told us, he gave his tutorials. He was very friendly, welcoming and encouraging. As the others left, I hung back for a moment to explain to Dr Bradley that I had not been to school in the UK but had arrived as a refugee from Afghanistan. I listed my AS-level grades. Would the university consider me?

'Yes, you should apply,' he told me. 'And I do hope you will think about applying to Trinity Hall.' He shook my hand warmly.

I made up my mind at that open day. Trinity Hall was the place I wanted to be. I didn't really dare to hope I might get in but nothing ventured, nothing gained. I was going to give it my best shot.

10

Cambridge

'PLEASE, WILL *SOMEONE* HELP me with my UCAS form!'

It was in trying to make the step up to university that the flaws in my piecemeal approach to gaining my qualifications began to appear. Although the UK had spread before me all the opportunities I could have hoped for, to reach them I'd had to swim against the tide. At the key moments when I needed support, I couldn't find it. What I had been lacking in my life ever since my arrival in London was someone I could look up to, who could offer me some guidance. Those closest to me – Sharif, Khalid, even my parents – were looking up to *me*. Everybody in my limited social circle was driving a taxi or working in a shop or restaurant, coasting along taking each day as it came, and I hadn't been able to forge the deeper connections that might have brought me within the orbit of a potential cheerleader or mentor.

In addition to Trinity Hall, Cambridge, I had decided to apply to three London universities: King's, Imperial and Queen Mary's. I was becoming increasingly frantic as I went from one college department to the next in an effort to drum up decent references from people who didn't know me and assistance with drawing everything together for my application form. It wasn't the fault of any individual: I was an anomaly in the system and I was falling through the cracks.

As A-level grade predictions had to be made on the basis of AS-level results, Westminster Kingsway was nominally in charge of supervising my university application, but of course I was no longer a student there and out of sight, out of mind. The teacher who was supposed to be my tutor was a bit happy-go-lucky about everything. He kept delaying help with my personal statement and references and, as the submission deadline approached, he said he couldn't supervise my application because I'd left the college.

Looking at the one sketchy, boilerplate reference I had so far, I had become tearful. I was going to be competing with privileged students from world-class schools who would be showcasing glowing references, expertly tailored to their chosen courses and ambitions, and this was the best any of my teachers could come up with?

In desperation I had gone to the Westminster Kingsway staff room to plead for help. They all stared at me, bemused, until one of the English teachers took mercy on me. 'Come with me,' she said. 'I'll help you.' She listened to my tale of woe. 'OK. You will need to collect references from the other colleges, but you can bring them to me and I will help chase up what you need from Westminster Kingsway and collate them all. We can go through your personal statement together and I will arrange for a teacher here to prepare you with interview practice.'

The interview practice did not go well.

'What do you want to do at university?' asked the teacher, leafing through my UCAS form.

'Medicine.'

He raised his eyebrows. 'Where are your GCSE results?'

'I don't have GCSEs. But I have done the work, and I have AS-levels.'

'I think it would be a mistake to apply to Cambridge. It's extremely unlikely you will get in. Most Cambridge students come from private schools and they are all going to have benefited from dedicated Oxbridge support, which we don't have in colleges like ours. You'll be doing very well to get yourself accepted by any medical school.'

He then moved on to the general interview preparation, which consisted mainly of picking up on all the shortcomings in my application and educational background. I was shaking and on the verge of tears. I just wanted to get out of there as quickly as possible.

I can see with hindsight that he had been speaking with the best of intentions. By listing Cambridge as my first choice, he believed I'd be burning one of my university chances, and he was being honest about what he saw as my most realistic route to medical school. But at the time I was devastated. In suggesting that I'd be lucky to get in anywhere he was casually uprooting the ambition I had nurtured my whole life.

Afterwards I walked around King's Cross trying to calm down. I'd driven myself to this point on pure adrenaline and I had plenty of heart for a fight. I was exhilarated just to be alive and to have the means to fight. I wouldn't have had those in Kabul. 'I've survived being shelled by the Russians and every rebel group under the sun,' I told myself. 'I've come all this way. I'm not going to give up now.' I went ahead and applied to all the medical schools I'd decided on, including Cambridge, and did the rest of my interview preparation on my own in the library.

Such low expectations can be explained, though not excused, by the fact that the college was not used to preparing students for any medical school, let alone Oxford or Cambridge. But instead of encouraging my ambition – I did, after all, have some excellent AS-levels – the teacher saw only what I couldn't offer. This was, it seemed, as new to Westminster Kingsway as it was to me. When I arrived to sit my Cambridge entrance exam under their supervision, I found I was the only candidate. The teacher roped in to invigilate did not hide his surprise. 'You're taking the *Oxbridge* exam?' he asked me in amazement as he unsealed the first paper.

The entrance exam consisted of three parts: a science test, an aptitude test and essays. I could have done better if I'd had more time. As ever, working in English slowed me down. I answered the questions in the first half of each paper thoroughly but had to rush the rest. It was terrifying, and afterwards I tortured myself by going over all the things I knew and would have included if only I'd had longer.

The English teacher who was helping me with my university application asked me to meet her at Waterloo Station just before the deadline so that she could hand over the finished paperwork. She had come into London specially, turning round to take the train straight home again. 'I have to say that this isn't something I'd ever do normally because you are not one of my students,' she said. 'But your situation was just so heart-rending. I wish you the very best of luck.'

I'd had the additional problem of how to put as positive a gloss as possible on my patchy early education. If I got this wrong I might find myself rejected right at the start. It had been a scramble, but in the end I'd gathered references that were appropriately detailed and encouragingly enthusiastic, including one from the lovely Mr Evans at Maida Vale describing me as 'exceptional' and predicting an A grade at A-level.

A book I'd found about how to get into medical school advised that evidence of relevant work experience was important in demonstrating your commitment. I had nothing medicine-related on my CV and no familiarity, even from a patient's perspective, with hospitals or surgeries in the UK. I'd never been near a British hospital. I hadn't even got round to registering with a GP.

I'd set about trying to catch up well before submitting my university application but it was still a race against time. In clinical settings, hands-on work experience wasn't permitted but you could make arrangements to 'shadow' staff. I had looked up the hospitals closest to me and secured a shadow placement at the Central Middlesex Hospital for a couple of weeks. I was struck by the cleanliness of the wards and the volume and variety of equipment, right down to the delicate, modern instruments they had at their disposal just for simple tasks like taking blood. 'What is that called?' I would ask, pen at the ready to scribble it down in my notebook. 'What are you using there? How did you do that?'

'All these questions!' one doctor remarked drily. 'I thought you were just here to observe.'

In the course of a few months, I shadowed a pharmacist, Mr Ashkan-Nejad, at the ABC Drugstore in Portobello Road, and sat in with Dr Lucy Abraham at her GPs' surgery in Willesden, not far from Khalid's school. Lucy, it turned out, actually taught at Imperial, one of my university choices, which may have resulted in her looking kindly on my request. Mr Ashkan-Nejad was courteous and friendly, and I learned a lot from him about how doctors work with pharmacists and how drugs interact with the body. I was impressed by how warm and compassionate Lucy was with her patients. Both professionals gave me supportive references.

I also volunteered briefly at a care home run by a charity for the disabled. The disabled have unique medical needs, and I thought it would be a good idea to show my awareness that medicine is not just about hospitals. Although there wasn't much I was allowed to do as an untrained assistant, I spent an uplifting and rewarding few days watching how the care workers managed their charges with skill and consideration, and helped out by fetching, carrying and making tea.

I didn't quite complete my placement with Lucy until after I'd sent in my UCAS form. I phoned the admissions office at Trinity Hall to ask if I could submit further work experience references to support my application. 'No harm in it,' they said. 'We can attach them to your file.'

I wrote a letter to all four universities, explaining the reasons for the absence of secondary education certificates, and attached my practical references. I could do no more. Now I just had to sit back and wait.

I couldn't quite believe it when Trinity Hall invited me for interview. By the time I boarded the train for Cambridge on a rainy morning, smartly turned out in my British Gas salesman's suit, I was a bag of nerves. I was as ready as I could be, given that I had no idea what specifically I needed to be ready for. It was perhaps just as well that, at this stage, I was only vaguely aware of how thoroughly many other candidates would have been coached. Those coming from schools accustomed to hothousing pupils for Oxbridge had been working on practice questions for weeks. At Westminster Kingsway, preparation for my Cambridge interview had consisted of completing the UCAS form, sitting the entrance exam and being told I hadn't a hope of getting in.

In a welcoming waiting room at Trinity Hall, supplied with coffee, tea and water, other students were going through copious notes. I fished around in my bag for my tie. I had worn one sometimes for my British Gas job, but tying it did not come naturally and I was so jittery I couldn't remember how to do it. A mother who happened to be present saw me struggling and took pity on me, smiling kindly as she effortlessly produced a perfect Windsor knot.

My first interview was with Professor Thomas Körner, an eminent mathematician. 'How was your journey?' he enquired politely, directing me up an antique staircase to his room. On every wall there were shelves full of books. There were books on every surface. There were books in piles on the floor. There was only just enough space for the table and two chairs where he invited me to take a seat. My eyes darted around the room, taking it all in.

Professor Körner's genuinely friendly demeanour could not prevent him from seeming pretty intimidating. The first few questions were along the lines I had anticipated, but then the grilling started to become slightly surreal. One question concerned vaccination strategy in a region where a disease was endemic. I talked about the importance of containment, of preventing movement in and out of the area, and of the need to ensure that those who couldn't afford to pay for the vaccination were not excluded. Every answer I gave,

Professor Körner interrogated, pressing me to come up with alternative pathways or solutions, exploring different angles, some academic, some practical. If he countered, 'Ah, but that might not work because this might happen,' I said, 'OK, maybe then I would look at doing X, Y or Z.' He kept firing back at me, drilling down, never leaving a response unchallenged. It was relentless and I had to think fast.

At last he stopped. The interview was over, it seemed. *What the hell was that?* I thought as he thanked me for attending and escorted me back to the waiting room. I didn't have the first idea whether my answers had been right or wrong, or even whether there was a right or wrong answer. Nothing in any of the advance reading I had done had equipped me for this curious test of my abilities. When I went to interviews at the London universities I'd applied for, none of them were anything like this. They were more or less what I'd expected, questions around medicine, on ethics, general knowledge, and I was better prepared because I knew what I had to be prepared for.

Next up was Dr Bradley, the director of medicine, whom I'd met at the open day. His approach was more academic and I felt I was on firmer ground with biology. He began with pictures of cell types, slowly stepping up his line of questioning to get me to show my scientific knowledge in my responses. But again it was deeply probing and I really had no clue as to how I had done.

At the other universities I got a sense that I'd acquitted myself well. But after my Cambridge interview I didn't know what to think. For now I mostly felt immense gratitude that I had been given this opportunity and glad that I had seized it with both hands. Glad, too, that I hadn't listened to anyone along the way who'd suggested that perhaps this ambitious plan wasn't for someone like me.

The day I opened the letter that confirmed my offer from Cambridge was one of the happiest of my life. Delirious with excitement,

I phoned my parents. 'Amazing! Great!' my dad exclaimed. Of course he understood that this was a good English university but, having never heard of Oxford or Cambridge, neither of my parents had any idea of what it truly meant – the ferocious competition, the prestige, the privilege, the sheer improbability of an uneducated boy from Kabul being accepted there – and, try as I might, I couldn't adequately convey a sense of just how special it was.

My mum said: 'I'm so happy. I always knew you were going to do great things. When are you coming home?'

Khalid, who was with me when I opened the letter, was the only one who got it. He was utterly thrilled for me.

My place at Cambridge was contingent on three A grades in my A-levels, the highest marks it was possible to achieve as the A* grade didn't exist then. I knuckled down. As the exams approached, so my anxiety escalated, and with it the horrors that plagued my dreams and my waking hours. I cut back on my British Gas work as far as I felt was economically sustainable. The lamp burned through the night at Ravensworth Road as I studied furiously, mechanically picking at whatever Khalid presented to me on a plate when the others were eating or whatever I found in the fridge.

I was full of trepidation as I headed into college to find out my results. So much was riding on them. A beaming tutor I saw there already knew: three As, he told me. I had done it. I managed an A, too, for my GCSE English written paper and a B in the oral exam.

I'd had offers from each of my chosen universities, and they all invited me to apply for scholarships or other financial assistance to supplement my student loan. At Cambridge I was the recipient of the Isaac Newton Trust Award, in the gift of neighbouring Trinity College. I went on to win it again for the next two years in succession. This was a bursary for students from low socio-economic backgrounds, for which I was competing with others. I had to submit an essay making a case for why I deserved the bursary, what I proposed to use it for and so on. I had no trouble expressing myself on the matters of war, hardship and separation from my family when required to write about them for a concrete purpose. But talking about them remained beyond me.

The colleges where I'd sat my AS- and A-levels all saw it as a great boost to have a student going to Cambridge. The head of City of Westminster said they appreciated where I had come from and were ready to give me any help I needed. The teacher from Westminster Kingsway who had advised me not to apply was gracious enough to apologize. 'I underestimated you,' he said. 'I'm sorry.'

'It's OK,' I told him. 'It just made me more determined.'

In truth I was still bruised by that episode but I reminded myself that it is from experiences like this that we learn. We can't achieve our dreams without taking risks. If we fail, we may well find another route to where we want to go, or perhaps even another destination, in the attempt. Not making the attempt in the first place gets us nowhere.

It was a busy summer. I put in a lot of hours for British Gas to make up for lost earnings and there were forms to be filled in and arrangements to be made for my move up to Cambridge and for Khalid, who was still only fourteen. I had spoken to Trinity Hall about our situation and I was touched when they offered to accommodate him with me, but he wanted to stay in London. He was making his own life and his own friends and he was settled at school. There were discussions with the local authority and it was agreed between us all that, while I remained responsible for Khalid, they would find foster parents to care for him while he finished school. He was placed with a nice family and I would keep in regular phone contact.

Before going up to Cambridge I was reunited with my parents for the first time in four years. I flew out to Pakistan and they came to meet me in Islamabad. I didn't have a passport until 2008, when I decided to apply for British citizenship, so I had to obtain documentation from the Home Office in order to travel. There was no bar to me going anywhere – except to Afghanistan, the country where my life was deemed to be at risk and from which the UK was giving me sanctuary.

My parents were waiting for me with Mahvash at the airport. We all wept as we flung our arms around one another. We spent a few days in Islamabad and then went to stay with Khala Jan at Shamshatoo. I found my parents in good spirits. In the honeymoon period that had followed the arrival of the Americans in Kabul, life had changed rapidly for the better. People were excited by the possibility that there might finally be peace. Aid and donations were coming in, the economy had been resurrected and there were more job opportunities, especially in construction. There was so much rebuilding going on that Pakistanis were coming across to work in Kabul after nearly twenty-five years of all the human traffic moving in the opposite direction.

Of course, these times were not to last. The rival warlords, the Taliban and Al-Qaeda might have been lying low, but they were still very much present and the Taliban maintained their grip on many other areas of the country. There was resistance to the presence of the Americans and their allies from the start. It would not be long before the same warlords responsible for the suffering of the past reappeared in positions of power in the interim government and Kabul became enmired in corruption, political horse-trading and renewed bloodshed.

But thanks to the new atmosphere of hope and regeneration, my father was starting to get the family back on its feet. After selling our home to fund my escape, and with Shahre Naow in a poor state of repair, he'd had to rent somewhere for the family to live. The money I'd been sending back had helped him to buy another house in Kolula-Pushta. Acquired before the Taliban had been driven out, this, like its predecessor, had been bought very cheaply, but it, too, needed a lot of renovation. Almost every house in Kabul was damaged in one way or another. If it hadn't been bombed, it had been peppered by shrapnel or stripped of pipes and wires. Wooden fixtures such as window frames had been ripped out of most unoccupied buildings to fuel fires in the bitter winters of the civil war.

With Shahre Naow once again viewed as a prime location, property there was in high demand and Dad was doing up the shops to get them ready to rent out for the first time in years, along with our old home behind them, in order to provide an income for the family. Money was still needed for these projects, but the taxi and the carpet-weaving equipment were gone and my youngest brothers and, for the first time, my youngest sisters were going to school and doing well. They would become the first of us all to receive an uninterrupted education through to the end of high school and that felt like real progress. The rent from Shahre Naow would ultimately pay for education and healthcare for the whole family. My married sisters and their husbands and children had begun to return to Kabul. Eventually they would all settle there.

It was wonderful to see my parents. Our time together was full of laughter but the memories it stirred of Kabul, the refugee camps and the trauma of the flight to the UK left me feeling off balance and exposed on my return. Back in London, I tried to put the emotions that had resurfaced into a box and close the lid on it.

Russell Steadman, pretty amazed, I think, by my achievement, drove me up to Cambridge in his old Volkswagen Scirocco to help me with my stuff and lend some moral support. I was allocated a beautiful room in an old part of the college. As we entered the Front Court I still couldn't quite believe I was here, either, walking the same paths around the college frequented by the young Stephen Hawking. For weeks I'd been waking every morning fearing for a moment or two that I'd dreamed the whole thing.

Through the window of my room I could see students coming in and out of the courtyard on their bicycles. It felt like the beginning of the life I'd been striving for, as if everything that had gone before had been leading up to this point. My concept then of life at a top university was based mainly on the depictions of Princeton in the film *A Beautiful Mind*, about the American mathematician John Nash, which I'd recently seen: a liberating, rarefied existence amid hallowed halls and lecture theatres, devoted to pure study.

In my four years in the UK I had been on a steep learning curve, but I believed I had smoothed off my rough edges, loosened up and was ready, at last, to become the person I'd always wanted to be. I was looking forward to making friends among like-minded students. But at twenty years old, with as yet no real cultural or social understanding or experience of the country I was living in, I was still searching for my identity. And I was bringing with me that box of unresolved parts of myself and my history. All this made it very hard for me to connect with anyone.

Looking back, I suspect I stood out as different from that very first day. When all the other freshers are arriving with their doting parents and you turn up with your barrister, it can't help but set you apart.

Most of the new undergraduates came from very similar backgrounds: traditionally English, well-to-do families and prestigious schools where they were top of their classes. They had so much in common and some of them already knew each other or had mutual friends. They gelled easily in halls, drifted together to watch a movie, went out with each other and gravitated into groups naturally right from the start. I wasn't in any of these.

In an attempt to create a persona for myself, I began to dress better, investing in some more stylish clothes. I tried my best to join in. I went on a freshers' pub crawl, drinking orange juice at every port of call. I went to parties, standing to one side, silent and enigmatic, and leaving early. The other students thought I was, or was trying to be, cool.

In truth I struggled to sustain an informal chat of any length. I hadn't seen the films they'd seen or read the books they'd read; I couldn't contribute to comparisons of summers spent in Europe or gap years travelling the world or activities and celebrations with their close-knit families. My conversational English wasn't as good as I thought it was, either. I didn't get jokes or understand colloquial language. I remember at one freshers' party, a girl in a lovely dress swayed up to me and announced, 'I'm pissed.'

'What?' I said, outraged. I'd never heard the expression before and thought she meant that somebody had pissed on her. 'Who did that to you?' I was all fired up and ready to leap to her defence.

She looked at me, puzzled. 'No, Waheed. Nobody pissed on me. I'm just *pissed*.'

I was none the wiser.

The old rituals and traditions at Cambridge colleges can wrong-foot any new student but they were always going to be more alien to me than they were to anyone else. At formal dinners, you'd be faced with five knives and forks on each side of your plate. I was clueless about dress codes. I didn't know when or how the academic gown should be worn or what 'black tie' meant. Early on I didn't possess a bow tie and wouldn't have been able to tie it if I'd had one. Invariably, I turned up to college events in the wrong clothes, which only added to my reputation as an international man of mystery. The other students interpreted it as an act of rebellion, assuming that I was making some kind of anti-establishment statement.

I didn't even know how to wear everyday clothes. This resulted in some eccentric choices and random combinations, which were also perceived as a sign of my individualism. In fact it was just ignorance. I was still learning how to put Western garments together. I once attended an anatomy dissection demonstration in a dinner shirt. I had no idea it was a dinner shirt: I'd just seen it in a shop and liked it. The instructor didn't say much, merely commenting, 'That's a *really* nice shirt, Waheed. Where are you off to tonight?'

Many teenagers and young adults establishing themselves in the world can seem aloof to their peers while underneath they are unconfident and fearful of rejection. The heartaches of growing up can be even more acute these days, with social media offering a shop window where people can present airbrushed versions of themselves and their lives. It can seem as if everyone but you has everything sorted and is having an amazing time. In my case, these growing pains were exacerbated by the trauma I carried and by the cultural and social barriers that left me isolated.

If I found it difficult to mix, the academic work I was there to do was a source of deep joy. The three-year Medical and Science Tripos, my degree course, formed the academic, or pre-clinical, stage of my six-year training and consisted of anatomy, biochemistry and physiology. Not surprisingly, the facilities and quality of teaching at Cambridge were second to none. I marvelled at the state-of-the-art labs with their array of gleaming hardware. I'd been impressed by the labs at my FE colleges, but these were something else. The biochemistry lab, run by white-coated technicians whose sole job it was to look after it, boasted all kinds of specialized, high-tech equipment, including everything required for electrophoresis and other genetic testing and analysis.

Professors and clinical doctors came in to work with the students, and there were lectures and demonstrations by teachers of world-class calibre, some of them Nobel prize-winners, who engaged us with a humility and approachability that belied their international fame. Dr Bradley showed us round some of the departments at Addenbrooke's, the main hospital in Cambridge, where he was a consultant physician and nephrologist, and we undertook projects there with individual patients.

In our first year of anatomy we had our own human cadaver to dissect over the course of a term, shared between four or five students. Dissecting a human being takes a bit of getting used to. But you become absorbed by the need to focus on what you are doing and by your curiosity and fascination. Models, diagrams and computer graphics are all vital to our understanding of disease but there is no substitute for being able to learn, from a real person who once lived and breathed, how the complicated three-dimensional structure of the body fits together and what all the parts actually look like. It was touching to think that this person had decided to donate their body to science to help train new doctors: their own quiet way of giving something back to society.

It was quite a leap up from A-level biology, for which I think all we dissected was a frog. I thought back to my refugee camp 'medical school' where, in our foundation year, we had been given one rabbit between twenty students to dissect. In our first semester of anatomy, we had been excited by the prospect of watching a teacher dissect an animal heart to show us the valves.

'Wow,' I said to myself. 'Now this *is* medical school.'

Our tutors were fantastic. My personal tutor, Dr Nick Bampos, an Australian of Greek extraction, showed me great warmth and used to try to put me at my ease by chatting to me as a fellow exile about how he missed his family or complaining about the British weather. Dr Bradley would invite his students to casual dinners at his house and used to hold a regular informal end-of-year pool party where he got us together with his wife and children. They both went to a lot of effort over our pastoral care. At Christmas there would always be personal cards from them, and from the Master, in your pigeonhole.

At this level students must research a lot on their own, with less input from their tutor. I had been used to studying independently all my life, so this was one of my strengths. I was good at research. I liked finding my own resources and digging deep into a subject.

And I was good in the practical classes. Encouraged to discover that I was also capable of shining when we analysed topics among our small tutorial groups, where I had time to think and compose what I wanted to say, to discuss and debate and show my understanding of the subject, I grew in confidence.

But I still found large classes uncomfortable. I'd sometimes feel the stress symptoms setting in the moment I took my seat and I was distracted by the awareness that I was more concerned about how I was coming over to others than about learning and processing. The professor would be running through some huge and complex topic and I just couldn't follow what he was saying or take notes quickly enough. I couldn't believe how fast the other students were writing. Working in their first language, they were also, not surprisingly, much faster at reading and absorbing material. There were weekly individual supervisions where we discussed our progress and preparation for exams and were given the opportunity to clarify anything we didn't understand or raise any other issues.

Committing everything to memory and writing it out was not going to hack it any longer. It was not about short answers now. I researched obsessively but I had no experience in how to sift my findings effectively, and I was trying to put practically everything I knew into my essays. You need to be able to assimilate, select and reject. I was at a disadvantage in analysing topics geared to developed countries. And the hour and a half we had to complete essays was a tall order when you were mentally translating everything into Pashto or Farsi and back again.

Every two or three weeks, and for at least some of the holidays, I'd go back to London, put in some hours for British Gas, catch up with Khalid to make sure he was doing OK and train at the Single Arm Kung Fu Club. I'd earned a black belt in kung fu the year I went to Cambridge. I'd been unable to find much common ground with my fellow students even when it came to sport. A lot of them played rugby, which they'd learned at school, or rowed, many to a very high level; I did martial arts on my own. In general, student participation in sports seemed to revolve around strange traditions and rituals and almost always finished up in the pub.

None of the university societies were on my wavelength, either. In a bid to counter my social isolation, I set up a martial arts society. It was not as grand as it sounds – a proper club would have meant premises and those cost money. It mainly consisted of me sending an email round to my year group whenever I planned to train in a corner of one of the parks, inviting anyone who was interested to join me. A few guys did come and I would coach them in what I had been doing at the Single Arm club on my previous visit. It helped me to make some friends, if only on a superficial level. I also tried to set up an Afghan Society, but nobody responded. I concluded that I must have few, if any, fellow Afghans at Cambridge.

I spent most of my time outside lecture theatres, tutorials and organized events on my own. I loved walking round the town, exploring, absorbing the history. I smiled at the amateurs trying to punt on the river, pottered around the city library or sat, solo, reading in a café. The coffee shops were my favourite places. I enjoyed people-watching. I found it comforting to feel life going on around me without having to make the effort to interact with anyone.

In the evenings I worked late in the Trinity Hall library or walked by the river, taking in a beautiful sunset. I might go to the student common room late, when it was quiet, after everyone else had finished drinking and watching their soap operas, to catch up with the news. There were movie nights at the college but it was more relaxing to go to the cinema by myself and escape into the imaginary world created by a thriller or an action movie, or give myself a good laugh with a comedy. It was lonely, particularly in the holidays, when everyone went home to their families or away, leaving only the international students and postgrads.

A late-night run always helped me to consolidate my thoughts and would lift a melancholy mood or ease escalating anxieties. I gave myself pep talks, reminding myself every night how lucky I was. I had my problems, certainly, but I was grateful, always, for all that I had. Drifting off to sleep in my private space within the walls of one of the world's finest universities, I still sometimes found it hard to believe that I was actually there, and on my way to making my life's vision a reality. When, amid the hopelessness of the civil war, I'd imagined that room of my own, with its desk and books, I couldn't in my wildest dreams have foreseen how my prayers would be answered.

11

Belonging

AS THE YEAR WORE on my grades started to dip. Instead of the predicted firsts or 2:1s I was getting thirds. This plunged me into a state of extreme anxiety and had my tutors scratching their heads and wondering if they had got me all wrong. Although I doubt I had stood out on the basis of the entrance exam, I learned later that, on the strength of my interview, I had been rated among the top five of the forty or fifty applicants considered. As I had discovered, the interviews were not designed to produce pat answers but to reveal your ability to think and solve problems. So the staff couldn't understand what was happening now, especially when I was doing so well in tutorials, which confirmed to them that I belonged on the course and had the aptitude to handle it. And I could handle everything orally. It was in written work in exam settings that my performance was taking a dive.

I had a better idea than my tutors about why things were going wrong, if not precisely how. I had passed all my previous exams with flying colours through sheer effort and hard work, but at this level my lack of fundamental education was being exposed. In addition to the language problem, I had never been mentored in exam technique. Multiple-choice questions were new to me, as was negative marking, whereby you have marks deducted for a wrong answer, which means that if you don't know the answer, you are better off not addressing the question at all and settling for zero.

My tutors would have been only vaguely aware of my background. The details I had disclosed in writing on various forms and applications would have been sitting in a file somewhere in the admissions office, but they were not something I discussed with my teachers. On my UCAS form I'd had to take one or two liberties with the truth on the question of my secondary schooling and the extent to which I was self-taught, and I lived in constant fear that if the inadequacy of my formal education was exposed I would be 'sent down'. In other words, thrown out.

It was this fear that underpinned my reluctance to open up about my history, along with the stigma attached to anyone perceived to be struggling academically. However sympathetic our tutors, no medical student was prepared to admit to that. We were all highly competitive: you had to be to have won a place at Cambridge, or indeed any medical school, in the first place. I wouldn't have been the only one to have been feeling the strain. Students who were used to being top of the class had arrived to find that, for the first time in their lives, they were not, and that is a hard adjustment to make.

My mental state was working against me. I shut myself away to prepare for exams and wouldn't speak to anyone on the phone for two or three weeks except Khalid, not even my parents. I never slept the night before. I would be compulsively going over and over material I already knew off by heart. And yet the next day information I knew would vanish from my memory. My anxiety reached the pitch where I would be telling myself that if I didn't get top marks my whole life would fall apart.

Everyone gets stressed at exam time, but in my case the anxiety was out of all proportion. I didn't understand that this was an aspect of PTSD. I thought it was just the way I was and I had to live with it. Beneath it lay the trauma of my past and the worries of the present: the sense that I was in some way leading a double life, the pressure of the obligations I was putting on myself as the family's eldest son, the deep-rooted desire to make my parents proud, the duty to make the most of a once-in-a-lifetime opportunity.

I had meetings with Dr Bampos and Dr Bradley. Distressed and emotional, I opened up to them a little. I spoke of how heavily the need to help support my family in Afghanistan and the welfare of my dependent brother in London weighed on me and of how desperately I missed them all. I did not speak of my academic weaknesses.

Dr Bampos made it very clear that I had to quit my job. The Medical and Science Tripos was so incredibly intense, he said, that I would not succeed if I was effectively trying to earn a living at the same time. If I was worried about money, there was help available. Although I was already benefiting from some bursaries, there were further options. 'Come and see me any time if things are getting on top of you,' he said. 'You don't have to make an appointment.'

Dr Bampos was right about the demands of studying medicine. Five or six years is a very long course and those demands only intensify as you progress. Medical students are particularly vulnerable to anxiety and other mental health problems, and there are regular reports claiming that the attrition rate is increasing. At least two people from my course dropped out. One of them I'd always held in awe for his brilliance. A couple of years later, after graduating with a first, he told me that he was going to give up medicine. 'I can't take the pressure,' he said. 'It's just too much.'

I realized I had to act quickly to turn things round. Academic work doesn't define intelligence. In real life, adaptability, perseverance and the capacity to use that intelligence to solve problems are more important. But academic work was the measure by which my ability had to be judged at this stage, and I had to get to grips with the nature of the exams and to pinpoint what it was they were designed to elicit from me. I knew the 'why'; I just had to figure out the 'how'.

I was concealing my lack of secondary education so successfully that I'd started lying about it even to myself, but it was making me question my intelligence. I had to accept and get past the deficiency of my schooling. The fact that English was not my first language was always going to make me slower than others in exams and that would be reflected in my marks. I needed to acknowledge this difficulty and work with my tutors on the best way to manage it.

Above all, I needed to start believing that I had got to Cambridge on my true merits and was entitled to be here. I wrote down a list of reasons why I was worthy of my place, why I should do well, why I should not accept that I should be getting a third in exams and recited my responses in my late-night pep talks to myself. I read Tony Buzan's books on mental literacy and 'mind mapping' to gain an understanding of how learning works. They helped me to teach myself how to summarize and to tackle the requirements of the exams in a practical way.

And I did, mostly, comply with Nick Bampos's order to give up working. I gradually stopped sending money home. It was hard to let go of my image of myself as the family's saviour. But I knew that my father, who consulted me regularly as the eldest son on all family matters, was on his way to re-establishing their life in Kabul and I could see how senseless it would be to put everything I'd fought to achieve at risk at this crucial stage of my education.

Through a combination of addressing these problems myself, the personal attention of my tutors and the help of a couple of senior medical students who were very supportive, I managed to get over this bump and went into my second year comfortably achieving the grades that were expected of me.

By this time I had got a little better at putting on a front. I was learning how to appear to be mingling socially with my fellow students even if it was all on the surface. Interacting with the boys was more straightforward than with the girls. If girls showed an interest in me I was not sure how to read the signals, and I didn't want my intentions to be misinterpreted. While I was keen to have girls as friends, I wasn't looking for a girlfriend. I was certain that, whatever the future held, I would be embarking on it with an Afghan wife by my side, someone who spoke the same language and shared my culture, values and religion.

My mother was already asking questions about what qualities I was looking for in a wife. I was not yet ready to start thinking about marriage, but in the meantime I was cautious about unintentionally finding myself getting too involved with anyone in the UK. It wouldn't have been fair on her or on me.

I would go to a café sometimes with a mixed crowd. We had our university experience in common now and I found it easier to chat about films, TV, our lectures and tutors, and day-to-day life. But quite a few of my contemporaries seemed very young to me. With some groups the conversation would revolve around school jokes or childhood references beyond my experience, or trivia about what was happening in *Home and Away* or *EastEnders*. Then I would feel the odd one out and it would discourage me from meeting up with them again.

I got on better with the postgrads I came across, and the reality is I sometimes felt I had more in common with the porters, who were friendly, greeted me by name and were always up for a chat. My best friend at university was probably one of the kitchen porters, a lovely guy from North Africa. His outlook was one with which I could identify: the outlook of an immigrant who was doing what it took to make a decent life for himself and to support his family, just like the Afghans I'd met who worked in the chicken shops in London.

At the local mosque I made some Afghan friends with whom I would get together for a game of pool or to watch a film. Some were at the Anglia Ruskin University in Cambridge and others were employed in local shops or restaurants.

I also signed up with a student visiting service formed to combat loneliness in the city's elderly and housebound. Every week during term-time I spent an hour or so with an elderly widow, just to chat and keep her company. I enjoyed these visits. I was touched by how trustingly she welcomed a stranger into her home and it was rewarding for me to feel I was brightening someone's day. I encouraged her to talk about her life and her husband, and her reminiscences about the Second World War, unfamiliar to me with my different national history. My reluctance to give much away about myself made me a good listener. She would play the piano for me. She suffered from rheumatoid arthritis and complained that this had affected her ability to play, but it sounded beautiful to me.

These moments of connection helped to sustain me, but mostly, as ever, I had my head down, working furiously. In my third year I'd been allocated one of the best rooms in the college, overlooking the lawn and library, which was such a tranquil place to study.

I gained my honours degree with a 2:1 for my written exam and a first for my pharmacology research project ('The role of human sterols in cell membrane transporters'). This felt like such a huge triumph that it is hard to put into words how much it meant to me. I sat outside the Senate House reflecting on how far I had come, pride mingling with a sense that I was somehow living in some parallel universe.

The head of pharmacology told me he was extremely impressed by my defence of my thesis and would be delighted if I chose to remain in the research arena. I loved academia and I think in many respects the life would have suited me, but deep down I was driven by a visceral need to be active on the front line of medicine; to be responding in the moment, helping to heal, to improve and save lives.

Graduation day was a bittersweet occasion. I was so happy, but here I was, experiencing the proudest moment of my life to date, and I had nobody to share it with. It hadn't been possible even for Khalid to be there. Seeing all the other students celebrating with their families was painful. It underlined the absence of mine and made me miss them even more. I brought a little camera with me to take some photographs to send home but even to get those I had to enlist the help of a passing student or their parents.

I could have stayed on in Cambridge to complete my medical training but I decided to return to London for my three clinical years. The big city had the advantage of the widest range of teaching hospitals and I wanted to be closer to Khalid, who would be studying for his A-levels. I wanted to make sure he had more support with his exams than I'd had at his age.

I had opted for Imperial College, a world-class medical school whose students learned their trade across London at large hospitals such as Charing Cross, Chelsea and Westminster, and Hillingdon. Imperial, which had offered me a scholarship on my original university application, had made the same offer again. This would be of great assistance to me financially, although it was gratifying to me that this scholarship was based on 'exceptional interview performance' rather than hardship.

I was desperately sad to leave Cambridge. Trinity Hall had looked after me so well and studying there had been an amazing experience. But it was good to be back in the buzz of the capital. It was quite a contrast to Cambridge, mainly because of the switch of focus from academic to clinical work. The landscape changed continually with our rotations and an array of lecturers who came and went. We did our clinical attachments in small units and I'd spend three or four months with the same group, start to make friends and then move on to my next placement. By its very nature the system was not conducive to building relationships with either teachers or fellow students.

Professor Karim Meeran of Imperial and Charing Cross Hospital presided over our initial year. An endocrinologist, he was the head of medical education at the college and a friendly, approachable and inspirational figure. Before we were let loose on the wards, he taught us how to carry out examinations and basic practicalities such as taking blood and giving injections, which he demonstrated on a dummy. It brought back memories for me of practising on my dad with that heavy syringe in our mud room at Badaber and his black-and-blue arms.

I relished this new hospital life and was in my element on the wards. It was a joy to be able to apply theory to real-life situations and I loved the human contact. I was at ease talking to patients and interested in them as people as well as in their diseases. The students were often asked to take down patient histories, which enabled you to see the bigger picture and how the current problems fitted into a patient's general health and life story. The patients were, on the whole, very tolerant and nice to us. Most of them understood that we were still learning and some rather liked the additional attention.

It was in the interaction with patients that the rewards of the job were immediately tangible. Sometimes the smallest changes in medication or drips, drains or tubes could make them more comfortable and raise their spirits. The smile of relief or gratitude that confirmed your actions had made a difference said it all. For the first time, my vision of what being a doctor really meant was coming to life.

I was surprised, in the capital of such a wealthy country, to encounter some of the conditions and problems associated with poverty. Charing Cross Hospital, in west London, had an excellent pulmonary department and I came across patients with TB who were suffering just as I had done as a small child in a refugee camp. TB is a disease that the medical profession had hoped to be able to eradicate in the UK in the twentieth century, until cases began to rise again in the 1980s. At Charing Cross, patients with chest problems were questioned on countries they had visited recently and screened for TB. As the COVID-19 pandemic would later starkly highlight, high rates of disease in any region cannot be ignored on the grounds that it is 'not our problem'. It is in the interests of us all as global citizens to address these issues, not only out of compassion for our fellow human beings but because what happens anywhere in the world has an impact everywhere.

There was also a high incidence of other lung conditions seen disproportionately in those from low socio-economic backgrounds, such as COPD (chronic obstructive pulmonary disease) and smoking-related cancers, and a lot of patients from ethnic minorities, often Indians, Pakistanis or Arabs. As many of the elderly, especially the women, spoke no English, my languages came in useful. Whenever a grandma held out her hand to me and said in Urdu, 'Son, how are you?', the other students would leave me there chatting away to her. Being able to communicate directly with a 'doctor' reassured these patients at what could be a confusing and frightening time for them. And I was good at understanding social problems. I understood them in my bones. I was determined I would never look at a patient and see only a medical condition.

I enjoyed attending case discussions and the regular multi-disciplinary team (MDT) meetings, where clinicians from the various departments assembled to report on the different aspects of a patient's treatment and agree on the path forward. At these meetings, everything started to fall into place. It was when we had to present cases after a ward round that the anxiety began to kick in. I'd feel the telltale sweating palms and racing heart. But most students find it stressful presenting to consultants and I knew it was something I was going to have to adjust to.

I got on well with my fellow students although these relationships, founded on workplace gossip and banter and mutual support in the face of the wrath or the foibles of our professors and consultants, tended to last only as long as the clinical attachments that sustained them. But I was slowly making some real friendships, too, which have stood the test of time. Mark Jennings, one of my house-mates at the place I shared with a revolving cast of med students, arrived to do a PhD at Imperial from Stanford University in California. Half American and half Irish, he had a warmth to him and understood the kind of culturally split life experienced by most of us living in a foreign land. I talked to him a bit more about my childhood than I had to anyone up to then. Masood Soorie, an Afghan I'd met by chance in London when I was at Cambridge and he was at Imperial, was working in research after completing his PhD. We would have dinner from time to time and discuss politics, our families and personal lives, the challenges faced by Afghanistan and ways in which we might be able to help our country.

So much of what I was learning brought to the surface thoughts of Afghanistan and what a huge difference the resources of the UK's renowned National Health Service would make to the people there. In Year 5, I did rotations in paediatrics, obstetrics and gynaecology, and psychiatry. My paediatrics placement was in the top-class unit at Chelsea and Westminster Hospital. It was a wonderful experience working with babies and children, although, inevitably, there were some scary moments. I remember the first time I saw a toddler having a convulsive seizure. I was so impressed by how the consultant dealt with it. Everybody else was panicking – the parents, all of us students – but he remained utterly unflustered, coolly putting in a line and getting the fit under control before instigating calm discussions with the parents and doctors to try to determine what the trigger had been and what to do next. I remember reflecting that in Kabul that toddler would probably have died.

I thought of my parents, and what they must have gone through when they lost my two youngest sisters, whom I never met. My mum had given birth to her last two babies, twin girls, after I came to the UK. They had both died of whooping cough. The more I learned, the more it dawned on me how incredibly lucky my own family were to have come through so much: TB, malaria, wartime injuries and, in my mum's case, delivering thirteen babies in conditions ranging from merely inadequate to positively dangerous.

I was thinking a lot about the future and how best I would be able to make any meaningful contribution in my homeland. My dream had grown out of the desire to take care of my family first and then those suffering around me, but my vision went much further. It seemed to me that when it came to trying to help the people of Afghanistan, if I returned to Kabul I'd be just one more unsupported doctor battling to do my bit in a non-existent healthcare system. I would have access to far better resources, and more scope for making an impact, from the West.

I did my psychiatry rotation at St Charles Hospital, just round the corner from Portobello Road, which brought back memories of my early days in London. Hakim had gone back to Afghanistan to work in the family gem business and there was nobody I knew left now at the flats where we'd lived, but I strolled around checking out what had happened to the shops I remembered and treated myself to fish and chips from George's Portobello Fish Bar.

I was on familiar territory in more ways than one. In the psychiatry department, where I saw at first hand some severe cases of mental illness, signs of PTSD, depression and anxiety struck a chord with me. But I was still blocking my own bad memories and denying to myself that several of my own symptoms could have their roots in named and medically recognized conditions.

It was during my time at Imperial that the struggle to find my identity and the effects of my suppression of the past really began to assert themselves, coming to a head in my final year. My values were Afghan, but my way of life was British. I felt torn in two. Though I still didn't know where I belonged or where I saw my future, it seemed increasingly unlikely that it was going to involve living in Afghanistan on any long-term basis.

The question of marriage was gnawing away at me. My parents were not deliberately putting pressure on me to marry: they had talked to me about whether I would like them to find a young woman to whom I might be introduced, I had said yes, and they were simply acting on what had been agreed. I wanted to do the right thing as their eldest son, and to please them; I wanted to do the right thing for myself, too, and that was to settle down and have my own family. I had never wished it any other way. But now I was having difficulty envisioning how this was going to work when I had a foot in two continents and cultures.

I played out different scenarios in my head. If I married in Afghanistan and brought my wife to England, how was that going to pan out? A domestic set-up that slotted easily into family life in Kabul would not be as straightforward here. What if my wife wasn't happy in the UK? What if she didn't speak English? My parents would probably have that on their list of requirements, but I knew only too well how isolated a new wife would feel if all the English she actually had was a few words. Afghan women are wonderfully strong and capable. Historically, they supported men in battle and sometimes took up arms themselves. I had grown up witnessing their astonishing courage and resilience in wartime, not only in the example of my mum and sisters but in women from all over the country.

In Afghanistan, though, they are functioning within robust and secure family networks. I thought of all my grand plans and pictured what it would be like to feel tied down by a sense of responsibility, guilt even, for a wife who might find herself removed from that environment and heavily reliant on me only because of where I had decided we should live.

Taking time to get to know each other isn't part of the Afghan courtship protocol. In Afghanistan, I would get to meet my future wife maybe only once, with her family, before formally asking for her hand and setting in motion a chain of events it would be very hard to pause or stop without causing offence or distress. It is not done to go back on your word. It would create problems for the family and probably result in you being blacklisted in the marriage market. But I wasn't in Afghanistan. This was going to be incredibly difficult for me to micro-manage from a distance of 4,000 miles.

Should I try to meet someone in the UK? I didn't know any girls, or at least not any with whom I felt I had enough in common or the type of friendship that might blossom into a closer relationship. In the meantime, the questions from home kept coming and photographs of eligible women were beginning to arrive. Instinctively, I vetoed them without even looking at them. It was a delaying tactic. I just didn't know what to do for the best.

In Year 5 we had the option to apply for an elective, a period of up to three months away from our medical school, usually abroad, which offered students an opportunity to broaden their horizons in different healthcare settings, to gain experience relevant to the specialties they were planning on pursuing, or perhaps to come to a decision about how they wanted to specialize, and generally to enhance their CVs. Those who were intending to go into research could make an early start. Others chose hands-on relief work in low-resource countries. I already had direct experience of poverty and the health problems it created. What I was looking for was a way of providing solutions.

I was thinking about specializing in cardiology or general surgery and I wanted to go to America. It would also be a great chance to check out the US healthcare system to see whether working there was something I might consider. Needless to say, America is always one of the most popular choices for electives and places would be at a premium. I made sure I put in my application as early in the year as I could. I looked at various possibilities, all of which would have been fantastic, but my heart was set on one institution: Harvard. I was in awe of the reputation of this world-famous university and the prospect of being able to add the name of such a prestigious Ivy League medical school to my CV was irresistible.

Another Imperial student had been to Harvard Medical School the previous year and he gave me advice on how to apply and some useful general information. I had to finance the trip myself and there were fees involved, but there was a hardship fund available to which I applied at the same time. I was accepted for a month's 'clerkship' in the autumn of 2008. Harvard waived the fee.

That May I became a British citizen. My main motivation for taking this step was practicality: it would ease my passage across borders. In my career I would need the freedom to travel and it would allow me to return to Afghanistan. But gaining my citizenship had an emotional resonance for me as well, one that perhaps I hadn't anticipated. It told the world that I was no longer a refugee and that Britain was my home.

I was heading to the airport for my flight to Boston when I took a call from Kabul. 'Mum has not been well for a few days. She is OK, but one side of her face and her body are paralysed.'

It was obvious to me she'd had a stroke. 'I'm on my way to catch my plane to the US. Shall I come home?'

'No, no, you go ahead. That's the reason why we didn't phone before. She told us not to say anything to you because you'd only worry and rush over. But we thought you should know.'

They put Mum on the phone. She insisted that the paralysis was minor and that she was all right. She knew the elective was important to me and it seemed that it might cause her more stress if I dropped everything and diverted to Kabul. 'I will call every day,' I promised. Nevertheless I spent the whole journey fretting about my mum and how I was failing in my duty to be with her.

I arrived at Logan Airport in Boston on a bright morning in late October, my head stuffy from the flight and a scramble of mixed emotions. I inhaled the sharp, energizing air of the American East Coast and took a taxi into the city. The taxi was big, the cars were big, the highways were big. Everything was big. It was amazing to see the kind of landscape so familiar from films and TV programmes passing the car window in real life.

I had rented a studio flat through a landlady recommended to me by the guy at Imperial. It was in the middle of town, almost opposite the hospital. I found the landlady, collected the keys, dumped my bags and went out to explore the hilly local streets. I had a few days to acclimatize before I was due to join the November surgical rotation at Massachusetts General Hospital. I checked out the restaurants, cafés and food shops and found a Starbucks and a cinema. There was no TV in my room and I was going to need something to unplug me from medical life. The people were friendly and picked up on my accent. 'You're British, huh?' they would say. 'London? We love London!'

I remember going to the cinema one night to see *RocknRolla*, which had just been released. I was on my first, exciting trip to the USA and here I was watching a British film set in London. It was strange, after all the years of missing Afghanistan, suddenly to find myself feeling what seemed suspiciously like homesickness for Britain.

During my clerkship, while remaining officially enrolled at my own college, I would have the same responsibilities and privileges as final-year Harvard students. My American colleagues were all very friendly and welcoming and chatted easily with me in the locker room, but they came from another world, an Ivy League idyll of expensive educations and summer weekends sailing off Martha's Vineyard. They were seriously focused, clean-cut and always smartly turned out in their crisp Brooks Brothers shirts. A couple of the doctors were from Ireland and Germany respectively. They took me under their wing and gave me their phone numbers. 'We know what it's like,' they said. 'Just call if there is anything you need. We Europeans have to stick together!' I reflected on the irony that in the UK I was Afghan, whereas on the other side of the Atlantic I was European.

The main hospital was huge and the workload bigger than I was used to, with a long daily production line of surgeries. If you wanted to assist at a particular operation, you just scrubbed in and went for it, and the consultants – known here as attendants – allowed you to float between surgeries. You were expected to be very hands-on: it was all hold this, press that. I relished being a part of it. The Irish doctor, who was a really bright clinician and had a great sense of humour, guided me through the suturing and other practicalities.

Off duty, I worked in the hospital library or in the internet cafés. I roamed Boston on the trams, trolleybuses and the subway, the 'T'. I went to the Prudential Tower, with its rooftop observation deck and 360-degree view across the city and beyond. It was wonderful to be in New England, celebrated for its rich autumn colours, in the 'fall'. The landscape was stunning. During breaks at the hospital I would interrogate my Irish and German colleagues, and some of the Americans, about the US training pathway. Might working in the States be for me? I was tempted.

It wasn't until I got back to London that I realized quite how much I had missed it and how British I had become. I'd had a brilliant time at MGH and gained unparalleled practical experience. America had so much to offer and the career prospects there were second to none. But I'd worked so hard to climb up through the UK system. It didn't make sense to start all over again. And I loved England, loved its people and its deep history. Britain was where I belonged.

12

The Doctor

IN 2008 I RETURNED to Afghanistan as a British citizen, having not seen my parents since 2005, ahead of my last year at Cambridge, when I'd met up with them in Pakistan. Top of the agenda at home was the marriage issue. My mother and sisters had been busy. Mahvash and Shabana had been identifying suitable candidates among girls they knew from school and the quest was uppermost in my mum's mind at every wedding she attended. My sisters told me that if an eligible young woman was pointed out to her she would get out her specs for a closer look.

My mother had been receiving a higher number of callers than usual who just 'happened to be passing' and took the opportunity to casually mention their daughters. Marriage is, in Afghanistan even more than most societies, a marriage of families, and the means by which their stability is ensured. I imagine a doctor trained in the UK with the potential to earn a good salary would have ticked off one or two of the attributes required in a son-in-law. I discovered that I was also something of a local celebrity on the strength of an article about me that had been published in 2007 in the education pages of the *Guardian*. No doubt my dad had been showing this to everyone he knew.

My mother would then visit selected families to meet their daughters. She approached her mission with characteristic practicality. My sisters gave her pep talks beforehand ('Mum, please make sure you stay long enough to finish your tea!'), fearful that if the potential fiancée didn't meet with her approval she would just get up and leave and inadvertently give offence.

Through these time-honoured rituals they had come up with two or three young women they thought I might like to meet. My role in this intricate choreography was to be present somewhere in the house when they called on us with their families in order to be 'accidentally' encountered in the hallway on their way out. The daughter and I could then be introduced, exchange greetings and get a good look at each other. I would pay a return visit with my family to their house, where a similar rendezvous would take place.

It was only after participating in a couple of these meetings that it dawned on me I was no longer comfortable with the idea of marrying someone I didn't know. It was nothing to do with the women I met. They were warm, educated, engaging and from lovely families. The problem was me. It came as something of a shock because it had never occurred to me I might feel like this. It was an instinctive response, not the result of some inner debate. Although I had been worrying a lot back in London about how to approach this important step, I'd been worrying largely over practicalities. I had always expected to get married this way and it was not until I put my toe into the water that the reality hit me. The person I was becoming, and was still struggling to inhabit, had been shaped, as we all are, by my environment, and it was inevitable that growing up in another country was going to change me.

Now what was I going to do? My parents were in no particular hurry for me to settle down. Their view was that, above all, I must be certain in my own mind that whatever decision I took was one that would make me happy. This was pressure I had been putting on myself. My mum's stroke had disturbed me. It forced me to face my parents' mortality and brought my responsibilities into sharper focus. The stroke had been caused by high blood pressure – without medication my mum's BP was always through the roof. I was genuinely worried that any undue stress might kill her.

It wasn't hard to shelve the dilemma, saying that I wasn't sure about any of the young women I had met and that I felt I needed to consolidate my future plans. Inside, though, I was in turmoil. I didn't want to tell my parents how I felt until I could get it straight in my own mind. If doing the right thing in their eyes was not the same as it was in mine, how was I going to reconcile the two? And what *was* the right thing for me?

In Kabul I was swimming in a sea of muddled impressions and recollections. I walked around my old haunts in Shahre Naow, looking at what remained, what had gone and what was in the process of being rebuilt. When I was caught by a wave of memory, I couldn't be sure if it was true or a fragment of a dream.

Seven years after the Americans had arrived, it was clear that nothing had really changed. The economy looked good on paper but all the money was going into the pockets of a few wealthy men. The rebuilding was being carried out by private concerns, so although it created jobs, it was not benefiting society as a whole. Corruption was rife. Letting out the house and shops was a full-time job for my dad, who had to deal with different people coming to him every week demanding bribes for this or that. He had to pay somebody just to have his tax declarations accepted.

The only money genuinely boosting the economy had been brought in by the international community, the NGOs whose staff rented houses and bought goods and services. My dad had let the Shahre Naow house to tenants working for EMERGENCY, an Italian NGO that provides medical treatment for victims of war, poverty and landmines. They were very active in Kabul and had set up a surgical centre on the site of a former nursery school destroyed in the war by a rocket.

Underneath it all lay the same lack of government competence. The same people who had done the damage were still there and the ruined infrastructure was not being regenerated in the way everyone had hoped. Education was on its knees, healthcare was on its knees. It was confirmation for me, if any were needed, that there was more good I could do for Afghanistan from the UK than in Kabul.

I sat with my parents and brothers and sisters and reminisced. These were emotional days. We laughed, cried, remembered good times and bad. Was that true? Had this really happened? 'Look how far we have come!' someone would say through their tears.

I would return to Kabul regularly from this point on, usually a couple of times a year, but leaving my family behind always unsettled me. It still does, to some extent, to this day. In Afghanistan my protective mask slipped and I flew home to London feeling emotionally and psychologically drained.

I put my mask back on. I made an effort to dress smartly and socialized with the other medical students in the students' mess. By this time I had learned how to engage in conversation about families and future plans, as well as films and rotations, and I was as at ease with my female colleagues as I was with the men. But nobody knew the real me. Not even I, it seemed, knew the real me.

In the clinical arena, everything went very well in my final year. My general medicine and general surgery rotation was at St Mary's in Paddington, where I shadowed the general surgery, urology and vascular surgery teams. I loved the routine of gowning up, the smell of the theatre, the adrenaline rush. I assisted with operations for conditions such as acute appendicitis, bowel cancer and bladder cancer, which required a high level of skill. I still had my sights set on specializing in general surgery, widely viewed as the most exciting discipline, or cardiology, the coolest.

At Northwick Park Hospital in Harrow, I learned about many infections familiar from my childhood. Geoffrey Pasvol, the inspirational clinical dean of the faculty of medicine at Imperial, was the infectious disease consultant at the hospital's specialist department for infectious diseases and tropical medicine, the largest in the country. A South African from Cape Town, Professor Pasvol had studied at Oxford as a Rhodes scholar and worked in Gambia and in Boston. We saw a lot of TB, hepatitis and, of course, malaria. When patients were rushed in from Heathrow, straight off flights from malarial regions, their temperatures oscillating wildly, the initial diagnosis was usually 'pyrexia (fever) of unknown origin'. The first test was usually for malaria. Treatment was with anti-malarial drugs unheard of at Shamshatoo camp in the 1990s.

During my time at Imperial, and beyond, I took courses with the Royal College of Physicians and some external academies. These courses are not restricted to clinicians trained to any particular level, but because they have to be done on top of your regular work, at weekends and in your time off, they tend to be taken mainly by qualified doctors with specific requirements in mind, and course leaders are always a bit surprised to see medical students in attendance.

In keeping with my policy of extracting the maximum value from every opportunity, I did loads of them. I chose courses with universal themes that could be applied across all specialties so that they would be useful whatever direction my career took: leadership, clinical governance, teacher training, research, scientific training. In Year 5 or 6 I even did a course aimed at cardiology registrars. If the leaders were a bit taken aback by the presence of an unqualified student, they seemed impressed by my enthusiasm. For me, going the extra mile was what you did. It was not enough just to scrape by. And when it came to choosing my specialty, I wanted to get in, not to be at the back of the queue.

In my final year I was getting top marks in my clinical attachments, especially for skills such as communication, clinical management and bedside manner. Academically I was doing OK, but not as well as I should have been. And yet I was no longer struggling with my written work. I'd had that problem figured out by my second year at Cambridge. It was my attention span that was causing the trouble.

This felt so wrong. Here I was, on the last lap of my long road to qualifying as a doctor, and yet somehow I couldn't seem to muster the energy and focus I needed to study. I felt disconnected, almost uninterested. As I tried to read, all the deeper concerns I carried around with me would come surging into my consciousness. So I was almost a doctor. But what was I going to do next? My parents were not going to be around for ever, and while five of my sisters had their own families, I might still be responsible for two sisters and three brothers. As I went over everything my mum and dad had done for me, memories were starting to resurface, which I did my best to suppress. The blank canvas of my life that stretched out in front of me seemed more bewildering than exciting. What was I going to do about settling down? I couldn't ignore indefinitely the little biographies and photographs winging their way over from Kabul.

By the time I had completed all my rotations and the exams loomed on the horizon, the mental strain was manifesting itself physically. Crippled by back pain, shoulder pain and sciatica, I couldn't even sit down to prepare for my exams, let alone concentrate. I felt my whole future was on the line. In the end I went to see my tutor, Dr Michael Schachter, clutching a sick note from my GP, and more or less crumpled in front of him. I told him I thought I was on the verge of a breakdown. I felt under such pressure and I had no family here, nobody to talk to about it. He gave me a consoling hug and took me for a coffee. It was the first time any of my tutors had done that. But it was also the first time I had ever really levelled with a tutor. In this less formal setting, and loosened up by the warmth of human contact, I poured out my heart.

Dr Schachter was a senior lecturer in clinical pharmacology, not only a terrific teacher but one held in great affection by generations of students as a mentor and counsellor. When he sadly passed away in 2020, colleagues and former students alike remembered his remarkable qualities of perception, humanity and kindness. He listened patiently. 'You need to acknowledge the stress you are under,' he told me. 'I've never had a student battling with pressure on this scale. Take it easy this year. You don't have to do everything at once. Students think the world is going to end if they don't complete their training on schedule but you have a long career ahead of you. Give yourself time to evaluate how you want it to go, to heal and to sort out your issues.'

He sent me to see a college counsellor. Medical schools have a higher than average number of suicides, and perhaps he felt I should be assessed by a professional to be on the safe side. But that was something I would never have contemplated, no matter what. I had come to understand how precious life is, to ourselves and to those who care about us. I had simply run out of steam. The counsellor referred me to an outside therapist. I spoke to the therapist of my marriage dilemma and my confusion about where I belonged, which I believed to be at the root of my problems.

'Do you see yourself going back to Afghanistan?' she asked me. 'Are you marrying for your parents or for yourself?'

Taking a step back and articulating my feelings freely helped me to untangle them. I needed to work out whether I was living for my parents, for myself or whether some kind of happy medium was possible. Post-medical school training was long and I wanted someone to share my life as it was, here and now. Marriage was not a box to be ticked. A husband and wife must be solidly compatible, to really like each other, and for me that meant getting to know someone properly first. It would not be fair on any woman to marry her and bring her to the UK without being sure I could love her. The decision had to be about me.

As the counsellor tried to get to the nub of my identity crisis, she asked me about the war. I said a little about that, but I was unwilling to speak much about it.

'From what you have told me,' she said, 'and from what I can see, you have symptoms of PTSD and anxiety. I think it would be useful to talk some more about these. Would you like to come back and do that?'

It was the first time anyone, including me, had come out and named these conditions. I'd always taken the view that they went with the territory and that eventually they would just go away. The flashbacks had been fading since Cambridge, but it was true that I still suffered from nightmares, stress and hyper-alertness in crowded areas. I had my own form of cognitive behavioural therapy which alleviated the symptoms, underpinned by my faith, positive thinking and exercise. I didn't want to address them by digging down into my childhood and my wartime trauma. But the therapist said that I had bottled everything up and she believed that my childhood and war-time trauma were precisely the issues that were affecting me now.

I did return for a couple of sessions but I did not continue with them. Trying to access some of the memories I had repressed and to acknowledge and mourn the loss of my childhood was just too painful. When you have therapy you are warned that, although it is ultimately a good thing to bring all this stuff to the surface, and you will feel better in time, the process will be tough. I was creating a new persona and a new life and, as time passed, I felt I was putting the trauma of my early years further and further behind me. It seemed so much easier and so much less torturous just to move on with the alternative, 'normal' life I was constructing than to start raking about in the ashes of my old one. But the little therapy I accepted did help: it unlocked that box in which I had hidden all the baggage of the past, enabling me, very gradually, to begin to unpack and acknowledge it. I had a long way to go before I really opened up, but it was a start.

One step forward I was able to take was to call a halt to the marriage mission in Kabul. I came clean to my parents. If they were a little sad and disappointed, they were perhaps more relieved that I was being honest about what I wanted. But they were clear that they felt the right thing now would be for me to look for a wife in the UK. Nationality was not important. 'This is someone who has to be your friend for life,' they said. 'We trust your instincts. Just as long as you are compatible and she shares our values.'

Having their blessing lifted a weight from my heart.

I took Dr Schachter's advice. Although I did manage to sit my exams and took the results of most of them forward with me into my career, I stayed on at Imperial for another year to repeat one of the courses, medicine, doing the clinicals again and retaking the written papers in 2010.

It wasn't an easy option financially. I had no student loan any more, no grants or bursaries, and the sciatica and back pain, which went on for months, were too severe to allow me to get a job. I had to claim unemployment benefit, which felt like a backward step.

Benefits are there to offer a safety net when trouble strikes but grappling with the system can make you feel like a failure. It was depressing having to spend so much time every couple of weeks standing in a queue of claimants worn down by frustration or despair, all of us waiting to jump yet again through the same hoops. I was interviewed initially by a surly man who barked questions at me and generally treated me as if I was trying to defraud him. When I said that I was a medical student, his whole tone changed. I felt sorry for anyone else reliant on his help and understanding who did not happen to be a medical student. I was lucky, too, that my landlady already knew me and was OK with me staying on in my room. Many landlords will not accept tenants who are on benefits.

But it was the right move. I had been studying at breakneck speed ever since I embarked on those first two AS-levels and it gave me time to take a breath, to digest what I had learned and to process everything that had been happening to me. It was only after I eased off the accelerator a little that I realized just how ever-present and debilitating the tension and hyper-alertness had been. I'd been like a coiled spring for nine years straight.

I added to my collection of Royal College of Physicians courses and in the vacation after the first semester I took a short break with my family in Kabul. While I was there, I wanted to look at how I might be able to use my medical training and my presence in the UK to help improve healthcare in Afghanistan.

All of that obsession with gaining maximum value from my education was driven by the need to give the maximum back. At this point my access and experience was limited to education, so that was the direction my thinking was taking. Afghanistan had for decades suffered a continuous brain drain of medics and teachers and generations of students had been denied a proper education. Developing medical expertise in Afghan hospitals was not so much a matter of making up lost ground as scaling a mountain.

How could I share data or research? Could I somehow transfer the curricula from which I was benefiting to Afghanistan? Might I be able to forge links through my connections with Cambridge and Imperial? I knew nobody at Kabul University.

An opportunity to meet some clinicians arose when I accompanied my mum to an appointment at a private diagnostic cardiac centre. Perhaps there was a route in through the independent sector, I thought. I spoke to a few of the doctors and the centre permitted me to give a poster presentation of a cardiac infarction case study – a big deal for an as yet unqualified medical student. On the basis of my presentation, and our discussions afterwards on the ways in which our research could be mutually helpful, they sent me home with a letter confirming that we had agreed on a collaboration to further strengthen our co-ordination in cardiology and other medi-cally researched parameters. Maybe it would be a foot in the door.

In the spring of 2010, I worked in the college library to refresh my preparation for the medicine exams. This time I was calm and focused. I gained the straight As of which Dr Schachter had known I was capable and emerged that summer a fully fledged doctor, men-tally and physically ready to begin the career I'd set my heart on at the age of five. I could hardly believe my dream had finally come true.

Before beginning my first paid job as a junior doctor, I made another visit to Kabul. At Heathrow I spent my first month's salary in advance on my credit card to buy two beautiful watches for my par-ents. I wanted to give them each a keepsake of this milestone in my life, something that would remind them daily of my gratitude for their unfailing support and all the sacrifices they had made for me. It mattered to me that these gifts came from me as a doctor, bought with money I earned as a doctor, and that they came from the coun-try that had made it possible and which I was now calling home.

In August I began the first of my two foundation years of medical training, FY1, at the Basildon and Thurrock University Hospitals NHS Foundation Trust in Essex. I moved out of London and into the doc-tors' accommodation in Basildon. Junior doctors' hours are famously long and yet, as you are getting to grips with the work, you are also expected to be researching and deciding on your specialty. You there-fore have to be thinking right from the start about the courses and projects you should be doing to gear your CV to your chosen field. I had concluded towards the end of medical school that general surgery probably wasn't for me and was veering more towards cardiology.

We began a fresh round of rotations: urology and general surgery, endocrinology and general medicine, paediatrics. This is when you begin to find out all the stuff they don't teach you at medical school. One of the first lessons is that you need to learn things you never even knew you needed to learn, many of which are nothing to do with medicine itself. In my case it was how to manage my time successfully and how to be a team player.

I'd always enjoyed interaction with patients. In order to make everything as perfect for them as I could, I wanted to know everything about how they were feeling and made sure I went back to them with the result of every last little test. That may have been great for the patient's mood and morale but it was perceived to be not so great for the efficiency of the team I was a part of. A doctor's time is not limitless and you must achieve the right balance between how much you devote to the patients and how much you need to give to the team when there are other jobs to be done.

On one rotation word got back to the consultants that I was not spending enough of my time with the team. In those days I was sensitive to criticism and I felt this to be an injustice, but I had to take a step back and figure out whether perhaps they had a point. I sought feedback from other colleagues and one doctor defended me to the others, telling them that, far from being ineffective, if anything, I was too thorough.

Deep down, though, I knew I had a tendency to fly solo and tried to do too much. I had a competitive nature and I always wanted to be the best at everything. I had to acknowledge that the other doctors were just as good as me. To be effective as a unit we had to share the tasks and I had to learn to listen and to compromise.

Junior doctors often have a sense that they are marginalized and it is not uncommon for them to feel bullied. They are learning on the job and under a great deal of pressure to get everything right. Responding to a resus call for a cardiac arrest, for example, it can be very hairy to witness a senior doctor taking charge and trying to put in a cannula while everyone else is jumping the patient's chest. It takes experience to cope. In FY1, you are stressed before you even start your shift. I used to get nervous just writing up a patient's meds.

And so, after a couple of rotations, I had recognized the need for good teamwork and time management. I had also learned the hard way that it irritated nurses to be asked more than once to do a job. Nurses are vital members of the team and usually have a lot more practical experience than junior doctors. Until FY1, I hadn't really appreciated just how much is expected of them and how heavy their workload is. Once I did, I tried to do what I could to help before adding another task to their to-do list. My nursing colleagues have been a great support throughout my career and I have learned a huge amount from them.

More broadly, FY1 taught me early on how important it is for junior doctors to feel supported by their seniors and to have good, constructive communications with them. Just recently, in the accident and emergency department at the Royal Shrewsbury Hospital, where I work part-time today, a junior colleague ended up spending three hours with a single patient. It was a very tricky case and there were multiple issues to be dealt with, all while following COVID-19 protocol – a psychiatric patient who was autistic, aggressive, had taken recreational drugs and had beaten up a security guard. He also had a stoma needing care.

What the junior doctor should have done in a situation like this was break down the issues in order of medical importance, attend to the immediate requirements and then delegate, in other words, refer, further management to the most relevant department. Instead he had found himself caught between all of them. In the meantime, we had four or five traumas piling up and not enough staff to cope. What I needed to do was not to tell him off for spending too long with a patient while the rest of the team were run ragged but to acknowledge that this was a difficult case and thank him for sticking with it. I then highlighted the lessons he could take from this experience to help him move on a complex patient from A&E more quickly next time.

We have to be open to making mistakes and finding a way to

learn from them. It isn't always helpful even to categorize every unsuccessful decision or action as a mistake. I prefer to call it 'trying different methods'.

I loved the FY1 clinical work. I was always enthusiastic and adrenaline-fired, even when I was tired. Unlike some doctors, I enjoyed being on call. I loved learning, even more than I had at medical school, now that I was immediately applying what I was learning in real life and real time.

Khalid was by this time away studying. He had made it to Leeds University and would end up with several degrees on his way to fulfilling his own dream of becoming a dentist. Before I began my foundation year at Basildon he had come with me to Cambridge, the first time he had ever been there, to a ceremony in which my BA was upgraded to a masters degree, as is customary at Cambridge. I was so pleased to have a family member with me this time, to be able to show Khalid round the magnificent college he'd heard so much about and to introduce to my tutors the little brother for whom I'd been responsible as a student. And they were pleased to see that he, too, was achieving his goals within the UK higher education system. But no one was more pleased than I was.

Since receiving my parents' blessing to pursue love and marriage in my own way, I'd also been going out on the odd 'date'. I'd met up with one or two young women for coffee and if we got on well, and it seemed from our conversation that we were on the same wavelength, I might progress to inviting them to dinner. I enjoyed talking to them, finding out about their jobs, families, and their hopes and dreams, and generally gaining an insight into the female perspective on life without feeling under any pressure.

My approach, it occurs to me now, was a kind of hybrid of the Afghan style and what I understood of Western ways: I was almost taking on the role my parents would traditionally have performed, as well as my own as a 'suitor'. In truth, for the moment, my career was too all-consuming to accommodate a real social life, but it was good to feel free to make friends and potentially to develop a relationship at my own pace.

Each rotation was a chance to spend time with senior doctors and delve into the positives and negatives of their specialty. One of the jobs that tends to devolve to the juniors is requesting scans, and it was through handling X-rays, MRIs and CT scans that I got to know Dr Sami Khan, the senior consultant radiologist. I would pepper him with questions, which he always took the time to answer. Sami is a keen educationalist, with hundreds attending his seminars in person or online. He took an interest in me and asked me questions in turn, about my life and family, as well as practical and medical matters.

I identified with Sami's work ethic, commitment and energy. He put in too many hours: he always seemed to be around, whatever time of day you went looking for him. Originally from Pakistan, he had previously practised in Saudi Arabia, where there was better medical treatment available for his wife, who had been diagnosed with multiple sclerosis fourteen or fifteen years earlier when their first son was only seven months old. He had then brought his family to the UK, where he had come to Basildon as a consultant. As he chatted to me, I began to share a little of my background with him.

For Sami, the purpose of life was giving, a philosophy that chimed with mine and inspired me. Giving to his family and his students was both his motivation and his reward. For years he went back to Pakistan for a week every month or so to take care of his parents, sharing the duties with other family members in spite of living so far away, and reporting on scans remotely. When his father died, he brought his mother over to the UK to live with him.

At the end of each rotation our supervisor would go over our portfolios to check that we were keeping up with the work that would be essential to securing our specialist training placements.

With cardiology top of my list, I was immersing myself in a broad range of medical, surgical and practical procedures while I made up my mind. I had a lot in my portfolio, but it was too diffuse. I needed to settle on my specialty.

'Why don't you consider radiology?' asked Sami.

It wasn't something I'd really thought about as a specialty. And yet radiology was pivotal to almost every case that came through the doors of a hospital.

I explored the idea further. Sami helped, advised and invited me to talks and classes. As well as using imaging to diagnose and treat disease, radiologists are qualified to perform a range of minimally invasive medical procedures guided by imaging technology, such as the insertion of stents into vessels to alleviate blockages, and he allowed me to drop into theatre whenever I liked to observe.

I was excited by radiology. It was such a huge subject, broad as well as deep, encompassing and tapping into every other medical discipline. It entailed five years' training to consultant level. The career prospects were excellent. As a result, placements were highly sought-after and there was a lot of competition.

But I'd never yet been deterred by a challenge.

Part Three

13

Giving Back

IN THE SPRING OF 2011 I met Davina, my future wife, and the jumbled pieces of my life started to fall into place. It didn't happen overnight but this was a crucial turning point. Having someone by my side I could trust, who trusted me, who came to know everything about me and didn't mind, changed everything. With Davina's love, understanding and support, the two different people I had always felt myself to be began to resolve themselves into the person I was now and, very gradually, I started to open up and to heal.

Our paths converged when I was meeting up one evening in London with my friend Mark for a coffee and a catch-up at the Berkeley Hotel in Knightsbridge. Davina was working there as a supervisor. She chatted briefly with Mark and me and, as well as being beautiful, smart and funny, she had a warmth and openness about her that struck a chord with me immediately. Instinctively, I felt I wanted the chance to get to know her better. I was too shy to ask her outright for a date. Before we left I enquired about how I might contact her, trying to give the impression that I might want to do so in a professional capacity, and she offered me her business card.

When I texted to invite her to dinner, she told her colleagues, 'It's a guy who was in the other night. I gave him my card. He's a doctor. He lives in Basildon.'

'*Basildon?* He's an Essex boy! Are you sure he's a doctor?' said one of the waiters.

'Well, he was very nicely dressed: crisp shirt, lovely jacket, beautiful shoes.'

'Perhaps he's a crime boss,' somebody joked.

'Oh, don't!' Davina laughed. 'He was very well spoken, and he had such lovely manners.'

'You should go for it. Just make sure you tell one of us where you are.'

I took Davina to a smart Indian restaurant in Marble Arch. I was trying to impress her; I also wanted to see if she liked Asian food. Her appetite belied her slender build. After eating everything on her plate, she asked me if I had finished and polished off the rest of my meal as well. My God, I thought, admiringly, she eats like an Afghan!

She told me a long time later that I'd seemed nervous, a bit too polite. And she thought I was putting on a posh accent. I wasn't. I just spoke English the way I had learned it. But she must have sensed something of a kindred spirit in me, just as I did in her, because our relationship blossomed from there.

I found out that Davina came from a comfortable background and had been privately educated. She was outward-looking, with lots of friends from different cultures, and well-travelled. She lived alone with her dog, a chihuahua named Louis, in Parsons Green in west London and, until recently, had worked regularly as a model in the advertising sector – fashion shoots for newspapers and magazines, mainly, but also in TV commercials and occasionally as a film extra. The modelling had fizzled out since she'd been at the Berkeley because the role was full-time and she was hardly ever available. She enjoyed her job. She was earning a good salary and it was an opportunity to develop her people skills and to manage staff to meet the challenges of dealing with all sorts of interesting and influential people, from business tycoons and foreign royalty to celebrities. But she was thinking it might soon be time to move on. It involved a lot of late shifts and in the longer term she wanted a normal, nine-to-five lifestyle.

Davina found out rather less about me. I talked to her about my day-to-day life as a doctor, about Cambridge and Imperial and the work I was trying to get off the ground to help with medical care in conflict zones, but not, for a long while, about my deeper history. I was afraid that it would scare her off. I had told her when we first met that I was of Persian heritage and that an uncle had sponsored me to do my medical training in the UK. These were my stock responses in casual conversations. They saved me from having to field questions about Afghanistan and gave the vague impression that my origins were well-off but ordinary, not interesting enough to be worthy of further discussion. As Davina and I saw more and more of each other I realized that at some point I was going to have to backtrack and tell her how things really were.

I would test the water by offering snippets of information to see how she reacted. She was always unfazed and, gradually, I would elaborate. As I came to trust her, I came to appreciate that it was not in her nature to shy away from hard truths or to judge. 'I'd rather you just told me,' she would say, but, sensing that my reticence was not due to any deliberate dishonesty and that there was so much I found it difficult to speak about, she allowed me to open up at my own pace.

She saw signs of my PTSD before she knew enough to make any specific connections. We had gone for dinner at a place in the King's Road and had been seated in an underground part of the restaurant. Dark and windowless, it was crowded and quite noisy. She noticed that I seemed nervous and was sweating a bit.

'Are you OK?' she asked.

'I just don't like confined spaces.'

It was not until I told her several years later about the hours of terror in our bomb shelter as rockets crashed down on Kolula-Pushta, and the choking black hell of that bread oven in which I was almost killed, that she thought back to that evening and put two and two together.

For my second foundation year I would be back in London, at the Royal Free Hospital. Before starting there in the summer, I went to see my family in Kabul. During my foundation programme it was hard to push forward with my ambitions to make a difference in Afghanistan. Any research I wanted to do or ideas I wanted to take further had to be tied in with my leave, and with the additional work I was taking on to enhance my career prospects, which ate into my time off. And I didn't really have a clue where to start.

I had made contact with the Association of Afghan Healthcare Professionals (AAHP-UK), a British-based organization that supported the health sector back home, and had been invited to attend their conference. Chatting with a few doctors there, I told them I was keen to contribute and asked what I could do. They had links with a couple of US-run hospitals in Kabul, CURE and HOPE.

'What about Afghan hospitals?' I enquired. 'What about the university?'

'The Afghan hospitals are very difficult and so is Kabul University,' I was told. 'They haven't been receptive to our approaches. They don't like people coming from abroad and telling them what to do. They see it as patronizing.'

I notified the association of the dates of my trip to Kabul and they arranged for me to give presentations as a guest lecturer at the HOPE International Hospital and CURE, operated by a small American charity. At HOPE I offered an introduction to radiology. I delivered my presentation at CURE International, on research and clinical audit (improving patient care and outcomes through systematic review), at 7am, the only time of day that gave all the staff the chance to attend.

My hosts at CURE invited me to a dinner at the hospital to allow me to chat more informally to their doctors, who'd all had to rush off to attend to their patients after my presentation. At the dinner I was introduced to another guest, a very distinguished one: Dr Faizullah Kakar, who was at that time the government minister advising the president on health and education. I revealed to him that we had met before, when he was chancellor of the Islamic University at the Shamshatoo camp and I was a thirteen-year-old refugee student. He was surprised and delighted to find that the visiting speaker of whom he had heard good things was one of his alumni. He gave me his card and said that he would like to talk to me some more about the ideas I had floated during our conversation.

'Come and see me tomorrow. You can either come to the Presidential Palace or to my home.'

The hospital chief couldn't believe it. 'I've been trying to get him here for three years and here you are with an invitation to the palace on your first meeting!'

I was really excited by this unexpected opportunity. Whatever the shortcomings of the government, I knew Dr Kakar to be a man of global vision with a genuine vocation to improve health and education in the country. And he had the ear of the president, Hamid Karzai.

Back at my parents' home, my dad was thrilled by my news. 'Go to his house, not the palace,' said my mum grimly. 'It's safer.'

I needed to gather my thoughts before visiting Dr Kakar. I hadn't come to Kabul with any firm proposals in mind, but this was a chance I couldn't afford to waste. My ideas were developing as I gained experience. As a medical student I'd been focusing on the input needed in the higher education sector. Now that I was putting into practice what I had learned in the real world, I'd been looking more towards addressing what was lacking in the hospitals. I didn't see why we couldn't establish direct links with the struggling Afghan healthcare system. There was no point in offering help to hospitals run by NGOs, which were well-funded by donations, comparatively well-equipped and staffed by international healthcare professionals who provided adequate training. Those weren't the hospitals that needed the help.

Surely there must be a way of setting up a channel of communication between the medical community in Afghanistan and their counterparts in the UK? Perhaps some kind of exchange scheme whereby volunteers could come over to educate, train and deploy their expertise at the sharp end? The clinicians were the people who could tell us exactly what it was they needed most urgently, but, given the complexity and volatility of Afghan politics, government approval would be required for such a project. Dr Kakar had the influence to get it.

I arranged an appointment with him at his house in an upmarket suburb of Kabul. On arrival I was vetted by his security people and shown into a comfortably furnished meeting room, where Dr Kakar joined me. As tea and sweets were brought, we chatted about the Islamic University, and he was intrigued to hear how I had got from there to qualifying as a doctor at two of the UK's top medical schools. The Islamic University was still going: it had been relocated, initially to Peshawar and then, in 2008, to Khost province. It was now called the Sheikh Zayed University in recognition of the founder of the United Arab Emirates, which had funded the move to Afghanistan.

Dr Kakar listened to what I had to say. I told him there were hundreds of skilled doctors in the UK who were ready and willing to give up their spare time to come to Afghanistan and share their expertise with the clinicians in government-run hospitals if the connections could be put in place to facilitate it. Of course, I had no idea how many volunteers there might be, but medical professionals are a humanitarian and philanthropic bunch, and I was confident that, if presented with a firm proposal, the volunteers would be there.

Dr Kakar understood that direct links with hospitals would be necessary for such an idea to work. We discussed it in principle: how many hospitals it would be practical to involve, numbers of volunteers, rotas and frequency of visits. The biggest issue was safety. It would not be possible to bring foreign doctors into the country without being able to guarantee high-security accommodation and transport for them, and such accommodation would have to be purpose-built. Dr Kakar gave me his permission to pass on a report of our meeting to the AAHP-UK, and I left feeling that, at the very least, there was the outline of a project in his mind and in mine.

I dropped into one or two of the local hospitals at random and introduced myself to some of the doctors. I asked how things were going, what they were short of and how I might be able to help. Far from feeling patronized, the clinicians on the ground were pleased to see me. Smart, compassionate and dedicated, they seemed glad of a sympathetic ear, someone to moan to about how this machine didn't work, that machine didn't work and how there had been no power on one of the wards all day. Some of the tests they were using were years old.

I flew back to the UK to give the AAHP-UK the good news about my meeting with Dr Kakar. I put them in touch with his office before turning my attention to moving into the doctors' accommodation at the Royal Free and preparing myself for my second foundation year.

FY1 is stressful for every junior doctor. You are more of a supernumerary in clinical situations and the trainees tend to stick together, working as a pack and distributing the tasks between them. FY2 was a step up.

I was in charge of my own section of about seven beds on the wards and the rotations – cardiology, general medicine, neurosurgery and acute medicine, including A&E admissions – were complex fields with inbuilt learning curves. The hospital is located in one of the nicest parts of north London, right next to Hampstead Heath, and it was a lovely place to live.

I was maturing as a doctor and a person, and growing in confidence. Feedback from the consultants was consistently good. I was enjoying the social side of life more and learning to control my PTSD symptoms better. My heart still raced when I had to speak up in front of groups of people on ward rounds, but on the outside I was composed. And after putting in such long hours I still found it hard to get to sleep before 1 or 2am and be back for the ward round at 8am. I used to take a short cut in the mornings round the back of the hospital where the maintenance people would have their equipment, sidestepping and jumping over all their stuff in my rush to make up the five minutes' extra sleep I'd allowed myself.

But I felt on top of things. I never hurried off when my shift officially ended. I'd usually be there for a while, chasing bloods or X-rays and generally satisfying myself that all was in order before the night staff took over, in case anything went wrong in the small hours. My instinctive thoroughness served me well. It's what good care is built on. You can't get it right all the time, but as long as you have given everything your full attention you have no reason for self-reproach.

When you are treating the sick every day it is inevitable that you will encounter death, especially in the acute departments where I was working at the Royal Free. I remember being heartbroken to lose a woman who had been brought in after suffering a heart attack. She had not received CPR in time so she had already sustained global brain damage when she arrived with us. She was breathing, but not much else. Our cardiology department was amazingly high-tech and well-equipped and we had one of the country's top heart consultants, but there was nothing anyone could have done. It was just too late.

On my neurosurgery rotation I was at the cutting edge of medicine, involved in theatre in tumour removals and other procedures. After one patient who had been well on admission had a brain aneurysm, a stent was inserted, but there were complications. I was looking after her at her bedside when she had a stroke. I could see the fear on her face as one side began to droop. She was transferred immediately to ICU and placed on life support, but in the end the machine had to be turned off.

I was very upset. She was only in her forties. You can't help but be affected. You wouldn't be human otherwise. But you have other patients who need you and you must train yourself to compartmentalize and move on. We are all going to die and no doctor can prevent that. It's the untimely deaths that get to you.

You focus on what you *can* do, on the many positive outcomes: the potentially fatal cardiac problems resolved; the brain tumours successfully removed. Even when death is inevitable, when you are caring for a patient whose cancer has spread everywhere, you can help to keep them comfortable and take away the pain. I don't think the violence and loss I experienced as a child made me any more susceptible to the trauma of death than any other doctor. The evidence before my eyes that the skills I was honing were saving or improving lives made me, if anything, calmer and less prone to stress and anxiety. I was taking my experience of the world and working with it. The sense of reward inspired me daily and reassured me that I was in the right job.

At the end of FY2, my supervisor flipped through my portfolio, bulging with all the courses, presentations, audits and research I'd done going back to my medical student days. I expected a pat on the back. I was surprised to see a frown on his face.

'This is overloaded with stuff,' he said. 'You need to condense it. You're only an FY2 and you look like a professor!'

I had to narrow the focus and start tailoring the contents to what had most relevance to my specialty. But I have never regretted all the courses, research and presentations. They would stand me in good stead in the future.

In acute medicine, doing night shifts on my own built my confidence. As I gained experience I was becoming more dextrous. At Basildon it had taken me a lot longer to do everything. Here the pace was faster: patients were moved in and out quickly, either on to another department or to go home. You have to learn how to perform tasks correctly and proficiently before you can learn how to do them with speed. When I found I was combining the two, I had an exhilarating sense that everything was coming together.

By the time I left the Royal Free, the worries about my lack of education that had lurked at the back of my mind through medical school had begun to recede. In the practical setting of the hospital, everything I had learned at Cambridge and Imperial came back and made complete sense. All those months I'd been afraid that I was floundering my brain had been acquiring the terminology, the science, the understanding of diseases, and it had no trouble at all retrieving it on demand. I was good at problem-solving in real life and unfazed by heavy workloads or emergencies. I had made it. I was a doctor. Not a nervous trainee, but a good doctor, on a par with other doctors and even better than some. It was a fantastic feeling.

It must have taken me over a year to really level with Davina. I had met her parents a couple of months into our relationship, when they invited us down to their lovely house in Surrey. Welcoming and hospitable, they wanted to know all about my education at Cambridge and my work as a doctor and chatted to me about their own interests. I was pretty vague about my family for a long while. Big families are common in Afghanistan where, culturally, they form the bedrock of society. But you don't meet too many people in the UK with ten siblings and I had no idea what Davina, who had just one brother, would make of it.

It wasn't until the prospect of her actually meeting my family became a real possibility that I decided I'd better prepare her. I approached full disclosure in my usual way: by testing the water.

'There are a few things I need to tell you.'

'OK.'

'What would you do if I told you I had seven sisters?'

'What do you mean, what would I do? I wouldn't do anything, obviously. Have you got seven sisters?'

'Yes.'

'Wow. Well, that's good to know. I just don't understand why you thought it was something you felt you had to keep from me.'

She was right, but these were personal details I'd never discussed with anyone in England and I was still learning how. With her help, I was gradually coming to accept my past, although she still only understood the half of it.

I knew that in Davina I had a partner who was emotionally giving, empathetic, independent, strong and practical. We were on the same page in our outlook on life. It didn't matter to either of us that she had been brought up in the Christian tradition and I was a Muslim. We were united by the common human principles that underpinned both religions and by our shared values as individuals.

I could not yet know what fulfilling my dreams was going to involve, but I knew that our relationship gave me the space and freedom to find out. There is no question that I would not have been able to go on to achieve what I have without her support.

It was important to me that Davina was in tune with the need for me to go back and forth to Afghanistan. She was encouraging and engaged, taking an interest in what I planned to do there and wanting to hear about everything. When I had my first meeting with Dr Kakar in 2011, she was almost as excited about it as I was.

On my trips to Kabul I was dismayed to see how little was changing in the hospitals. It was over a decade since the Taliban had been driven out, and billions of dollars in aid had been pouring in all that time. In 2004 it had been calculated that there was only one medical centre for every 27,000 people in the country, with some hospitals serving up to 300,000, and yet not a single new hospital was up and running. Where had all that money gone?

The initiative I had discussed with Dr Kakar was not progressing as fast as I wanted or thought was achievable. The AAHP-UK were supportive, but my ideas fell outside their areas of activity and their mission, which made it difficult for them to take it forward. While they were doing great work with one-off projects, my vision of a scheme with the potential to have a national impact was something different.

A partnership involving an agreement with Afghanistan's health authorities would have been considered impossible by any UK charity at the time. It would have been the same story with any politically unstable, low-resource country blighted by ongoing conflict and galloping corruption. This is why so much of global health becomes about helping those who don't particularly need it. In the end it is just easier to go and give a lecture at an international hospital where they lay on a lovely dinner and the lights work.

I had remained the main point of contact with Dr Kakar and so I started to keep in touch with him directly. For political reasons, the go-ahead to build the secure accommodation that was essential to any plan to bring in foreign volunteer doctors was not materializing. Dr Kakar thought it best to hold on until after the presidential election, due to take place in 2014. Dealing with a new administration actively looking for new initiatives to help make its mark was likely to be more fruitful.

In the meantime I continued to do what I could. I had organized and chaired a mother and child health conference for AAHP-UK in 2011 and raised money for a charity-run clinic in Afghanistan. In Kabul, I gave presentations on an ad hoc basis and visited the local hospitals to connect with the doctors, help out in any way I could and keep the flame of my mission alive.

Conditions in the provinces were terrible and, waiting in the corridors of the city's hospitals, I would see people from the countryside who had saved up, perhaps sold their cattle, to bring a sick child to Kabul to visit a specialist. When I looked at the hospital's ancient X-ray machine and thought of all the high-tech equipment we had at our disposal in the NHS, it made me want to weep. And yet better imaging technology would not, on its own, have solved their problems. Even if they'd had up-to-the-minute CT and MRI scanners, there wasn't anyone who could accurately interpret the images because there were no qualified radiologists in the state hospitals.

Scans are not actually difficult to come by in this part of the world – provided you have the money to pay for them. They are available at private clinics or from entrepreneurial individuals who have invested in an X-ray machine or a CT scanner and set up shop in a marketplace, where you can go and get a scan, or indeed a blood test, while buying your vegetables. But, not surprisingly, the quality and relevance of the images is variable and they are not much use without a radiologist who can tell you what they show.

Medicine is a field of rapid advances and although the medical schools had been re-established they were still following old-fashioned curricula which had not been updated to match standards now considered the norm elsewhere. And there simply weren't enough doctors, nurses or other clinicians. The new Jamhuriat Hospital in Shahre

Naow, funded by the Chinese government to the tune of some $15.5 million, was a case in point. This had apparently been completed and equipped by 2009 but had still not been opened because sufficient staff could not be found to run it.

Nobody who could afford it had non-urgent medical treatment in Kabul. People didn't trust the healthcare or the diagnoses and there was no such thing as a second opinion. So they continued to travel to Pakistan or India, as many had been doing ever since the outbreak of the civil war. Afghan medical tourists were big business for Pakistani doctors: you would see long queues of them lining up at the border. That included my family – my parents, my sisters and their husbands, their children. It was an inconvenient and costly exercise, involving three or four days away and medical, travel, visa and accommodation expenses, and tiring for my parents as they began to get older.

My mother had a heart condition, and went to Pakistan for a checkup and treatment every six months. By now her movement was hampered by arthritic joints, which resulted in her putting on weight. In 2011 my dad, too, had suffered a stroke. Time is of the essence with stroke yet he was in hospital in Kabul for two days before he was given a scan, by which time it was pretty pointless. He could have died. He was left with enduring weakness in his left arm and hand. The less visible legacies of their traumatic lives were the bouts of depression my dad suffered and my mum's anxiety. After a lifetime of hypervigilance, she needed sleeping pills to get any real rest.

While I was applying for radiology posts in the UK, I returned to Basildon for a couple of years as a trust grade doctor, the NHS term for a non-training position, an option often taken by doctors who are trying out different specialties before committing themselves. I was working in orthopaedics and general surgery at senior house officer level as a locum, on a regular rota just like the other SHOs.

I treated this as an opportunity to continue my training on my own initiative. I mapped out my way through the core surgical training curriculum and found a supervisor to make sure I was hitting the same levels of competency at the same time as colleagues who were already receiving specialist training. By 2014, my supervisor had signed me off as having completed the equivalent of two years' core surgical training.

I had spread my net wider by working a few shifts on my days off and at nights as a locum in A&E. In surgery and orthopaedics, I had a lot of dealings with A&E and I was interested in the limitless range of diseases and injuries encountered there. It was a great way of broadening my experience of the role and application of radiology in diagnosis and emergency interventions.

Emergency medicine satisfied that deep desire in me to be able to provide aid quickly and to see the results of my efforts. The human contact with patients and their families is heightened in emergency situations, the variety of cases stimulating. On one shift you might be dealing with anything from a child with a bead stuck up his nose to multiple casualties of a serious road accident. You are learning constantly. I have been serving in A&E departments, on and off, ever since. It remains the thread that connects me with my dream and my purpose.

14

Building the Future

DAVINA AND I WERE happy together and secure, and I felt it was time to move things to the next level. And so, in 2013, I asked her to marry me. She said yes.

Sami Khan and his wife Teenat were delighted when I told them our news and invited us to celebrate our *nikah* at their house. This is the contract considered integral to an Islamic marriage. Until we got round to formalizing our union under UK law with a civil ceremony, Davina and I tended to describe ourselves to our non-Muslim friends as engaged, but in the eyes of Islam we were legally married. With an Islamic scholar officiating, you each declare three times before witnesses (in our case, Sami and Khalid) that you accept the terms of the marriage, then there are lots of sweets and that's more or less it. The Khan family decorated a room in their house for the occasion, made all the preparations and provided a handsome spread. It was such a special, happy day.

I was touched and a little surprised when Davina said she was up for coming to Afghanistan with me to meet my family. My parents were over the moon. It was strange and moving to see my homeland through Davina's eyes. It was wintertime, and she had never experienced such low temperatures. The moment we stepped off the plane, her feet turned to blocks of ice, despite her fur-lined boots. But she was enchanted immediately by this new and unfamiliar landscape; by the scent of woodsmoke and lamb sizzling at the food stalls.

In Kolula-Pushta, she was delighted to be enthusiastically greeted by an avalanche of women and children. A feast had been laid on for our arrival and some twenty or thirty of us, crammed into one room, sat down to eat. My mum and sisters, in the belief that European women in general were not big eaters and that, because she was slim, Davina would be no exception, had solicitously prepared a smaller plate for her – complete with her own knife and fork, in case she was not at ease eating with her hands.

'I think I can manage a bit more than this,' Davina remarked to me, enviously eyeing everyone else's heaps of food.

'What is it, Waheed? Is something wrong?' asked my mum.

'She wants a bigger plate!'

'Ah!'

'She eats like a goat!' my mum declared later. Which, in Afghanistan, is a compliment.

Davina was happy to be enfolded in the warmth of my big family, with everybody bending over backwards to ensure her every comfort. The language barrier didn't prevent her and my sisters from quickly discovering that they shared a similar quick-witted sense of humour. Shabana and Mahvash can speak a little English. My brothers are fluent and so are all of the kids, who were keen to try out their translating skills.

It touched my heart to see the protective cordon my parents had always held around us all extended to my wife. They understood how much I had suffered from trying to do the right thing on my road to marriage and any concerns about culture or religion had been swept away. They were just overjoyed for me.

Davina was eager to see Kabul. She was accompanied by my family wherever it was considered safe for her to go. A trip to the market involved a group of my sisters surrounding her on all sides, escorted by one of my brothers. She would be dressed in Afghan clothes and a headscarf but her height drew attention to her European looks, which marked her out as a prime target for kidnap or attack by insurgents. She didn't fully understand at first why my sisters insisted on hurrying her when she wanted to browse at a stall.

She was appalled at the sight of small children begging in the snow with nothing on their feet but flip-flops and agog at the cars on the streets so laden with passengers, all sitting on top of one another, that the kids' faces were squashed flat against the windows. To us that was normal: the definition of a family saloon in Kabul.

Before our trip Davina had put out a call on Facebook for second-hand clothes, shoes and so on and had brought with her two huge suitcases stuffed full of donations. I remember her holding up a jumper in the flat at Parsons Green and complaining, 'This one's got a hole in it.'

'That doesn't matter,' I said. 'If it's warm, bring it. These people have absolutely nothing.'

With my dad and my brothers, we visited a refugee camp for dis-placed people on the outskirts of the city, where Davina distributed her supplies. First one wide-eyed child would emerge from a small mud house, its frozen mud floor furnished by a gas stove and a cou-ple of pots, followed by another and then another and another . . . Davina was, we were told, the first female Western visitor they'd ever had. 'My God, how many people are living in there?' she asked as other families ran from their huts towards my dad and my brothers, who were surrounded by hands grabbing for the few afghanis they had brought to share out.

One of the mothers took Davina's arm to lead her into her house.

'Don't go in,' I warned her.

Davina glanced at me questioningly.

'It might not be safe.'

Kabul and the areas immediately around it were relatively calm at this time but that didn't mean it was beyond the realms of possibility that there was a guy with an AK-47 hiding behind the door.

'How on earth are they surviving here?' asked Davina.

'We lived in a house very like this when we were refugees. Maybe even a little worse than this. When I was five, and very ill with TB.'

For a moment, she was speechless.

'People can survive,' I told her. 'They just need someone to give them a chance. It's why I do what I do.'

That year my application for radiology training was successful. I was on cloud nine. Specialist training posts were like gold dust, few more so than in radiology. The pick of the deaneries was allocated according to a ranking of the selected applicants and my first choice, to remain in London or the south-east, where Davina and I were settled, was not available. But my top choice outside the area was. I'd heard great things of the radiology training at the North-West Deanery, where I was offered the position of registrar in clinical radiology, starting in August 2014. These posts provided 'run-through' training, a guaranteed route all the way to consultant level, as long as you continued to meet all the necessary criteria and passed the relevant exams, which was why they were so coveted.

As we had always been aware that my radiology training might involve relocating we were primed to take the decision to move north. I would be doing six-month rotations at five hospitals in the Merseyside area, beginning at the Royal Liverpool University Hospital. The north of England was new territory to both of us. We warmed to the calmer pace of life, the space and the countryside. We decided to make our home in Chester, a picturesque little city steeped in history. Right at the end of the year, we had a quiet civil wedding at the local register office, attended by a few friends and family, with a reception at home afterwards.

I was passionate about radiology. It was at the heart of all the decisions made at MDT meetings and I loved its range and its depth. The level of detail involved in every case suited someone like me, who likes to dig down into everything.

It was at the Royal Liverpool that I began to pay attention to the ways in which telemedicine was being used to share scans within the hospital and beyond. Some radiology work is routinely outsourced to save the NHS time and money, to clear backlogs and when results are needed urgently out of hours, which makes the system particularly useful in A&E departments. In the evenings images are transmitted securely to a hub which allocates them to a remote consultant radiologist, who reviews them and returns their report to the referring clinician, just as they would do within the hospital. Scans might be reviewed by a radiologist based elsewhere in the UK or in Europe. Some London hospitals even send them to Australia.

I would chat to my colleagues and consultants about the links I was establishing with Afghanistan. Initially, I'd found that doctors were keen in principle on the idea of volunteering for a stint there but increasingly reactions were sceptical. Travelling to and from the country would not be straightforward and since doctors can't just take leave at the drop of a hat, arrangements would have to be put in place a long while in advance. It was looking expensive and generally logistically difficult to set up such a programme even for Kabul, never mind the provinces and conflict areas.

As ever, the prime concern was safety. At this point I was still hopeful that the promised doctors' accommodation would appear, but just how safe could it be, realistically? Only that spring, the US-run CURE hospital, where I'd given my presentation three years earlier, had been attacked by a rogue member of the security forces and three Americans, one of them a paediatrician, had been killed. And this had been the second such incident in a month. The one thing I simply could not do was put the lives of volunteer doctors at risk.

I was beginning to see the limitations of my project and, as I watched radiology work being outsourced, I was starting to think about how it might be possible to use telemedicine to support emergency departments in Afghanistan. The snag was that our hospital systems were complex and they cost millions.

A colleague suggested I talk to Dr Elizabeth Joekes, who was very involved in global health. Dr Joekes, who was from the Netherlands, was a senior radiology consultant at the Royal Liverpool. Although we were working in the same department our paths hadn't yet crossed. I discovered that, before coming to Liverpool, she had been head of radiology at a teaching hospital in Ghana and that she was an external radiology adviser for Médecins sans Frontières (MSF), or Doctors Without Borders, one of the best-known humanitarian medical NGOs, which has been operating across national boundaries in conflict zones and areas of endemic disease for forty years.

When I happened to find myself on ultrasound duty with Dr Joekes one day I seized the chance to ask her about her work in Africa. Between scans, we spent the whole session talking about the capabilities of telemedicine. From their clinics on the front line, MSF sent Dr Joekes radiology images for review, along with the relevant clinical information, by photographing them against a white background and transmitting the picture. My mind was whirring with ideas about how I might be able to deploy a system like this to exchange scans and reports with hospitals in Afghanistan. Dr Joekes was so enthusiastic and committed. After the session was over she invited me to come to her office to discuss telemedicine in greater detail. I had further conversations with her about the fundamentals, she connected me with others interested in global health and I did some research of my own.

Telemedicine falls into two distinct categories: live and interactive (synchronous) or time-delayed (asynchronous). The platform that linked Dr Joekes with MSF, which I discovered could be trialled free on a small scale, used the asynchronous store-and-forward technique employed by our hospital telemedicine system, whereby data are temporarily stored before transmission. The image is uploaded from the camera, captured on a digital file, sent to a hub and allocated by a co-ordinator to a remote radiologist.

It is a method that has many advantages, especially in communications with areas where internet access is patchy, and it is suited to non-emergency medicine, where you are dealing with one issue at a time and there is no need for an immediate response or an ongoing dialogue between the same specific doctors. In her role as an external radiology adviser, Liz was supporting the MSF staff, not working directly with local medics, so this ticked all the relevant boxes for her. Emergency medicine, however, requires live support and the capacity to exchange data in an uninterrupted thread and in real time.

I wasn't optimistic that anyone in the Afghan hospitals would have the skills to operate these systems, even if they could get the necessary equipment. Still, I was excited to establish that, in principle, all that was basically required to put Afghan hospitals in direct contact with specialists in the UK was an internet connection, some computer monitors and a few laptops. This would be enough to enable UK doctors to report on cases and potentially to supervise live emergency treatment as the technology evolved. Such a network might also provide a video-conferencing platform in the future for training and lectures for both clinicians and university medical students.

Afghanistan now had a new president, Dr Mohammad Ashraf Ghani. After the elections in the summer of 2014 resulted in a stalemate, the US had brokered a national unity government in which his opponent, Dr Abdullah Abdullah, took on the new role of chief executive officer. An anthropologist by profession, Dr Ashraf Ghani had a masters degree and PhD from Columbia University in the States and was a former chancellor of Kabul University. He and his family had settled in America, but he had renounced his US citizenship to allow him to stand in the Afghan elections. His wife, who was of Lebanese Christian origins, was similarly highly educated and, as first lady, was establishing herself as an advocate of women's rights in Afghanistan.

With two camps in the government, it had taken until 2015 to confirm the cabinet. Dr Kakar was retained as the minister advising the new president on health and education. Eager to try to engage this new cohort of politicians to make progress with my healthcare initiative, I booked some leave and flew out to Kabul in June.

I had not abandoned the idea of bringing specialist volunteers to Kabul – I was hoping we could do that as well – but I put it on the back burner to concentrate on what could be accomplished on the front line more immediately by telemedicine. My priority was to find a way of providing help now, not in ten years' time. The solution therefore had to be simple and based on the resources already available, not reliant on an infrastructure from the government that might never be delivered.

I prepared a detailed proposal for a charitable project and sent it to Dr Kakar. He was due to be away in the States but before leaving he smoothed a path for me to the minister of public health, Dr Ferozuddin Feroz, and Professor Mohammad Osman Babury, the deputy minister for higher education. 'Please give this young man your support,' he asked them. 'He has made a great success of his medical career in the UK and he wants to help.' With such a message coming from the office of the president, the ministers were more or less duty-bound to give me a hearing.

Ahead of my arrival in Afghanistan I had been put in touch with the deputy minister of public health, Dr Ahmad Jan Naeem. In Kabul he introduced me to their adviser, Dr Mamosai Zewar. A meeting was arranged at which they would both be in attendance, along with several of their departmental colleagues.

They were all curious about how a refugee from Kabul had ended up as a doctor in the NHS and my story prompted general reminiscences of the war. Everyone had stories of their own and quite a few of those present had been refugees, too. I told them that my family was in Kabul and how my youngest brother was training to be a doctor. Our shared experience was a great ice-breaker. There was a palpable collective pride in what we had all managed to achieve and a feeling in the room that I was one of them, someone who empathized with the pain and suffering of the Afghan people. The power of common ground to open up an effective diplomatic channel made a big impression on me, which I filed away for future reference.

Although this created a welcoming atmosphere, at the outset there was nothing forthcoming from the government side. As I would learn in the years that followed, sometimes it seems that no donation but money is seen as a kindness. This response is not unique to Afghanistan: it happens with governments in many low-resource regions and it comes from the top, not from the people on the ground.

It is this, rather than any practical or technological problems, that makes implementing solutions from the outside so challenging and why so often a diplomatic approach has to be taken to achieve results. Governments tend to be unwilling to countenance any foreign collaboration in their healthcare systems, let alone something that potentially permits outsiders to penetrate their whole medical network through direct hospital-to-hospital co-operation. Without a proper agreement in place, it may be illegal for a doctor from another country to contact you for advice.

'Does your charity donate money or equipment?' somebody asked.

'I am not here to give you money or equipment,' I said. 'What I can bring you is expertise. What I would like to discuss with you is how we could best use this expertise to support your hospitals.'

'That won't work in Afghanistan,' one adviser cut in. 'We need more machines, instruments, tests.'

'I don't have money for tests,' I insisted. 'I have doctors who want to help.'

I knew that this health ministry's flagship project was to build, or rebuild, fourteen hospitals across the country, to include the provision or upgrade of emergency and intensive care departments. Some of them already had facilities described as emergency departments but they were antiquated and poorly equipped.

It beggared belief that it had taken Afghanistan fourteen years to get round to delivering primary and emergency healthcare, which should have been the first priority once the donations had begun to flood in. Funds allocated for building hospitals had disappeared under the previous administration. But at least we were here now. All new elected governments want to present themselves as new brooms, sweeping away the errors of the past, and I needed to convince them that I could enhance their political showpiece.

I outlined how the upgrades could include a few computers and monitors to accommodate a telemedicine system that would enable remote specialist volunteers to assist with emergency and intensive care management, perhaps, in due course, in real time. Otherwise the only prerequisite was the internet. To be honest, I hadn't a clue about the technical side, but I was confident that those details could be worked out back home. It was a huge deal even to have got this meeting and I had to use it to secure some kind of agreement in principle before I could do anything. I could worry about the practicalities later.

I made it clear than neither I nor anyone else would be taking a salary from this charitable endeavour or profiting from it in any way. Nor would we be seeking any financial contribution from the Afghan government, beyond the provision of the basic equipment I'd mentioned.

My proposal was to trial the initiative in two or three of the hospitals that were being redeveloped. Dr Zewar was key to this plan as she oversaw all the hospitals and had been appointed head of emergency and intensive care nationally. She and Dr Ahmad Jan Naeem responded very positively, quickly understanding how such a venture harmonized with their project and could be of real benefit at minimal cost to the government. She arranged for me to survey five city hospitals the following day.

I went back to my parents' house drained but exhilarated. Then it was jacket off, shoes off ready for an evening of chit-chat with my family. My mum did her best to make sure everyone was happy, which was a full-time job in a family the size of ours. She had two mobile phones and often had one clamped to each ear, listening to two daughters talking to her at once. 'She ought to be head of the UN,' said my dad. By this time he was the proud owner of a red Toyota, which we'd all pile into, seven or eight of us, to visit a sister or an auntie. I sat in the front with my father and my brother Javid, appointed by Dad as the family driver, with Mum, Farid, a couple of sisters and whoever else was coming squashed in the back seat.

At my sister's house the kids would all be jumping on me – 'Hello, Uncle!' – and several of them invariably wanted to come back with us to stay overnight with their grandparents. The overloaded car would crawl home at a snail's pace, its undercarriage virtually scraping the dusty, potholed road, grinding to a halt at checkpoint after checkpoint. These were golden times with my family, everyone in high spirits, cracking jokes and laughing.

In the morning it would be back on with my best *perahan tunban* and jacket, and Javid, who had studied economics at university and was working as an English teacher, would take time out to ferry me around from one meeting or hospital to another, waiting outside in the Toyota to drive me on to my next destination.

The day after my meeting with the ministers and advisers he took me to the five hospitals selected by Dr Zewar. These included the rebuilt Jamhuriat, which had finally opened the previous year, and Wazir Akbar Khan, which had already been extensively repaired, under the direction of the International Committee of the Red Cross, and handed over to the Ministry of Public Health ten years earlier with, among other things, a waste system and maintenance workshop installed by the Danish Red Cross and central heating provided by the Norwegians. The others were Ibn Sina, Khair Khana and the Indira Gandhi Children's Hospital.

I was shown round the new emergency departments being set up. When I say 'set up', they were clearly thinking about it – there were certainly plans in place. However, as yet there was no sign that anything was actually being done.

I looked about me at the patients waiting, many of them still flocking in from rural areas, where conditions were so much worse, some clearly suffering from chronic pain, others almost at death's door. A lump came to my throat. In the four years since I'd first started visiting these hospitals unofficially, absolutely no progress had been made that I could see. With the glacial pace of change in Afghanistan, how long was it going to take for even the modest plans I was proposing to get off the ground, let alone the new units? These doctors and these patients needed help *now*.

I took rough inventories of the equipment and human resources they did have. Understanding the problems was key to understanding the requirements. In Afghanistan most emergency and intensive care medics received only six to twelve months of specialized training. It wasn't nearly enough. Neither did they have the opportunities enjoyed by other clinicians to travel abroad for training or conferences.

I talked to some of the doctors, when they were able to stop for a minute. They were so stretched, rushing from one place to another, under stress and on the back foot the whole time. Those I spoke to all said, as Kabul doctors had been saying to me off the record for four years, that it would be great if they could be linked up with experts in other countries.

There were the perennial complaints about scarcity of equipment. 'Let's look at what you have got,' I said. 'You have an X-ray machine, that's good.' I made a mental note that volunteers at home would need to be briefed not to expect to see high-tech MRIs or CTs from this hospital. When I mentioned the internet, one or two gave me a cynical glance. The government had been promising the internet but networks had yet to be installed.

On my whistle-stop tour of the hospitals I was getting more real information from the clinicians about the types of diseases and conditions they were dealing with and the medical specialties in which they were desperate for expertise than it was possible to acquire from hours' worth of meetings with government departments and administrators.

At one of these hospitals I had the lightbulb moment that changed everything. It dawned on me that, everywhere I went, nearly all the doctors were using social media on their phones to keep in touch with one another, fix meetings and so on. I began asking people about their apps. 'Viber,' some told me. It rang a bell. I realized that this was the instant messaging app my nephews and nieces were using to exchange texts, images and video calls with their friends. Everyone had a smartphone, mostly cheap replicas of the leading international brands, and access to the internet via the mountain-side masts and inexpensive deals on offer from their phone companies.

Could we tap into this Viber? Why couldn't doctors just snap photographs of radiology images, like the MSF clinicians did for Dr Joekes, only on their phones? A number of doctors were on Skype, more familiar then in the UK. Both networks were common in Afghanistan. The means to bring live telemedicine to Kabul was right there in front of our noses.

I was euphoric. 'I have figured out how to do it!' I announced at home that evening. Of course, there would be myriad legalities and practicalities to negotiate – matters of clinical governance, patient consent and confidentiality, data protection, language, to name just a few – but the key thing was that we could make use of the technology most of the doctors already possessed and didn't have to be trained to operate. If the government came through with the computer equipment and connections, all well and good. If there were problems and delays, we would have options. Either way, these social media apps would give us an instant, direct communication channel with the medics doing the actual work.

I started collecting phone numbers from individual doctors. I needed more time to talk to them and their department heads before I left Kabul. Time was something they didn't have in the hospitals and there was always someone whose input was necessary but who wasn't around. My best move was to get the clinicians out of the hospital setting. I asked the ministry for permission to give a teaching seminar. 'What do you want to talk about?' they asked guardedly.

'Emergency medicine and trauma management. It will be a good fit with your emergency and ICU programme.'

With their blessing I organized a half-day seminar for the coming Friday, a day when a lot of hospital staff were off. I invited doctors, nurses and other clinicians from all over Kabul. This gave me a good opportunity not only to give a talk and discuss case management but to meet more doctors, to build a rapport with them and to get a feel for how medics in the UK would be able to co-operate with them effectively.

I spoke in a mixture of Dari, Pashto and English, trying to gauge the general standard of language skills, and chatted with people informally to gain a sense of the level of medical proficiency. I was meeting a young demographic of dedicated healthcare professionals, some of whom had quite good English. The influx of international organizations since 2001 had brought with it previously unknown opportunities to learn English and other European languages. This was a very talented bunch of clinicians, bright, capable and eager to learn. All they lacked was the training they needed and deserved.

On the higher education side, I'd had meetings with Professor Babury, and with the chancellor of Kabul University, where we discussed providing e-learning modules and video-conference lectures by science and medical experts in the UK and Europe. Dr Kakar had also put me in touch with the Ministry of Defence, who were in charge of the military hospitals, but in the end I decided not to arrange a meeting with them. In a country as riven by factionalism as Afghanistan, political sensitivities were acute and, as I reviewed the progress and responses to my ideas, it was clear that if this partnership was going to work, on our side it had to be strictly humanitarian and philanthropic, untainted by any perception of political, cultural or religious bias.

By the time I left Kabul I had the go-ahead from the ministry for a six-month trial with the five hospitals I'd surveyed. Officially, they would be appointing one English-speaking doctor, with emergency and trauma experience, from each hospital to translate if necessary. But I had already been working to directly recruit all of the doctors with whom I'd interacted in each of the emergency departments. I'd gathered a long list of contact details and when I got home this was indispensable in helping me to figure out who was using Viber and who was on Skype.

I wanted to start the clock ticking on those six months as soon as possible. Now I had to deliver on the promises made in my proposal. While I had discussed my project with a number of colleagues, as yet I had no firm roster of recruits or system in place. It was going to be a busy few months.

15

Healing

'DOCTOR SAHIB, CAN YOU hear me?'

The incoming video call was from Kabul. I realized that I had my first Afghan doctor on the line. I was so excited. But I kept my voice calm and measured and reminded myself that this was no time to be punching the air in triumph. First of all I had to solve his problem.

'This is Dr Arian. Tell me how I can help.'

I was at work and the doctor was phoning me direct from a Kabul emergency department. He was with a patient who'd been in a car crash, a young chap who was having difficulty breathing. They'd done an X-ray but were uncertain whether he might have a punctured lung.

As it was a radiology case, I would be able to review it myself. 'If you can put the X-ray up against a white wall, take a picture of it and send it to me on Skype with your case notes, we will give you the opinion of specialist radiologists here,' I told him.

If a patient has a significant lung puncture, you would put in a chest drain. But if he hasn't, or it is minor, inserting a chest drain could do him harm. There is a risk of puncturing the lung while you're performing the procedure. I took my break and examined the X-ray. It seemed clear to me that the lung was not punctured. I phoned Sami Khan, discussed the case with him and sent him the image. He agreed with my diagnosis.

I got back to the doctor in Kabul.

'No punctured lung. He has rib fractures but they are uncompli-cated.' Rib fractures with 'flail segments' might also have warranted

229

a chest drain. I suggested the type of painkiller I would use to make the patient more comfortable. He seemed grateful and relieved.

I went home high on adrenaline. Everything had gone like clockwork. 'It's working!' I told Davina jubilantly. 'The message is getting through!'

That summer I had started ringing round prospective volunteers. I had been keeping a list of consultants and other colleagues, past and present, to whom I'd spoken about charity work and who I knew were always ready to give a bit above and beyond. My first volunteers were drawn mainly from the emergency, orthopaedic, surgery and radiology departments in Basildon and Liverpool. I tried to make it easy for them to commit. I checked out the apps and media they used and asked if I could send them cases. 'You can help from wherever you are, just with your phone. It would be maybe an hour of your time every so often. Are you in?' They were.

The key to the success of this co-operation was my goal of a free flow of information from doctor to doctor. That and its simplicity. It wasn't about money or the latest technology. Innovation isn't about having up-to-the-minute tech or which app you choose. It's about employing original thinking to solve pressing problems in a user-friendly and efficient way. What works in one place on one day isn't necessarily going to be successful somewhere else on another. You need to keep your mind open to all the options, remain flexible and continually edit your solution as you understand more about the problem and the people experiencing it.

At the same time I stayed in touch with the doctors I'd met in Kabul to establish a relationship and to reassure them at regular intervals that the channels of communication were open. These harassed clinicians were weary of government promises and used to visitors trooping round their departments, talking the talk, and then never hearing from them again. I wanted the message to sink in that we were live, there at the end of a phone line, whenever they needed support, day or night.

Only a few days after that first case, I took a call about a patient in the opposite situation, an elderly man who had been injured in a fall. The X-rays of his lungs had come from outside the hospital, which evidently didn't have its own scanner, and were of poor quality. Even so, a large puncture was easily visible to the trained eye. After running the image past a consultant, I was able to confirm that the X-ray showed the patient did indeed have a punctured lung and suggest the insertion of a chest drain. Otherwise the pressure on the heart would have put him at risk of a heart attack.

Those two sides of the same coin are a simple illustration of the fundamental ways in which we were able to make a difference. If the opposite decisions had been taken in each case, it could have resulted in the loss of two lives.

Of course, things weren't always so straightforward. As the co-operation gathered momentum we would see more and more complex cases requiring a variety of specialists, and assessing images sometimes involved quite a bit of to-ing and fro-ing, as volunteers came back to me to say that a picture was not great, and could I ask the guys in Kabul to try to take a lighter one. But with the constant and rapid upgrading of smartphone technology, the phone photos were of a higher resolution, and by and large of a better quality, than those taken on the conventional camera normally used in the store-and-forward system.

From the outset I followed our agreed clinical governance: every report was monitored by a consultant. What we were doing had to be explained to each patient and their consent obtained by the Afghan doctors for their clinical information to be shared, strictly in relation to discussion of their case and for educational purposes. Our volunteers were required to maintain that patient confidentiality at all times. But when it came to the wider legal, security and privacy standards that needed to underpin the project, I was learning on the job.

In addition to protecting our collaboration from political influence, we had to be working in accordance with UK, Afghan and international law, medico-legal and general. It was essential that our social media exchanges were encrypted. Patients were not permitted to access a telemedicine network directly and it was the responsibility of the doctors on both sides to ensure that the images were not circulated on social media outside their groups. I received a lot of help and advice on all this from my colleagues and seniors at Aintree University Hospital, where I started a new rotation in August 2015.

Aintree was a fresh recruiting ground. In casual conversation with my fellow radiologists, I would mention my Afghanistan project and ask them if they might be interested in getting involved. 'Why Afghanistan?' one of them queried. I explained a little of my background.

'My God, that's amazing,' she said. 'Have you talked to Fin about your charity work?'

'Who is Fin?'

'Fin McNicol. He's the hospital communications director. I'm sure he'd want to know about it and he'd probably be a big help to you.'

I arranged a meeting with Fin and took along my weighty portfolio.

'What inspired you to do this?' he asked me as he looked through the details of my medical education. 'And why Afghanistan in particular?' Again I trotted out my potted history. He questioned me further and began to tease at the roots of the childhood I was lucky to have survived.

'You know what?' he said. 'This is a mission that needs a story and it has already got one – yours. It's an extraordinary story, and the more you tell it, the more you will bring out the stories of others on the front line.' He fished out a photocopy of the eight-year-old interview I'd done for the *Guardian*. 'You need to use stuff like this to recruit your volunteers. You can go a lot further. But you have to put your story out there, front and centre.'

I was a bit taken aback. Although all of this had been driven by my own intensely personal desire to help Afghanistan, the project itself had never been about me. It was all about the volunteers, the struggling medics in Kabul and relieving human suffering; about compassion for patients and solidarity between doctors; about healthcare professionals reaching out to each other across the world to save lives. The last thing I wanted was to draw attention to myself. There was something else that troubled me, too. Although I was reconciling myself with my past, I had never talked about it in any detail in the UK to anyone except Davina, and there was still a lot even she didn't know. And now here was Fin asking me to share it publicly.

Much as I shrank from that prospect, when I thought about it, I realized he had a point. I had already seen for myself how important my history had been in opening doors, with Dr Kakar, with the Ministry of Public Health, with individual Afghan doctors. If it could help to grow the charity, support more clinicians and save more lives, I had to let my story out into the light.

In October Davina and I went out to Kabul, where she was once again welcomed by my family like a visiting princess – especially when we broke the news that she was expecting our first child.

Co-operation with the hospitals was going well. By the end of the year it would have been up and running for six months – long enough for a pilot to produce results. I wanted to chase up the official memorandum of understanding that would give us the green light and to see how things were going with the installation of computer equipment in the hospitals.

I wasn't too impressed on that front. There were still no monitors and the ministry hadn't got very far with the internet connectivity. This was not their fault, to be fair. Installing internet networks is time-consuming and plans for their management and maintenance have to be put in place. It would not have been perceived as a priority by a department constantly distracted by having to fight fires. Every day there was an attack somewhere, or some other calamity requiring all hands to the pump. It was pointless waiting for input from them. I realized we couldn't be asking governments or organizations to bring in new resources, however modest. It either costs money or it takes too long, or both. You need to be ready all the time to adapt or change direction. It looked as if our best option was the smartphone route. It was working well, so where was the problem?

The beauty of smartphones was their versatility. They allowed us to use methods offered by both synchronous and store-and-forward telemedicine systems. We could manage cases by video call, text or in phone discussions. Video calls enabled us to see the patient in the background (with their permission). Once we no longer needed to be live, we could continue case management asynchronously.

As if to underline what the ministry were up against, a couple of days later we were in the middle of lunch with the family when the house was suddenly shaken to its foundations.

'Oh my God, it's a bomb!' shouted my dad.

'Bomb?' retorted my mum. 'Are you mad? It's an earthquake!'

'Everybody *run*!' I yelled. I bundled Davina, in her bare feet, and the kids outside while Javid was practically hauling my parents, neither of them capable of moving very quickly, towards the door. 'What about Davina's shoes?' my dad was saying.

Outside, as the world rocked on its axis, Mum wrapped herself round the little ones while my dad, still talking about Davina's shoes, had to be prevented from hobbling back into the shuddering house to fetch them. My heart racing, I had grabbed Davina's hand and dragged her into the middle of the stony road. I pulled her up and down the street, this way and that, running to get her clear of the taller buildings in case of falling masonry, desperate to protect her and our unborn baby.

It was a long while before it was deemed safe to go back inside the house. As we hung around in the street, one of my nieces lent Davina a headscarf. The presence of this bareheaded, barefoot European woman in the street was attracting stares.

'I've never seen you like that,' Davina said to me later.

'Like what?'

'Your whole face seemed different and I've never heard you shout so loud. You had hold of my hand like a vice and you were running so fast. You were looking up at those buildings as if you could predict which one was going to come down.' She didn't add what she was clearly thinking: this is how it must have been for you in the war.

It was a huge earthquake – magnitude 7.5 – originating in the Hindu Kush mountains and felt across South Asia. It destroyed buildings, triggered landslides and left some 400 dead in north-east Afghanistan, the federally administered tribal areas of Pakistan and India, including twelve Afghan schoolgirls in Takhar who, poignantly, were crushed while trying escape from their school building.

Although there was some damage in Kabul, there were no recorded deaths and the city got off lightly in comparison with other areas of the country. A seminar I was giving the next day with the chief medical officer of EUPOL, the European police mission in Afghanistan, was able to go ahead. EUPOL had agreed to share the trauma response training it provided for law-enforcement officers with local medical staff. The seminar was taking place inside their headquarters and security was tight: the Kabul clinicians had to register in advance and to be suitably vetted. Naturally, an organization like EUPOL was a prime target for terrorism. But it wasn't safe for any European to be on the streets. I was at risk, too, with my veneer of Western affluence.

Over coffee in the conference room, all the talk was about the earthquake. Like my dad's, the automatic reaction of most people had been that it was a bomb. Attacks and suicide bombings by the Taliban were a constant danger. By now Al-Qaeda had been weakened by years of drone strikes and special operations on the ground. The leaders were in hiding and their lieutenants had diversified into training Taliban fighters. But the threat they represented would soon be overtaken by a new and savage fundamentalist splinter group hell-bent on creating a caliphate across Iraq, Syria and beyond: ISIS.

I was pleased with the way the seminar went and pleased to see Dr Zewar in attendance. The news she had for me was all I could have hoped for. Feedback from the hospitals showed that our work was saving a significant number of lives and enhancing the education of our medical colleagues. The ministry wanted to continue the partnership. This was a major breakthrough and an emotional moment for me personally.

It was becoming clear that my plans to support students in higher education would need to be sidelined for now. I would remain in touch with the university and help where I could on an ad hoc basis, but this was a whole separate sphere and we couldn't do everything. Our priority had to be saving lives on the front line.

A letter of appreciation I received from Dr Kakar, sent on behalf of the president, was emphatic confirmation of the partnership with the Ministry of Public Health. I prepared a draft memorandum of understanding between the ministry and our charitable association, enshrining the use of social media networks, and we launched our charity. In keeping with the strategy of spearheading it with my story, we named it Arian Teleheal.

I had more discussions with the ministry, securing their

agreement to let us roll out the project across the country. We would also add the Malalai Maternity Hospital and other new or renovated hospitals in Kabul as they opened. I had to expand our team of volunteers, and fast. We needed cover in general medicine, intensive care, anaesthetics, neurology and neurosurgery, paediatrics and obstetrics and gynaecology, plus more radiologists and orthopaedics specialists. I stepped up my recruitment drive and managed quite quickly to grow our volunteer base, numbering perhaps fifteen or twenty volunteers by the end of 2015, to about fifty.

I approached more people I'd worked with, or was working with now, and maximized the contact networks of our existing volunteers to fill any gaps. Fin McNicol sent a press release about the work of Arian Teleheal, along with a brief summary of my background and Dr Kakar's letter, to some of his local media contacts, resulting in stories in the *Liverpool Echo* and *Manchester Evening News*. They brought us a number of NHS healthcare professionals working in the north-west. He was now talking about 'going national'.

The North-West Deanery was fantastically supportive. My radiology consultant trainer at Aintree, Andy Smethurst, who was also appointed medical director of the Royal College of Radiologists in 2015, asked the college to publish my profile in their newsletter to attract more volunteers. Andy, Elizabeth Joekes and John Curtis, the deanery head of radiology, all volunteered themselves.

Ahead of the launch of Arian Teleheal, I had put in a request to go part-time as a radiology registrar. As the charity gained momentum, the work was incompatible with the rigid rota. Instead I took on ad hoc work as an A&E registrar, picking up shifts in various places, which gave me the flexibility I needed. It kept me plugged into the buzz and immediacy of emergency medicine and helped make up for the reduction in my salary: essential now that I had my own generation of the family to support.

I was on call at the Countess of Chester Hospital the night Davina rang me to say she thought she was going into labour. We'd been exchanging texts in which she reported that all was calm and she was fine.

'Perhaps you're still in the early stages?' I suggested. 'Maybe you won't need to go into hospital until the morning?'

'No! I need you to come home, now!'

The change in her tone left me in no doubt that it was time to go. But when you are on call you can't just drop everything and run off. I was in the middle of dealing with an emergency scan. I finished my report, phoned my consultant, handed over to a colleague, dashed home and brought Davina straight back to the Countess of Chester, where she was due to give birth.

It was surreal seeing our baby born at my workplace, in a maternity ward just across the corridor from the on-call room where I was supposed to be on duty. But in the delivery room I was just another anxious expectant father. My medical training went out of the window. 'What do you want me to do?' I asked Davina helplessly.

'Just stand over there!'

And the first time I held our son Zane in my arms I was as awkward as any other inexperienced dad. It was absolutely magical.

There was nothing new about telemedicine. It was already being used in plenty of settings in the UK and internationally. But while it was not logistically difficult to set up, in many instances it was being operated without the proper governance in place. It was like the Wild West out there: users of some of these systems had no way of knowing exactly who it was they had at the end of the line. Arian Teleheal was doing telemedicine in a fresh and innovative way. We were the first organization in the world to offer live, 24/7 international support using encrypted social media channels at scale, in partnership with a government and in accordance with all the legal requirements.

We were covering almost all specialties and in emergency cases we undertook to provide advice within a four-hour window.

Social media have their limitations. Even though our system was encrypted, no app could be a 100 per cent secure. Users have to weigh up the benefits against potential breaches of data protection. In peaceful, well-regulated countries, data protection may be given greater priority; in war zones, it is a trade-off between watertight security and saving lives. And in Afghanistan, there was no other way of doing that.

It was a big help to us when Simmons & Simmons, a firm of top international lawyers, stepped in to offer us their services pro bono. They enshrined all the governance issues in a legal framework to safeguard the charity, the volunteers and me, which we incorporated into all the partnerships we went on to establish.

I created a group for each Afghan hospital and, where we had strength in depth, specialty groups for the volunteers. Our groups were composed primarily of senior registrars and consultants, with at least one consultant in each. Everyone had sight of each case to enable the seniors, or indeed anyone, to comment. If we needed an expert we didn't have, I'd put out a call to the groups ('Does anyone know a plastic surgeon who might help?') and, somehow, the appropriate specialist would be found.

As the middle man, I was effectively on call round the clock. All the requests came to me in the first instance. I notified the relevant group of an incoming case and a doctor would pick it up. 'I'm in the middle of a consultation,' one might say. 'I'll give you a call in twenty minutes.' Or 'I'm in theatre. I'll be in my office in an hour.' That was another great advantage of using phones. The cases could be reviewed wherever the volunteers happened to be – grabbing some lunch in a hospital canteen, at home, sitting on a train.

I would summarize the cases, and summarize the reports and

advice coming back from the volunteers for the doctor in Kabul. It helped to ensure speed, consistency and clarity in the absence of a common language and to keep the volunteers' phone numbers private. I didn't want to run the risk of some over-enthusiastic clinician in Afghanistan bombarding a volunteer with calls. It was also important to protect the system from abuse, for example, the hijacking of volunteers' details by some entrepreneurial Afghan to promote their business and line their own pockets ('Come to my clinic! I have connections with all these Western specialists!').

A single case could require the involvement of multiple specialists. I vividly remember a little boy who was brought into the Indira Gandhi Children's Hospital from one of the provinces after falling down a well. He was in a coma and had many broken bones. As well as a paediatrician, we provided a radiologist to examine CT scans, an orthopaedic surgeon to advise on managing his injuries and, because one of them was to his head, a neurosurgeon. Thanks to the teams in Kabul and the UK, the boy recovered.

We needed all the resources at our disposal in April 2016, when there was a massive explosion in a busy part of central Kabul. This was the worst single attack on the city in five years. A Taliban suicide bomber blew up a truck laden with explosives in a public car park next to a government building and a second attacker then engaged in a fierce gun battle with the security forces. At least twenty-eight people were killed and more than 300 injured. Many of the casualties were brought to Wazir Akbar Khan Hospital.

The doctors were overwhelmed. 'We have mass haemorrhages and so many patients with plummeting blood pressure but the hospital is running out of blood,' one of them told me. 'What should we do? Hold on for supplies of the right blood group, or start giving what we have got?' While some of our specialists helped with specific cases, others gave advice on medication that could be used to stop bleeding and how to manage blood pressure and maintain hydration while the hospital waited for more blood supplies to arrive. The answer to that doctor's question, by the way, is that if you don't have the exact blood group, you can administer transfusions of O negative.

This case illustrates the value of 'reverse learning' to our own team. No co-operation of this kind is one-way traffic. In practical terms, yes, the help is going in one direction, but there is so much that volunteering can teach our doctors in return. They find themselves tackling problems without the resources they are used to having at their disposal, often problems they would not normally face in their day jobs in the first place, such as extreme, untreated medical conditions or disabilities, injuries associated with war zones and diseases rarely encountered in the UK. Afghanistan suffers from bomb blasts on a level unknown in London, Liverpool or Leicester and the need for blood transfusions on a vast scale is just one example of the challenges they pose. Experience of handling them can be extremely useful to the NHS in dealing with mass casualties at home.

Complex cases provide feedback for every specialty involved. There will usually be multi-disciplinary discussions on the phone between volunteers, with the radiologists perhaps expressing one view and the orthopaedic surgeons taking a different line. And if option one is unavailable to them, they may have to try option two, or come up with an option three. It is fertile ground for everyone, consultants included. We shared case details with all the volunteer groups and with Afghanistan so that everyone could benefit from what had been learned.

I was passionate, too, about 'reverse innovation', the term used to describe the adoption by higher-income countries of solutions tried, tested and implemented in low-resource areas. Using cheap, simple tech, Teleheal was demonstrating the effectiveness of live telemedicine in emergency situations, pioneering principles that were transferable to healthcare providers like the NHS with access to a wider range of technology.

To highlight the charity's work and its links with the deanery and Aintree Hospital, John Curtis and Sumita Chawla, the radiology training programme director, nominated me for the *Health Service Journal* Rising Star award. Dr Curtis accompanied me to make my presentation to the panel of judges. With the lives saved by Teleheal now running into the hundreds, I spoke of what we were doing and why; of how our project could bring learning back to the NHS; of the solidarity of the exchange of experience. From twelve finalists in the Rising Star category of the *HSJ* awards – the biggest celebration of healthcare excellence in the UK, probably in the world – I was picked out for the highly commended recognition. This acknowledgement of Teleheal and its worth to the NHS was wonderfully rewarding for a network of volunteers which had, at that stage, received little publicity outside the north-west of England, and wonderfully rewarding for me. It motivated me to keep pushing forward.

The first time I had given voice publicly to my story was in a ten-minute speech in Liverpool earlier that year. It was just a local deanery event, not even regional, but it was such a big deal for me. I had long ago learned how to conquer my nerves to speak out in front of people, from the early days of presenting to consultants to giving talks to students or roomfuls of fellow clinicians. But that was me speaking professionally as a doctor. This was something else entirely, something intensely personal. It forced me to come out of my shell and expose my past. I tried to concentrate on the purpose of that exposure: to encourage more medics to volunteer. I didn't say very much – simply that I had been born in Afghanistan, had grown up in the midst of war and that seeing so much suffering had inspired me to become a doctor and to create a telemedicine platform. But just shaping those words brought everything back.

I was incredibly stressed beforehand and afterwards I felt a mixture of relief, disquiet and a strange numbness. And I was just so tired – exhausted for the whole of the next day. Yet I knew deep inside that it was something I had to do. While my motivation was to attract recruits, I realized that I also needed to do it for me; that publicly acknowledging the trauma was enabling me at last to acknowledge it personally and to process my emotions. For a long while I would feel like this whenever I told my story. In conjuring that five-year-old, eleven-year-old or that teenager arriving in the UK, I was reliving his experiences. But I became aware that, gradually, some weight was being lifted from me. Slowly, the impact of thinking about the past was growing less painful.

One of my former colleagues and volunteers in Basildon, Nick Aresti, then an orthopaedic registrar, mentioned to me that he was an organizing member of TEDxNHS, the annual conference staged independently by the NHS, for the NHS. 'I would like to put your name up as a speaker this year, Waheed. What do you think? Would you be prepared to give a TEDx talk?'

TEDxNHS provides a unique platform for staff and patients to come together to spread learning across the system. It is licensed by TED Conferences, the company that posts talks online for free distribution, and run according to their guidelines. It would mean a big live audience plus many more potential online viewers – all drawn from the NHS. I had to do it.

Nick helped me with my talk and my presentation. My first attempt he felt was too academic. 'We need more about you. People are going to be really interested in your background.'

I went away and worked on my talk and my technique. I studied the speeches of great leaders and politicians. By far the best and most impactful were those delivered from the heart. I wouldn't achieve that effect if I was reading from notes or reciting something learned by rote. I strove for a balance between painting a picture of war-torn Afghanistan, and professional clarity and coherence. I didn't want it to come over as too monotone, so I put in some lighter moments from my early days in the UK, making fun of some of my mistakes as a 'freshie'.

'That's more like it,' said Nick.

The TEDxNHS event was held that summer at the Campus, Google's London headquarters. I was one of eighteen speakers, and anyone and everyone from the NHS was there, including Sir Bruce Keogh, the medical director of the entire health service. It was intimidating facing such an audience, but I could feel in the room the power of the story to inspire as well as to build bridges. It earned me a hug from Sir Bruce and the list of prospective volunteers I'd hoped for. One clinician from Russia even came up to me, bless her, and apologized on behalf of her country for the Soviet–Afghan war. 'Your talk made me cry,' she said. 'I am so sorry.'

I already knew that what we give back also gives back to us. Holding out our hands to our fellow human beings not only improves their lives, it enriches our own, too. What I understood now was that Teleheal was enriching mine in a very specific way. It had become my therapy. In compelling me to speak out, it was continuing the process set in motion by the counsellor I'd seen so briefly as a medical student and nurtured in the years that followed by Davina. It was bringing together the two sides of my life. The charity I had founded was not only helping to heal others, it was healing me.

16

The Power to Touch Lives

FROM THE START, ARIAN Teleheal had been about one ordinary doctor engaging the Afghan government and medics on one side while trying to rally volunteers to their cause on the other. When I reflect on that now, I am mystified as to how it all actually worked.

We were setting up from scratch in the field of digital health, the umbrella term for the use of technology to improve health and well-being, of which telemedicine is one of the main strands. We were operating in places where there was no precedent or other support, without any of the foundations that underpin most other organizations, big or small – no structure, no board of directors, no backing and no money. In the engine room there was just me, bolstered by Davina.

As well as the day-to-day call co-ordination and troubleshooting, there were many challenges thrown up by cultural, language and religious differences. I was learning the rules of philanthropy, clinical innovation and international governance as I went along, and making up some of my own. Governance and engagement have been some of the biggest hurdles faced by private companies and NGOs, hence their limited penetration of the digital health sector in the international arena, particularly in theatres of war and low-resource countries. Since governance is so fraught with politics and potential litigation, unregulated networks can be dangerous, and they tend to keep their use of telemedicine to their internal communications.

Governments and big organizations have the capacity to create ultra-secure apps on the same principles as Teleheal has done, but this needs to be part of an overall strategy. Reaching those on the ground and keeping them engaged takes a lot of effort. Simply putting an app out there with expensive military-grade security and then sitting back and waiting is pointless if nobody uses it. Partnerships are not about technology. They are about trust, compassion and cultivating a relationship while adopting an adaptable solution.

Having said that, while nowadays we cover almost every province in Afghanistan, early on I would sometimes receive random desperate calls from isolated clinics excluded from our partnership because they were in Taliban-occupied areas outside the government's control. Struggling doctors would hear about us somehow, on the news or social media, and message me asking how they could send us a case.

We helped these doctors where we could. Many of them were working on their own, barely qualified, with no support and meagre facilities that would have made even Kabul's hospitals look state-of-the-art. A phone was practically the only equipment some of them had. A number of these cases involved casualties of conflict, often civilians caught up in fighting or crossfire.

In building our relationship it was essential to ensure the compliance of the doctors. For example, there could be no discussion of political or religious issues, or any other potentially divisive private debate, going on within the social media groups. Doctors can be opinionated, but they had to keep their opinions confined to the medical sphere. Even here, we never gave orders, we made suggestions. The last thing the doctors on the front line needed was to feel patronized or intimidated. So it was always 'I would do it that way', not 'You must do it this way'.

It was important to keep the energy flowing in one direction, and that meant getting on top of small things quickly so that we were all fixed on the same objective and working efficiently as a team. I may have been front man, case co-ordinator, diplomat and data manager, but I was not a solo performer. It took the combined talent of every volunteer to drive the mission forward.

We all have our strengths and weaknesses, and perhaps the most useful skill we can develop is the ability to recognize and distinguish between them. That allows us to capitalize on our strengths and get people on board who make up for our weaknesses or lack of experience. I knew I had the necessary determination, drive, leadership and problem-solving skills, and I honed those qualities and pushed them hard. But perhaps my most practical asset was the ability to persuade talented people who shared my vision to join Teleheal. I'd have got nowhere if I'd acted like someone who thought he could do everything. We all benefit from seeking the help and advice of those who are the best at what they do. Their empathy, enthusiasm and commitment keep me motivated and energized. Doctors are high achievers and I have found that the bigger the vision I present them with, the more it inspires them.

Inspiring and motivating others is not the same as nagging. Volunteers and supporters are already motivated and they are going to do what you need: it's just a question of when. You have to ask yourself, how can I move this from number three to number one on their list of priorities? Everybody is busy. You have to show tact and respect for whatever else people may have on their plate. The last thing you want is for a valued consultant to be questioning what they are doing this for when their workload is already so heavy. If someone can't help, I thank them and leave the door open. But it is testament to the compassion and humanity of the medical profession that hardly anyone says no and less than a handful of our volunteers have ever dropped out.

Our lack of funding was quite low down my list of priorities. The message I was trying to get across, and still am, was that, just as it doesn't take cutting-edge tech and equipment to make a difference in the world, it doesn't take pots of money, either. All you need is a vision, a good idea to make it happen, courage, imagination and the means to harness the power of volunteerism to get it off the ground. Arian Teleheal relied more on word of mouth than aggressive fund-raising. Donations to the charity were mainly individual contributions, including one-off gifts requested by supporters in lieu of wedding or birthday presents. Most of our original funds went on setting up our first website.

The crucial donations are the time and expertise of our volunteers. That hour a consultant gives Teleheal could be spent seeing two or three private patients, but instead they choose to use it to help those in the most need. In the course of a year, those gifts are worth hundreds of thousands of pounds.

As well as being determined, I was ambitious. I wanted to expand telemedicine into other countries that needed support, into areas of Africa where healthcare was almost non-existent; into Syria, where 5 million refugees had fled the savage civil war, with a further 7.6 million internally displaced. I wanted Teleheal to become a leading force in philanthropy and innovation. I wanted to spread the platform we had created around the world. I couldn't just coast along on what we had achieved so far. I could see endless possibilities up ahead.

By 2017 I was more than halfway through my five-year clinical radiology training. Within those five years you have to complete two Royal College of Radiologists fellowship examinations – among the hardest in medicine. There is a high failure rate and some doctors have to take them several times. I had got the first FRCR under my belt without a hitch and had passed the first of the six written components of the final FRCR as well.

So I was cruising, and on course to acquire my radiology

certificate of completion of training and a guaranteed post as a consultant. Yes, it would mean a good salary, a bigger house, a smart car, a private practice alongside my NHS work. But was that all there was? It wasn't why I had become a doctor. I still loved radiology but, on its own, being a consultant radiologist wasn't going to give meaning to my life. I wanted to give back more of myself than this.

As so often, I was moving sideways to go forward. The straight road just doesn't work for me. Who knows whether that is part of my make-up or whether it developed as a result of the mazy path my circumstances have forced me to follow since my childhood. Either way, it is how my mind works. I slow down to take stock, to reconnect with my passion, vision and potential, and I change direction when my instincts tell me that is the right thing to do. Now they were telling me to pause my radiology training to pursue my bigger humanitarian vision.

Davina was right behind me. She understood my dream, and she understood that I had only one life in which to try to achieve it. If I allowed Teleheal to merely tick over for another two years, the momentum generated by its early success would be lost. And so might countless lives that could be saved.

I felt that the value to the NHS of the Afghanistan project would carry some weight with my superiors and strengthen my case for taking a break. The *HSJ* award had been very significant for the deanery and Aintree Hospital. It had brought them important recognition for their training programme, for the impact our innovative telemedicine work could have on the future of the NHS and, I reasoned, it had put us all on the radar of the NHS hierarchy.

The reactions of most of my colleagues to my request ranged from puzzlement to downright indignation. Some couldn't understand why I would want to 'throw it all away'; others felt aggrieved on behalf of fellow doctors who would have given anything to have been offered my coveted training post. But Andy Smethurst, John

Curtis and Sumita Chawla got where I was coming from. 'With your history and track record of overcoming such major challenges,' remarked Dr Smethurst, 'you're probably the only person who could make this work.'

I totally understood the general consternation. Of course, I was taking a huge gamble, both professionally and financially. It could have spelled the end of my career. Although the door would be left ajar for two years for me to resume my training, we all realized that, whatever the future held, the chances were I wouldn't be facing it by looking backwards.

I have never been afraid to try new things. We learn so much from our experiences, even when they don't turn out quite as we intended. I have seen people too terrified to take a month, even a week, off to do something that has fired their imagination in case it interferes with the career path they have mapped out. How can we know what we might be capable of if we don't even try? We are so quick to put people in boxes. We say even of very small children, 'Oh, she is good at sport but not so great at maths.' We predict GCSE and A-level grades that become self-fulfilling prophecies. Kids grow up believing in these limitations.

In January 2021, a survey carried out in the UK by the Prince's Trust charity reported that one in four sixteen- to twenty-five-year-olds had felt unable to cope with life during the COVID-19 pandemic. It is vital that, as a society, we do not impose a culture of fixed short-term goals on our young people and their parents. This generation is our future. They need the space to build the resilience to overcome the disruption to their education and immediate job prospects and the positivity to see a world full of possibilities ahead of them. Education and experience are lifelong.

Perhaps, in one way, it helped me that I came from a place where any expectations were a luxury. I had grown up with no precon- ceived limits to my potential. With so few chances as a child, my response has always been to grab every opportunity and use whatever skills or tools are available to me to the greatest possible effect. From my perspective in 2017, my opportunity to make a real difference was now, not in two years' time. And so, against advice, I took a two-year career break.

With a full-time voluntary job and Teleheal commitments to fund, as well as a family to support, I picked up paid work at weekends to leave weekdays free for the charity, alternating between shifts in A&E and assignments for insurance companies as a flying medical escort. This involved accompanying non-critical patients home to the UK from abroad, mostly Europe, but I went all over the place – Australia, China, the US, Canada, Thailand. It was ideal for me because of all the spare time it gave me to do my Teleheal work. On outward flights, and in between my checks and chats with the patient on the return journey, I could deal with all my emails and draft letters and speeches, with time left over to think and plan. On layovers I would manage any live cases overnight. When travelling business class, where wifi was now widely available, I could often remain on call even during the flight.

The only downside of the long-haul trips was the jet lag and general exhaustion afterwards. When I got home I wouldn't know where I was. I once slept for eighteen hours straight and woke up in the middle of the night in my own bed in Chester convinced I was in New Zealand. But there was something wonderful about handling a live case in Kabul or Kunduz from 35,000 feet up in the sky, with no idea of what time it might be, either there or wherever around the earth I was. Now this, I would say to myself, really *is* global medicine!

Having help to offer does not make it easy to deliver. For it to be as effective as possible, it has to be channelled through a country's government. But often the governments of the people in greatest need, those whose lives are ripped apart by conflict, won't take your hand for political reasons. In Syria, where the civil war had been going on for six years, President Assad had allied himself with Russia, and his regime was apparently unwilling to engage with charities based in the UK.

Trying to funnel support via opposition parties or splinter groups in a hostile political environment, especially in the middle of a civil war, is not an option. It is just too hazardous. Some of those trying to help from within Syria may, rightly or wrongly, be linked by the UK or US governments with terrorism. Just one perfectly innocent exploratory email to the wrong people could land you in a lot of trouble.

On the news one day I saw a truckload of building materials and equipment being delivered to an NGO called the Independent Doctors Association (IDA), which was working with refugees on the Syria–Turkey border. They had raised the money to build a children's hospital through crowd-funding. I checked out the organization. It had been founded five years earlier by doctors from Aleppo in response to the crisis in Syria, with strictly no political, racial or religious affiliations. Satisfied that their mission was entirely humanitarian, and that their level of activity was significant enough to justify our involvement, I got in touch with their head of programmes and asked how we could support them.

The IDA were trying to serve 1.3 million people in Aleppo, residents as well as internally displaced refugees. We exchanged contact details and I set up a WhatsApp group for their doctors. The cases coming in from the IDA tend to be sporadic. They are firefighting, and don't have time to keep records of outcomes so it is hard for us to keep track of what is happening on the ground out there.

The plight of sick or injured refugee children never fails to strike an emotional chord with me whenever one of these cases pops up on my phone. I was away from home, nearing the end of a shift in

A&E, when a video message came through from Syria showing a little girl lying motionless in bed. She was a seven-year-old refugee with type 1 diabetes and she was in a coma. The doctor had little more information about her. 'What kind of meds and fluid should we be giving her?' he asked. The type and level of fluids used to treat a patient in a diabetic coma can be critical. Get the formula wrong and it may lead to brain oedema. I referred the case to our paediatrics specialist group.

I monitored the child's condition into the small hours back at the doctors' accommodation, speaking to our medics and the staff in Syria and relaying updates back and forth. The paediatricians provided fluid management for eight hours. Within the first hour the little girl was stabilized and the phone went quiet.

You never get much sleep in hospital quarters. The rooms are inclined to be old and uncomfortable. I dropped off in spite of the hard bed but was woken early by the dawn light shining straight into my eyes through the thin curtain, a knot of anxiety in my chest. I checked my phone to find a video message showing the little girl up and walking around, a cannula poking out of her arm and a piece of cucumber in her hand. On her face was the most beautiful smile. My heart lifted. This was what it was all about.

In Afghanistan, where Teleheal's relationship with the doctors on the front line was more firmly established, I could see on my regular visits what they needed and address any issues. I sat down and had meetings with them, did a little coaching on particular topics, gave opinions on scans and examined the occasional patient. Bonds were being forged between doctors on both sides and maintaining those was important, too. It reinforced the connection and boosted the morale of the beleaguered Afghan clinicians to see the owner of the voice on the phone and the face on the screen walking on to their ward and asking what he could do to help.

In March 2017, Davina and Zane came with me to Kabul. We had brought our son, about to turn a year old, to meet his grandparents and the rest of his Afghan family and to absorb a little of his heritage.

Two days before Zane's first birthday, the Sardaur Daoud Khan Military Hospital, right next door to the Wazir Akbar Khan, where I'd been meeting doctors twenty-four hours earlier, was stormed by a group of at least three gunmen dressed in white lab coats. They opened fire indiscriminately. The US-run hospital, the biggest and best-equipped in the country, was staffed entirely by Afghans. One of their junior doctors was my brother, Farid.

We watched the news on television, aghast, desperate for word from Farid as the gunmen battled the security forces for hour upon hour. My mother lay prostrate, distraught, crying non-stop and screaming, 'My son! My son!' Davina, white-faced and struggling to keep up with what was going on, just held her hand. She had never seen anything like it. 'What a life they have to live!' she whispered to me.

It seemed like an eternity before we heard that Farid was safe. Two of his colleagues had been shot in front of him. Powerless to help, he and a couple of others had managed to smash down a door and had run for their lives. They had hidden for hours in a deserted canteen, terrified that the gunmen would find them. In the coming days the death toll mounted. At least fifty people were killed. ISIS claimed responsibility for the attack.

'You must not come again,' my mum begged us. 'Not until the situation improves. It is not safe for Davina or my grandson. It is not safe for you.'

I was, as things turned out, back in Kabul the following month. The BBC were making a half-hour documentary about Arian Teleheal and I was going out there to film the Afghanistan segments. BBC North West's current affairs and features editor, Deborah van Bishop, who had run a news piece about Teleheal the previous year on the local current affairs programme *Inside Out North West*, and producer and director Ged Clarke had successfully pitched the idea to Nick Aresti's wife, Stephanie Constantine, a producer and television journalist with the World Service.

John Simpson, the veteran foreign correspondent and world affairs editor of BBC News, was signed up to narrate the film. This was a man who had reported from thirty war zones and interviewed countless world leaders. I had watched his dispatches in 2001, when he was famously one of the first foreign journalists to enter Afghanistan. He had won an International Emmy for his coverage of the fall of Kabul, not to mention three BAFTAs. I couldn't believe that such an eminent figure was going to be telling my story.

Ged and his team, which included the BBC Pashto and Farsi units in Afghanistan, interviewed colleagues such as Dr Zewar in Afghanistan and Drs Curtis and Smethurst at Aintree; they talked to my parents on camera, to Farid and to Davina. They filmed me all over the place: at the Malalai Maternity Hospital, at a Kabul refugee camp, at home in Chester, at Aintree Hospital, and in London and Cambridge. I was thrilled when Sir Bruce Keogh agreed to be interviewed. He described Teleheal's work as 'a glimpse of the future' and said he felt the NHS had a lot to learn from the simplicity of our approach.

Waheed's Wars: Saving Lives Across the World was shown that summer in the UK by BBC North West and on *The One Show*, across the World Service, on *BBC World News* and adapted for World Service radio. At Christmas it was picked out as one of the programmes of the year and screened another six times on *BBC World News*. I was so pleased for Stephanie, Deborah and Ged and their dedicated team when the documentary was shortlisted in the Current Affairs Programme of the Year category for the Royal Television Society's North-West Awards. But more important than anything, and my only reason for making the film in the first place, was the impact of the film's storytelling on hearts and minds.

Volunteers began to come forward in numbers. We were soon able to call upon around a hundred, including medical specialists elsewhere in Europe and in the USA, Canada and Australia.

In August, in the middle of a night shift on A&E, I received a strange email. It was from the Global Hope Coalition, under the patronage of UNESCO, and it invited me to receive an award at a gala dinner at the New York Public Library the following month. I had, it informed me, been selected as one of six 'heroes of the global campaign against extremism and intolerance'. I called the number on the message to check that this wasn't someone having a laugh at my expense. It was not a joke. The gala dinner, it was explained to me, was timed to coincide with the UN General Assembly, when the world's leaders would be in town. I listened in growing astonishment as the guest list was reeled off to me – heads of state, royalty, philanthropists, academics, celebrities . . .

I put down the phone stunned by the realization of what this recognition, and the access it would give me to some of the most influential people on the planet, would mean. I was so excited I burst into tears.

I called a delighted Davina. Then I called Fin. And then I was called back down to earth to attend to a chap who had been brought to A&E after falling two floors from a nightclub balcony. He had sat down on an ornamental bush, for some reason expecting it to bear his weight.

I still don't know to this day how I came to be nominated for the Global Hope Coalition Everyday Hero award, let alone chosen as the first UK citizen to receive that honour. Arian Teleheal was hardly an established name in the field of international humanitarian medicine. But I owe a debt of gratitude to whoever was responsible because it opened so many doors.

This was followed by another huge surprise: an email from the Bill & Melinda Gates Foundation. I had also been appointed a 'goalkeeper' for the UN's Sustainable Development Goals campaign to end world poverty. They invited me to two of their events taking place in New York, again being run in parallel with the UN General Assembly.

I made sure that Fin was on the guest list for the Global Hope Coalition ceremony. It was thanks to him that we had come this far. He was the one who had persuaded me to put my story out there and he had been absolutely right. Since the start he had taken on pro bono the role of the charity's communications director, the same job he did for Aintree Hospital, and the importance of the media coverage he had masterminded cannot be overestimated. There was always a spike in offers of support and enquiries about volunteering following any publicity.

On the day of the dinner I attended a Global Hope Coalition summit high-level panel discussion at the New York Public Library, where I had been asked to talk about the impact of extremism on women and children in Afghanistan, followed by lunch with the leadership council.

Davina and I met up with Fin before the dinner. I had been warned that afternoon by one of the doormen at the public library, where security was already tight, to come early as the streets would be under lockdown. He hadn't been exaggerating. Entire blocks were cordoned off. We set off on foot.

The incongruous sight of Fin – who I'd last seen a few days earlier at Aintree Hospital in his shirtsleeves – strolling through midtown Manhattan in his Scottish formal wear of Prince Charlie jacket and kilt set the tone for what would be a surreal evening. The air throbbed with the adrenaline pumping through the city as it played host to the profusion of events surrounding the UN General Assembly. Closer to the imposing New York Public Library, the wailing sirens grew louder and camera lights flashed as convoys of big, black, bombproof cars and their motorcycle outriders pulled up and disgorged an assortment of world leaders. Burly men in sharp suits talked into their sleeves. We all stood outside while a final security check of the building was completed.

'When they make the film of your life,' mused Fin, looking up at the helicopters hovering overhead, 'this would make a good final scene.'

'What?' I asked distractedly.

'You've come from Russian helicopter gunships trying to shoot you to New York's finest sweeping the skies for your protection.'

I wasn't listening. I was going over and over in my head what I was going to say in the three and a half minutes allocated for my acceptance speech. I had been working for days on how best to grab the attention of a roomful of 450 dignitaries with the power to change the world.

Inside I was caught up in a blur of introductions and congratulations. To be milling around in the orbit of presidents, influential UN figures and household names felt utterly unreal. At dinner, which I was too wound up to eat, I was seated between President Ashraf Ghani of Afghanistan and Gillian Sorensen, the former UN assistant secretary-general for external relations under Kofi Annan. President Ghani was there to present an award to former US first lady Laura Bush, also on our table. He told me how proud he was of the work I had achieved in Afghanistan and the world.

It was momentous to find my mission to help my homeland being acknowledged in person by its head of state. And meeting Gillian was both a privilege and a stroke of luck. We have kept in touch and her expertise has been invaluable in guiding me through the jungle of humanitarian politics and international diplomacy. This is an arena where I am not sure of my ground and to have the praise of such a senior figure, her reassurance that I am getting it right, and just to keep doing what I'm doing, has been immensely encouraging.

It was humbling to be recognized alongside some exceptionally courageous and inspired individuals. They included Dr Denis Mukwege, a Congolese gynaecologist and pastor who established a hospital for some of the hundreds of thousands of women raped and brutalized in his country's horrific war – he would be jointly awarded the Nobel Peace Prize the following year – and former gang member Sammy Rangel, co-founder of the Chicago-based NGO Life After Hate, which helps far-right extremists to transform their lives. But I could think of nothing but my sole purpose for being there: getting up on that stage and delivering my message. I spoke of how Teleheal was not just providing healthcare across the world but bringing communities together by changing long-held perceptions and breaking down division and distrust. I kept it short, direct and, I hoped, potent.

I left the New York Public Library still not quite believing that the evening hadn't been a dream. How was it possible that the boy who couldn't bring himself to raise his hand in class had just addressed an audience of presidents and policy-makers? It was only as the pressure began to ease that I realized how hungry I was. Davina and I rounded off the night wolfing down tacos from a Mexican food van in Times Square, almost empty now but still pulsating with neon lights. As we sat there in our finery, my award on the table between us, I checked my phone. Like New York, Teleheal never sleeps.

The Global Goalkeepers awards dinner the next night, staged, in partnership with UNICEF, by the Bill & Melinda Gates Foundation, was co-hosted by Melinda Gates and the film-maker Richard Curtis, co-founder of the British Comic Relief charity's Make Poverty History campaign, and recognized the contributions of some more extraordinary humanitarians. Their Goalkeepers 2017 conference the day afterwards brought together innovators and change-makers from all kinds of different settings. The speakers ranged from former US president Barack Obama and Canadian premier Justin Trudeau, to Queen Rania of Jordan, to Bill Gates and the musician will.i.am. The prime minister of India joined us by video link. There were films and appearances by live performers, global health experts and those working on the ground to eradicate poverty.

All of the groups represented here were powerhouses in their own right. My mind raced with thoughts of how significantly their individual achievements could be magnified by partnerships between them. Towards the end of the day, Stephen Fry, who was chairing the event, asked whether any of the goalkeepers wished to come up and share any ideas. Go on! I told myself. What are you waiting for? I raised my hand.

Stephen Fry waved me up on to the stage and handed me the mic. Standing there amid the bright lights, massive cameras and secret service personnel hovering in doorways, it hit me that not only had I not come prepared to speak but the former US president had been talking into this mic only moments before. You just stood up and issued a challenge to a bunch of statesmen, I scolded myself. You can do anything now! Explaining who I was and how Teleheal was saving lives with basic tech, I spoke up for the potential of collective strength in innovation, one of the sustainable development goals, and then, overwhelmed by applause and flashing cameras, returned, slightly dazed, to my seat.

Afterwards I found myself discussing ideas with so many amazing people whose missions intersected with mine. People such as Dr Raj Panjabi, who arrived in the States as a nine-year-old refugee from Liberia, became an associate physician in the Division of Global Health Equity at Harvard Medical School and returned to Liberia to co-found Last Mile Health, which builds community-based primary healthcare systems in Africa, and groups like Choose

Love, a pioneering, volunteer-led movement providing refugees with aid and assistance on the ground.

The connections I made in New York represented a giant leap for Teleheal. Not all of them bore immediate fruit – that would have been a practical impossibility – but several led to productive collaborations. Others may prove to be useful stepping stones, sometimes in round-about ways, towards potential future co-operations and partnerships as new crises strike and the humanitarian response evolves. No such brainstorming is a waste of time because no one person or organization can do it all. But together we have the strength to move mountains.

17

Going Global

OVER THE NEXT TWO or three years, I found the doors of governments and the leaders of global organizations opening up to me as Teleheal's heightened profile, and the networks it enabled me to build, began to extend our reach around the world. Our work was further acknowledged in the shape of the Rotary International Peace Award and the UK prime minister's Points of Light Award, which recognizes outstanding volunteers.

As the NHS celebrated its seventieth birthday in 2018, I was put forward to represent NHS innovation at a reception marking the occasion at 10 Downing Street. Approaching the gaggle of expectant photographers outside that famous front door, I couldn't help casting my mind back to the grim early days I'd spent incarcerated in Feltham Young Offenders Institution as a lone and almost penniless refugee. In the hallway I was taken to one side and told that I was one of a small group chosen to have a one-to-one conversation with Prime Minister Theresa May. It didn't seem possible that, nineteen years on, my efforts to give back to the NHS were being picked out for acknowledgement by the prime minister herself.

In my role of UN Goalkeeper, I had attended the Malaria Summit in London, co-convened by the Bill & Melinda Gates Foundation, held during the Commonwealth Summit in the spring. Most Commonwealth heads of state and their health ministers were present, as was HRH Prince Charles. In the lunch break I pitched the telemedicine message to several African ministers, all of whom connected me immediately with their teams. I also had the good fortune to be introduced to Dr Tedros Adhanom Ghebreyesus, director-general of the World Health Organization, at an opportune time when the WHO was very focused on digital health. As a result I later had a meeting at the WHO headquarters in Geneva at which a digital health partnership with Teleheal was agreed in principle.

It was back to New York that autumn in the week of the UN General Assembly, this time in response to an invitation to the Stop TB Partnership's UNHLM – United Nations High-Level Meeting – as an Afghan 'champion' and healthcare innovator from the UK. I called for digital health solutions to be used in the fight against TB, like malaria one of the world's top ten killers and, of course, another disease of which I have personal experience. There has to be a more effective way of channelling budgets of hundreds of millions into tackling TB, such as investing, in regions lacking trained radiologists, in artificial intelligence (AI) that can detect it from scans. Following my 'impactful contribution' to the meeting, I was appointed a TB global ambassador.

Everywhere I went I was networking and handing my details to a posse of ministerial aides and secretaries. If my mum had seen me, she would have said I was like a barber, wetting ten customers' heads before I started to cut anybody's hair.

Voluntary work inevitably entails financial sacrifice and none of us begrudges that. It has to be said, though, that for Davina and me it amounts to more than just loss of income. While the big organizations do take care of travel and accommodation expenses in connection with their conferences and events, for the most part, until 2018, when the charity began to attract enough modest donations to fund my out-of-pocket expenses, the cost of fulfilling my Teleheal commitments – all the travel, the meetings, the recruiting – had to be met by the family budget. That concentrated my mind on weighing up the potential benefit to the work of the charity of every invitation before I accepted it.

Teleheal's first foray into Africa was our ongoing partnership with Health Education England (HEE), whose director of global engagement, Professor Gerard John Byrne, bought into our telemedicine model and agreed initially to a six-month trial in South Africa. We support NHS doctors, known as global health fellows, working out there on six-month placements. Where the partnership has proved particularly valuable is on the educational side. We exchange cases with all of our groups, including the global health fellows, together with regular updates on guidelines and protocols.

In Afghanistan, we formed a new partnership with the charity Enabled Children Initiative (ECI), which was running the first residential home in Kabul for disabled children who had been orphaned or abandoned. It is now building a community centre for the disabled of all ages. Not surprisingly, Afghanistan has one of the world's largest populations per capita of disabled people, for whom there is next to no support. Decades of war have left hundreds of thousands with amputated limbs and problems with mobility, sight and hearing. Others have been permanently damaged by diseases such as polio or other untreated conditions. Many more suffer from the effects on their mental health of depression and PTSD.

Our involvement sprang from an introduction to Lael Mohib, the founder of ECI, at the Global Hope Coalition dinner in New York. We advise their medical staff directly and have an agreement with local hospitals for emergency cases to be treated there. A second opinion from one of our ENT consultants recently resulted in a four-year-old child with a severe hearing impairment being offered a life-changing $25,000 cochlear implant in Pakistan, thanks to the compassion of the International Medical Relief Agency, a UK-based charity. With the recent addition of mental health professionals to our volunteers, we are now able to assist on that front, too.

Of course, not all lives can be improved medically, but in some cases a second opinion from an expert in the UK or America can pave the way for people to begin to accept their diagnoses. Because of the lack of faith in Afghan healthcare, families may make huge sacrifices to pursue treatment or surgery in Pakistan even after being assured that nothing can be done. We can at least spare them that.

Our volunteers provide comprehensive and continuous support for as long as it is needed. This isn't always easy, but you are not going to be much help if you suddenly stop giving advice in the middle of an emergency. In one case this meant supervising a patient from Kandahar to Kabul on the phone from the UK. He had been knocked off his bike by a car and brought in a coma to a little local hospital in Kandahar. The only doctor there had our number and called me on WhatsApp. The poor guy was inexperienced and he was panicking. 'He is unconscious. This is just a basic clinic. I don't know what to do!'

We got him to confirm that the patient was breathing and then talked him methodically through the checks that would be second nature to anyone working in an NHS A&E department. Stabilize the patient, then check his observations: blood pressure, pulse, temperature, oxygen levels, breathing rate. All of these were within the normal range, but we could see on the photographs the doctor had sent us on his phone that the patient had 'panda eyes', a worrying sign of a basal skull fracture and a possible bleed on the brain.

He needed a CT scan. With no scanner at the clinic, he would have to be taken in an ambulance – most likely just a van – for a full body scan by a marketplace radiographer, but moving him was risky. We talked the doctor through how to make the patient safe, how to immobilize the spine with a collar and blocks around the neck, and warned against moving him around too much.

Next the doctor, who was relying on our guidance at every step, needed the expertise of our radiologists to interpret the scan. It confirmed a skull fracture and a huge bleed on the brain although, rather surprisingly, no other injuries. The patient required trauma care. His family were prepared to try to get him to Pakistan or Kabul to save his life. We knew that the new Shaikh Zayed Hospital, specializing in neurosurgery and neurology, had recently opened in the Afghan capital. The doctor didn't. And he didn't know how to get in touch with them.

We contacted a neurosurgeon there on his behalf, explained the case and the neurosurgeon reserved a bed. The hospital was some twelve hours' drive away.

'How do we get him there?' asked the doctor in Kandahar.

'The family will need to organize a private ambulance.'

We then spent a day out of communication while the patient was taken to Kabul, wondering whether or not he was going to make it. To our relief he turned up alive at the Shaikh Zayed Hospital and Teleheal switched its support to the doctors there. Updated scans were reviewed in real time by volunteers in multiple specialties and our neurosurgeon kept in touch with theirs, continuing to offer live opinion. He took the view that the bleed could subside. His advice was not to rush to operate but to keep the patient under observation for a few days and then to repeat the CT scan of the head.

And a few days later a video message arrived of this chap sitting up, alert, and engaging with the medics. Aware that our volunteers had been helping in the background, he added his own message of thanks. I passed on both to the whole team with my congratulations on a difficult job well done. And to one happy doctor in Kandahar.

It is in emergency cases like this one that any more complex app relying on the store-and-forward technique, with its time delays and practice of dealing separately with one question at a time, is just not suitable. Scans and clinical findings need to be reviewed urgently and repeatedly. The phone and WhatsApp were very probably the only tech available and our team had been able to use them to provide a seamless response.

Another example of the importance of a live network in a crisis is the occasion when dozens of people were brought into the Jamhuriat Hospital in Kabul with some kind of poisoning. They were all fighting for their lives in intensive care. It appeared that they had drunk an unidentified alcoholic concoction, perhaps spiked with opiates. Casualties involving alcohol are less commonly seen in countries that don't have a drinking culture, but this is a complex area even in the UK. If you don't know what the patient has ingested, it's like looking for a needle in a haystack. However, we have the advantage of TOXBASE, a database we can use to pinpoint a drug from the patient's symptoms, and which offers information on antidotes and management. We also have access to a 24/7 national helpline. The Afghans have none of that. They didn't know how to test for the poison or stabilize the patients, let alone find an antidote.

They were sending us videos of monitor readings while we were firing over questions – 'Is the breathing slow? Are the pupils dilated? Is the patient hallucinating?' – in a race to try to identify the cause and halt the deterioration. Our doctors got there in the end and most of the patients were saved.

Our doctor-to-doctor policy cuts through so much red tape and official posturing once it is up and running, but even after we have an agreement in place, internal politics can intervene. The Ministry of Public Health in Kabul went silent on me for a couple of years. In Afghan politics, the arguing never stops and the fact that I had been referred to the ministry in the first place by Dr Kakar, President Ashraf Ghani's adviser, whereas the health minister was one of Abdullah Abdullah's appointees, may have had a part to play. Dr Kakar was not on the scene any longer, as he was by this time serving as Afghanistan's ambassador in Qatar. Whatever the reason, when a minister takes a particular stance, all those under him have to protect their own positions. People won't even exchange emails because of the trail they leave.

In practical terms, this made little difference to our work there, as the agreement with the ministry was in place and our co-operation with the doctors on the ground required no governmental input. So we just carried on as normal until they resumed contact.

I was not travelling to Kabul at this time. The relationship with the doctors was now firmly rooted and, with the attacks in Kabul escalating, family visits were off the agenda. Only weeks after I'd last been there for the documentary filming, I'd been distressed to hear that my BBC driver in Afghanistan, Mohammed Nazir, had been among more than 150 people killed by a massive truck bomb detonated in the high-security diplomatic quarter. Instead we linked up with my parents on neutral territory so that they could see Davina and Zane in safety. In 2018 we had a wonderful holiday in India with my mum and dad and we met them several times in Dubai, where I could arrange medical check-ups for them while we were there.

Their travel was co-ordinated with military precision. One of my brothers would get them through the airport at Kabul, where security checks begin before you even reach the terminal, and Davina and I would meet the plane at the other end. In case of language problems, they carried cards written by the family – 'I need a wheelchair when I arrive' for my dad, and another one with my name and phone number on it. They were getting old and I needed to look after them as best I could. But, for the most part, that would have to be done from a distance.

I felt I was really getting somewhere with my ambition to take Teleheal global. Until 2018, I was focusing on activating the connections I had made to expand our own telemedicine service: to grow the tech, build more partnerships and bring more volunteers on board.

There was huge scope and enthusiasm for telemedicine in Africa and India, and I knew there was more we could do in Syria with better networks. Increasing the volunteer base was no problem, but to scale our operations in line with my big ambitions would require funding on the management, co-ordination and technology side. Negotiating the multiple layers that lie between governments and the front line is complex and time-consuming. I could not do it all on my own.

What made Teleheal different was that it was lean and innovative; too innovative, it seemed, to match up with the criteria or donor lists used by the UK government and other bodies that allocate public money to charities. This was available only to cover finite projects, not ongoing initiatives. So we could apply for funding to build one hospital but not to provide continuing digital health support, however cost-effectively, for a whole country. Disappointingly, without financial help with other costs, it just wasn't possible to scale our work to the rest of the world on the basis of our volunteer structure alone.

The solution was to change direction. We would concentrate on the innovation that could be achieved with our volunteer structure in the countries where we were already established, Afghanistan and Syria. What we were creating there were templates that could be transferred to all sorts of ventures, in healthcare and other sectors, which we could promote and share. We would use the model we had devised and refined to inspire and empower other, larger bodies with greater resources to adopt those templates and implement them across the world.

When deciding which speaking invitations to accept I prioritized those that would reach the most people with the expertise and potential influence to revolutionize the approach to global health.

In 2018, after participating in the NHS Clinical Entrepreneur programme – which trains clinicians in the commercial, technological and entrepreneurial skills of the business world to equip them to develop, scale and share innovative solutions in the healthcare field – I became one of its mentors. Through my involvement with the programme, I was asked to give a talk at the London headquarters of Bloomberg, the financial, software, data and media company, to an audience that included investors, innovators and journalists, as well as members of the medical hierarchy.

I addressed student conferences to pass on what I had learned to up-and-coming innovators. At Cambridge University I was the keynote speaker at the 2019 Model G20 Youth Leadership Summit, where international students participated in politically based problem-solving simulations in the roles of world leaders, diplomats and ministers. At Oxford I contributed to the student-run Global Scholars Symposium on the themes of cultivating innovation and charting unmapped territories.

Innovation is about identifying the problem, aligning it with your vision and looking first for the simplest way to solve it. You continually test and refine your solution – in our case, a handful of doctors in Afghanistan talking to a handful of doctors in the UK – until it is bulletproof, and only then do you scale it up. One size does not fit all, and you adapt your template to the context. India, for example, does not, like Afghanistan, suffer from a lack of technology, at least not in its major cities. But it does have a huge number of people living in rural areas with no access to a hospital or to specialists.

So many government programmes and big organizations with a genuine mission and meaty international aid budgets are not maximizing their resources or getting the help directly to where it is needed because they are using the wrong channels. Flying off to endless conferences or setting up webinars with other politicians and heads of NGOs is not the answer. It tends to result in everyone agreeing that something must be done, grand mission statements being issued and nothing much actually happening on the ground. The most you end up with is a few one-off projects in a few villages. That is not global health.

We had templates to share that demonstrated the success of doctor-to-doctor communication, incorporating all the associated lessons we had learned, and our refocused mission of empowerment has led to some important new collaborations. Today we are pushing for live networks in remote parts of Africa with the potential to help millions by providing access to world-class healthcare expertise, free of charge, from thousands of miles away.

As a partner in the West Nile Consortium, Arian Teleheal is working alongside HEE, THET (Tropical Health and Education Trust), the Uganda Red Cross and others in Uganda and its West Nile sub-region, where over a million refugees have fled from the civil war in South Sudan. We have an agreement with Wales for Africa, the global health arm of the Welsh government, to support and scale up digital health solutions in sub-Saharan Africa.

We have also formed a partnership with the British Association of Physicians of Indian Origin (BAPIO) in the UK in an exciting project with the All India Institute of Medical Sciences (AIIMS). Our goal is to connect doctors in India with a central telemedicine hub and an international volunteer network delivered by BAPIO, for which AIIMS will provide technical support. With the backing of the NHS and the Indian government, the impact of such a system in the near future could be enormous. BAPIO has 60,000 members, a huge pool of potential volunteers, and they do not, of course, all have their roots in India. Many have family backgrounds in Africa. So there is scope there for a very wide reach.

My message to them all is that the key to global health is relationship-building, from top to bottom, on the front line, demonstrating genuine appreciation for the work of those at the sharp end in challenging contexts, learning from each other continuously and adapting co-operations accordingly.

Technology, which is no more or less than the medium through which all of this is facilitated, should be a long way down the list of priorities. We might find that the situation on the ground is not what we anticipated. We need to fix our focus on the problem and find our solutions as we meet each challenge. My advice to anyone would be the same. Whatever your venture – business, personal, charity – just start somewhere and figure it out along the way.

What is most likely to hamper a telemedicine project is not the tech but medico-legal restrictions. On a trip to Dallas to speak at a graduation ceremony, I was invited to a telehealth demonstration at the neonatal ICU of the city's Children's Health Hospital where, from a state-of-the-art telemedicine suite, a paediatrician and an NICU specialist helped to manage a case in another Texas hospital. While I was amazed by their expensive system and what it was capable of, what the doctors found amazing was how on earth I had overcome the legal challenges to establish Teleheal's global links so quickly. In the USA a doctor registered in one state was not at that time allowed to use telemedicine to give advice in another unless they were licensed in both states. So, very often, the potential of all this superb tech to save lives could not be extended beyond state boundaries.

Personally, I am not bothered about having the latest tech for its own sake. I didn't buy my first laptop until I moved to Chester. As a student, I couldn't afford one. I just used the computers in college libraries and then I inherited hand-me-downs as Masood or Khalid upgraded theirs. As long as their old laptops did what I needed them to do, there was no reason to change them. It is only when I see some cutting-edge development with the clear potential to transform an area of medicine or digital health management that I get excited.

I am proud to have performed the world's first international telemedicine consultation using augmented reality on Microsoft HoloLens. The BBC tech people set this up for me while they were making *Waheed's Wars* and filmed me handling the case from a training theatre at the Aintree Hospital Simulation Centre, with an Afghan doctor at Ibn Sina Hospital in Kabul. It was an astonishing experience and I look forward to the time when technology like this is affordable for all.

Representing the Bill & Melinda Gates Foundation at CogX 2019, Europe's largest festival of artificial intelligence and emerging technology, at King's Cross in London, I gave a talk on the festival theme of how AI and emerging technology can support a better world. I urged the tech gurus listening not to steer away from humanity in developing AI but to factor in the challenges we face at the design stage. Too often we are looking through the telescope from the wrong end: trying to get the problem to fit the technology instead of the other way around.

To illustrate the point: I had an enquiry recently from the director of medical informatics at NASA, someone who would have access to a wealth of technological know-how. He was researching examples of successful ventures for a lecture on telemedicine principles and it was not, of course, the tech we used that interested him but our innovative approach to problem solving.

Automating everything is not the answer. Technology is a force for good, but when we focus on it too heavily we hit trouble. We need to understand and work to its strengths and its limitations while recognizing that human interaction should be at the core of our solutions to the world's problems. We should not forget, either, that so many of the regions we are trying to serve can't afford technology. Neither do they have the resources to teach people how to use it. To support a better world, we need to support it without discrimination.

18

Anything is Possible

AT THE START OF 2019 I took stock. We were expecting another baby and in February my two-year career break was coming to an end, requiring me to officially resign from my radiology post. While Teleheal was all-consuming, I didn't want to become detached from my NHS career altogether, or lose sight of the personal progression as a doctor that had been the backbone of my whole adult life.

Our daughter Alana was born in July and, that summer, I began doing regular weekend shifts for one hospital, the Shrewsbury and Telford Hospital NHS Trust, as locum senior doctor in the A&E department.

To me A&E is not like work. Whatever other roles I am performing, I am a doctor first and foremost and it reminds me on a weekly basis of why I first picked up a stethoscope. Emergency medicine feeds back into everything I am doing with Teleheal and keeps me on my toes, up to speed with radiology and connected to people in immediate need. It gives me an opportunity, too, to teach in a hospital setting. Thanks to my rather unusual career path, I have more training and experience than the average A&E doctor – not too many of us divert from specialist training only two years short of becoming a consultant – and I am always happy to share that experience and put it to good use.

Royal Shrewsbury A&E is a great working environment with a well co-ordinated team of friendly seniors and capable and committed doctors and nurses. My colleagues are fascinated by my other life on the front line of telemedicine. Some are surprised that I am so actively involved myself and still choose to work at the hospital. But no matter how busy I am with the charity, I want to be in A&E. By the time I start my shift, the adrenaline is already pumping.

During the week, while I juggle case management in Afghanistan and Syria, projects with our partners and all the conferences and meetings, I am constantly looking ahead to the next opportunity.

My life requires a high level of commitment and of course there are stresses, but I try to keep everything in balance. As I make daily lists of what is urgent, what can be delegated and what can be deferred, I motivate myself by visualizing the charity's ultimate mission. If we do not have defined goals, everyday tasks sap our physical and mental energy. I attend to the urgent matters, delegate what I can and ignore everything else. We need to have priorities otherwise it's too easy to feel overwhelmed and end up wasting hours on Twitter. But it is important to be flexible with those priorities. Certain tasks might be promoted or demoted according to how the day pans out, but I never look on emptying my inbox as a sensible objective. We all receive too much trivial and distracting information through our tech.

I try to fit in some regular exercise, mainly cardio workouts and weights, at home or at the gym, and I like to keep my hand in with martial arts.

Early in the evening, I spend time with my family. We eat together (I'm still a hopeless cook, so my job is washing the dishes and clearing up the kitchen) and after Davina and I get Zane and Alana bathed and into bed, I return to work. Late at night, when the house is at peace, is when I have most of my ideas.

Before I go to sleep at night I still spend a few quiet moments reminding myself of all I have to be grateful for: my survival, my dear family, what I have managed to accomplish.

Playing with my children, watching them grow and learn, is

special. Having had no childhood, maybe I am only now living mine through them. It brings it home to me just how remarkable my parents were. How they managed is simply astonishing. For me, as for them, family is a solid foundation. Having small children certainly helps you to retain your perspective. Their simple, black-and-white view of the world and the transparency of their needs and desires boils life down to its essence.

At the end of January 2020, I saw on the news a convoy of six coaches arriving from RAF Brize Norton at Arrowe Park Hospital on the Wirral, where I had worked as a radiologist. They were carrying eighty-three Britons evacuated from Wuhan, a city in China locked down by the authorities after being struck by an unknown virus, who were to be quarantined for fourteen days in an NHS staff accommodation block at Arrowe Park.

Soon people with the same virus were coming through the doors of A&E at Shrewsbury. My first COVID-19 patient was a young woman who was struggling to breathe. Oxygen didn't work. Inhalers didn't work. 'God, what is this?' I said. We had no option but to escalate to the medical and ICU teams. The most terrifying thing was not understanding what was happening. With asthma or COPD, we know what we can do to help. As A&E doctors, we see it all, and we are simply not used to not having the first idea how to respond. I began to imagine what life must be like for an undertrained Afghan emergency doctor.

My first patient did eventually recover, but some did not. Like other hospitals, ours was rearranged to cope with the flood of coronavirus patients. We had green, amber and red zones. Those confirmed or suspected of having COVID-19 were sent to the red zone, where full personal protective equipment was mandatory for all staff. Making that decision was nerve-racking. What if you put someone who had COVID in the green zone? Or someone who did not in with the infected patients? The acute medicine and emergency departments were combined and we all attended our patients in whichever zone they had been placed. Increasingly, it was in the red zone. Most of the patients went from there to ICU. This was the NHS front line as I'd never known it before.

The conditions were exhausting and uncomfortable. Full PPE was tight, claustrophobic and made it difficult to breathe. I cleaned my hands so often that they were red raw from the rubbing alcohol. You didn't touch anything unnecessarily with any part of your body, or your clothes. We hardly sat down all shift for fear that the virus might be transferred between scrubs and chair and were cautious about eating in case the cutlery was contaminated. We were anxious even around minor ailments in the green zone. Was this really just a cough or a cold? We searched the rapidly updated Public Health England guidelines for the latest advice on treating pregnant women and children. We searched for PPE and clean protective glasses.

I was worried about bringing the virus home to my family. I put on hand gel before opening the front door, peeled off clothes, shoes, everything, into a bin liner, got straight into the shower and scrubbed myself vigorously for ten, fifteen minutes. Even then I was nervous about playing with the kids. Two lovely colleagues I had worked with died of COVID that spring, a registrar and a nurse. It was the first time I had ever lost an NHS comrade.

I took heart from the positives. On the rearranged wards, all the staff worked together as one huge team. With no elective surgery taking place, the orthopaedics doctors joined us and helped with the minor traumas. People were retrained and redeployed. Everyone just got on with it.

The support from outside was so touching. The weekly 'clap for carers' all over the country, the food being brought in for us, the free tea and coffee. It kept up our morale and gave us a great sense of solidarity. But as the pandemic wore on you saw people burn out and rally, saw the effects of the constant shock and stress.

On the world stage, I was dismayed that some of the big organizations were not quicker off the mark to react and wondered where those millions of dollars of aid were going. The provision of PPE, ventilators, meds, testing and expertise was sluggish. In any emergency, and especially in a pandemic, you don't have time to create a perfect system. You have to activate a crisis plan that is as good as it can be, move as quickly as you can and make adjustments as you go along and the problem evolves.

The Ministry of Public Health in Afghanistan re-established contact, in urgent need of help with handling COVID-19. They did have some ventilators, but nobody knew how to use them. We could not supply equipment or PPE but we rose to the challenge and, once again, Afghanistan became our innovation ground. In contrast to some ambitious health projects that cost millions and took months to build, Teleheal, with no money and no external resources, was responding within a couple of days. We were the first in the world to implement a digital health capacity-building strategy for COVID to support an entire conflict-zone country.

We just threw everyone in and everything at it. With people clamouring for information and the virus affecting so many of the body's systems, help was needed from multiple specialists. I rearranged the groups, merging all the hospitals into one big WhatsApp group for COVID, served by a new configuration of ICU, acute medicine and paediatric specialist volunteers, supported by radiologists. We were now bringing almost every province into the network, which involved communication between around 240 COVID-assigned doctors in total. We dispensed with centralized co-ordination and put the groups in direct touch with each other.

To our case management support we added virtual seminars on our social media networks. This proved to be a very effective way of advising a large number of doctors simultaneously, enabling them to interact with our specialists and live questions to be asked and answered. Topics such as which oxygen-delivery system to use and when to use it were covered in our webinars, which remained available for reference on the app to all our partners. Within the groups the volunteers talked doctors through how to operate the ventilators, which settings to choose and so on. It complicated matters that many of the machines were different.

COVID-19 was something everyone in the world was trying to understand and control and, with our knowledge evolving on a daily basis, low-resource countries were particularly vulnerable to misinformation. I encountered advice being drafted at official levels that quoted speculative stories from Western newspapers or prematurely promoted the use of drugs such as hydroxychloroquine, on which the WHO had paused trials due to safety concerns.

We were receiving new protocols every week and initially we passed them on as soon as we had them, but simpler information was needed in Afghanistan, Syria and Africa on continuous update. So we summarized the guidance and circulated more concise bulletins regularly to all of our partners. Some of the information was extensive – the advice from the WHO, for example, ran to about 200 pages, which one of our specialists sat down and condensed into a more accessible thirty-five.

We later created another group for the Agency for Assistance and Development for Afghanistan, an NGO supported by the World Bank, and provided them with these three layers of support. AADA has a big hospital in Herat province and rapid-response teams which go out to treat patients in the districts.

In the UK, a study after the first wave of the pandemic found that almost half of NHS ICU staff had been left stressed or traumatized to some degree. Healthcare teams in countries without access to the same resources were suffering from even greater anguish and burnout as they tried to cope with the volume of cases while watching patients and colleagues die, and sometimes their own relatives, too. I enlisted the help of our clinical psychologist, Dr Deborah Thorp, who was on one of the faculty committees of the British Psychological Society. She adapted for us guidelines the society had compiled for professionals, families and communities on stress and trauma management during COVID. Deborah gave webinars designed to help those on the front line to recognize and understand signs and symptoms in themselves and their colleagues and to accept that, in order to take care of their patients, they had to take care of themselves first.

According to the UN, in 2020 the country in the most need of humanitarian aid was Yemen, broken by civil war and famine. I'd had no response to a previous overture to the health minister. Now, as the virus began to circulate, the government was denying that there were any cases in Yemen. We have a consultant in the US primed to offer live teaching in Arabic, but we are still exploring ways of getting help to the people through the thicket of diplomatic, political and cultural issues. In the meantime, I have been advising a group of expatriate Yemeni doctors and nurses more familiar with the territory who want to find a means of using simple tech to put out public health messages in their home country. Their ultimate goal is to set up a telemedicine network like ours, using Yemeni volunteers living abroad. They have an uphill climb, as they are starting completely from scratch. But that's exactly where I was. With passion, drive and a committed team, anything is possible.

At the end of 2020 I contracted COVID-19 myself. For five days I lay in isolation in a bedroom at home, every part of my body aching, swinging between fever and chills, my temperature periodically soaring to 40 degrees. My Teleheal ICU specialist colleagues were keeping an eye on me remotely and I monitored my oxygen saturation with a pulse oximeter. Early on it was quite scary: I was only too aware of the unpredictability of this vicious virus and I had no way of telling which way it was going in my case. Fortunately, my symptoms subsided, although for several weeks afterwards I would find myself hit by sudden waves of fatigue.

Any large-scale medical emergency provides science and medicine with huge learning opportunities and forces us to look for different solutions. This pandemic, on a scale unknown in our lifetimes, compelled everyone to innovate. Dedicated scientists across the world raced to produce and test vaccines faster than this had ever been done before. But as inoculation programmes were rolled out in wealthier countries, WHO director-general Dr Tedros warned that the world was 'facing a catastrophic moral failure because of unequal vaccine policies'.

COVID-19 has given us scope to rethink the way we run global healthcare, and that must include ongoing support for countries which can't afford vaccines. In many regions, vaccination is the only workable preventative strategy. People living in poverty or refugee camps can't self-isolate or improve their sanitation. It is not only a moral obligation; it is in all of our interests to come together to stop the virus because it will not be under control until it is under control everywhere.

The pandemic also brought digital health into the spotlight. The urgent need to adapt has accelerated the understanding of telemedicine and the role it has to play in the healthcare of the future, not just in conflict zones but by connecting the whole world.

Responding to COVID brought the best out of Teleheal. The different approaches we tried out to tackle the challenge gave us a new road map for the future. The direct communication between the groups and the webinars were very successful. We now host virtual seminars regularly for our partners. And providing mental health advice for the first time had been a significant step.

Mental health was already by far the biggest unaddressed health-care crisis in the world today. In England alone, one in four people annually experience a mental health problem of some kind. Services are over-stretched and insufficient. According to the WHO, in low- and middle-income countries between 76 and 85 per cent of people with mental health disorders receive no treatment and, when they do, it is often of poor quality. In war zones and among refugees, the numbers are off the charts. It was an issue that affected the population of every single region where Teleheal had a presence.

In Afghanistan, little had changed since I was handed sedatives for my depressive episode as a child. After forty years of war, a majority of people suffer from a mental health disorder, yet there is still only a handful of psychologists, most of them in the cities, to serve a population of around 39 million. The government, which put together a mental health strategy in 2019, has trained a few hundred psychosocial counsellors but, with no qualifications required beyond a basic education and training lasting only a couple of months, there is a limit to what they can achieve. Especially given that many people are reluctant to seek help: mental health is not well understood and sufferers are frequently stigmatized by their communities. Similar situations are encountered the world over.

The international donors who invested heavily in health services in Afghanistan focused their attention on physical rather than mental health, and that bias is at the root of the lack of mental healthcare everywhere. The outcomes of treating physical injuries and illnesses are easier to recognize and to quantify. And yet mental health problems are one of the main causes of the overall disease burden worldwide.

In the NHS we see countless patients with such problems who end up in crisis in A&E, because by this point there is nowhere else for them to go. Early recognition of many psychological conditions can prevent the need for escalation to specialist services. But our overloaded NHS mental health services are not as accessible as they should be, and waiting lists are long. Some patients are treated with drugs when psychological interventions could have helped them without medication.

This is a situation that long preceded COVID. In the post-COVID landscape, the world will be facing a tsunami of problems created or exacerbated by the many legacies of the virus: long COVID, front-line trauma, physical illness, bereavement, financial problems, job losses and the effects of the long months of social isolation required to combat the spread of the virus. These will be coming to the door of health services already buckling under the strain of the demand for mental healthcare and insufficient capacity to provide it. Most vulnerable are key workers dealing with the public day in, day out – including the health professionals on whom the NHS itself depends.

At the height of the pandemic, in A&E we were already seeing a sharp rise in attempted suicides and patients abusing alcohol and drugs as a form of escape. Some of this fallout is preventable. Taking care of ourselves and reaching out to support each other is a way we can all help. Demonstrating kindness and empathy is not just altruistic. Studies show that it makes us happier, too. So everybody wins. In general, fixating too much on ourselves exacerbates our own problems, as we tend to focus on the negatives. Turning our attention outward keeps us engaged, curious and inspired. Focusing on the good in our lives, rather than the bad, makes us feel more positive. So does having a purpose, whether that is one big ambition or a series of short-term goals.

Our minds and bodies are not compartmentalized. Our mental health is unlikely to be great if our physical health is poor, and vice versa, which is why good nutrition, exercise and learning to manage stress levels are important for our mental wellbeing. Over the previous couple of years I'd been approached by psychiatrists, psychologists, nurse practitioners and wellbeing experts, such as dieticians, who were keen to volunteer for Teleheal and I had been exploring ways in which I could use their skills to create a digital platform to address stress and mental health problems, particularly at the pre-clinical stage. As the COVID-19 pandemic bit deeper, intensified by new strains of the virus, it brought the inadequacy of existing resources and expertise into even sharper relief and people were turning to health professionals for help in increasing numbers. Now was the time to put my ideas into action.

My vision is mental healthcare on demand. I am developing a model for a holistic service offering consumers direct access virtually to a full range of professional help – a one-stop shop for mental healthcare, to be run alongside Teleheal. There are any number of wellbeing apps out there, but many offer merely pseudo-science or a one-size-fits-all approach. Arian Wellbeing will be scientific, personalized and supported by experts. The plan is for every case to be overseen by a qualified clinical psychologist, who will provide a comprehensive initial assessment in a phone or video call and advise on the next step. In some cases, this might be a referral to a specialist mental health expert signed up to the service; in others, for example, an obese patient with mild symptoms, it could be as simple as suggesting exercise and the support of one of our personal trainers or nutritionists.

The provision of an expert assessment is crucial. Most stress and anxiety is a normal response to life's difficulties, but complex cases require targeted referral and specialist support. Certainly no standard wellbeing advice on social media would be capable of addressing these. Simply being told to text a friend or go for a walk is not going to help anyone with severe issues – in some instances it might even make things worse.

This joined-up system has enormous potential to deal with mental health problems before they escalate while improving physical health. Easy access through mobile devices not only avoids lengthy waiting lists, it helps to normalize the process of seeking medical attention in the first place. Too many sufferers leave it too long because of the stigma around mental health. It will also enable the participating professionals to quickly identify serious cases in need of medical or psychological intervention outside the network. We aim to test and refine in the UK or elsewhere, producing a template that will be scalable worldwide.

We need to be looking for long-term solutions, not just plugging the gaps, some of which Teleheal was already trying to tackle, at home as well as abroad. During COVID lockdown in the UK, I was contacted by the clinical lead of a Manchester-based NHS service specially commissioned to manage the healthcare of around 200 asylum-seekers and refugees being accommodated by the local authority. Her team was fighting on so many fronts: coronavirus, physical illnesses, PTSD, grief, depression and the consequences of torture.

These people had been travelling for months, over a year in some cases, men, women and children escaping war, poverty and other horrors in their own countries and experiencing further trauma during their journeys. When they finally arrived it was to lockdowns, confusing bureaucracy, extreme uncertainty about their futures. Because of the COVID crisis they did not have access to the level of support that would normally have been available to them. As the survival instinct, determination and strength it had taken them to get to the UK in the first place began to crumble, so the traumas they were suffering began to surface. Some of the children were exhibiting symptoms that their parents were unable to understand. The staff delivering their care were themselves being affected by what they were seeing and hearing.

These reactions resonated with my own experience of arriving in the UK as a refugee and I was glad to be able to help. I set up a series of virtual training seminars, with Dr Deborah Thorp and our Teleheal psychiatrist, Dr Salman Karim, to coach the team's healthcare staff on how to listen to the refugees' stories, to empathize, to pick up on signs of trauma, manage and refer them and to build resilience in the refugees and in themselves.

Making it to your new country isn't the endgame, it's just the beginning of a long and difficult road to constructing a new life. We need to start looking at refugees differently, as an investment, not a burden. Their unique talents, fortitude and problem-solving skills can be of great benefit to their host countries, their homelands and the world at large.

In the early days of 2020, as COVID-19 began to stalk the world, I'd had a call from my brother in Kabul. My mum was not well. Her tummy had not been right for months and she thought she had an infection. I told him to get blood tests, take her to a sonographer for an ultrasound and send the scan to me. The image showed a mass on the liver. My heart sank. I advised a CT scan. When that came back I shared it with several radiologists, including Sami Khan. 'There's a chance it is cancer,' he said. 'You'd better get her an MRI.'

The MRI suggested it was a fifty-fifty chance. Mum needed a biopsy without delay. We made arrangements as quickly as possible to send her to the Mahatma Gandhi Hospital in Jaipur, India. I had been here with my parents a couple of years earlier, on the recommendation of one of my BAPIO colleagues, who had connections with MGH, to find my mum some help with her arthritis. It was a flagship hospital with its own telemedicine suite, which they used to enhance their high standard of care with the support of outside experts. The doctors had said at the time that my mother had the worst knee joint they'd ever seen. Yet she always kept moving. Her strength and courage were just astonishing. I contacted my BAPIO colleague and he swiftly sorted everything out with the hospital while, between us, my family and I got Mum on a plane to India.

The news from MGH broke my heart in two. She had cancer. And it was inoperable.

Living with cancer in Afghanistan is incredibly tough. So is dying from it. There is no real support and no chemotherapy. Although there was no treatment that would change the outcome for my mum, she needed palliative chemotherapy to be kept comfortable and that had to be brought from Pakistan. In the West chemotherapy is given in a carefully controlled way. Before every session, the patient is checked, blood counts are analysed and boxes ticked to confirm that the body can cope with the treatment. In Afghanistan it is a DIY business conducted largely by guesswork. My mum frequently ended up in hospital with bleeding caused by too low a platelet count. Getting hold of the chemotherapy drugs at all became increasingly difficult in the midst of the pandemic.

I was devastated but I had to take control of the situation and stay strong, for my mum, my dad and for the family. She had a skilled medical team looking after her from 4,000 miles away: radiologists, physicians to offer second opinions, surgeons monitoring the spread of the disease, an intensive care consultant, a pain specialist. There was a whole separate WhatsApp group just for my mum. And she was helping others by becoming a case study, which pleased her. The charity I had founded to help the world had now led back to where my vision had begun: with my family. Things had come full circle.

I managed my mum's care, with a volunteer ICU consultant on the end of the phone, until she drew her last breath.

'Shall we take her to the hospital?' my family were asking.

I had done everything possible. 'No,' I told my brother on the phone. 'We have to let her go.'

My mum passed away in May 2020 and, like so many others who lost loved ones in the time of COVID, I had to watch her funeral on social media. Acutely aware of how vulnerable my grieving dad was to the virus, I pleaded with my brothers and sisters not to invite people to the funeral. Many of them turned up anyway.

My mum was the lynchpin of the family and it would take a while for everyone to rebalance themselves around the gaping hole at its centre. With my dad bereft and becoming frail, I was now seen as the head of the family. I keep in touch and do the best I can to provide support and counsel. I video-call my dad every couple of days. FaceTime with Zane and Alana raises his spirits and they love chattering to Baba. I am so grateful that my mum got to meet Alana in person in Dubai a couple of months before she fell ill. 'You have one of each,' she mused. 'Perfect.'

My own grief was profound. Most bereaved people find that it comes in waves and goes through stages. The absence of a loved one is not something we 'get over'. Gradually, the raw pain will ease. We begin to accept our loss and to grow our lives around the gap they have left, but it will always be a part of us. To help the healing process, it is important not to try to deny our pain, to blot it out or bury it. That was one lesson I had already learned. We need to allow ourselves to mourn. And we need to talk. I talk often about my mum, and take comfort from the knowledge that I did everything possible for her, just as, throughout her life, she did everything she could for me.

Simple grief is a natural response to loss, not a mental illness, but its psychological and physical effects – depression, panic, a sense of isolation, changes in appetite, sleep problems – can be far-reaching. Being kind to ourselves and taking care of our physical and mental health will help us deal with bereavement, just as it helps us to build the resilience we need to meet life's other challenges.

I looked to the coping mechanisms on which I had relied for my survival since my childhood. They had kept my hopes alive during terrible times and helped me to overcome my stress and PTSD symptoms as I made my way into adulthood and beyond. In the post-COVID world, keeping depression and feelings of hopelessness at bay is going to be vital for us all.

Some psychologists suggest that trauma can have a positive legacy, a sense that if you have survived this far, you can survive anything, and a sharper recognition of the fragility of life which makes you focus on its meaning and what is most important. Perhaps that is one of the effects it had on me. I found my healing in giving back, in being able to make a real difference in the world, in Davina and my family, and in gathering my courage to tell and retell my story to real and effective purpose.

In Afghanistan, where it all began, doctors from around the world continue to handle cases together using the same simple tech, spurred on by a survey of our work there between 2016 and 2019 which confirmed that we have been instrumental in saving lives on an impressive scale.

While I remain available 24/7, I am pretty much able to step back and let the medics get on with it. Many of the volunteers and Afghan doctors are now on first-name terms. Their messages show them enquiring after each other's families and at Eid the greetings flow around the globe. It is amazing to see a critical-care consultant in the USA talking to a doctor in a village in Afghanistan like old friends. Our pioneering methods have broken down barriers and built bridges between people who would never meet in any other circumstances and who now stand shoulder to shoulder across the world to promote peace through saving lives and improving education.

By 2021, our nexus of wonderful volunteers had grown to upwards of 150 and counting, from across the world, in an increased number of specialisms and in non-medical roles, too: the support of professionals in fields such as law and management has been vital. There are others – radiographers, sonographers and specialist nurses, for example – waiting in the wings to step up as we take on projects that can use their skills.

Our work will never stand still. We are constantly creating new ways to use telemedicine, to share the expertise of our volunteers and to empower our partners to transform global health. It has captured the attention of governments, professional bodies and global health-care experts and has been peer-reviewed by academics.

It is a source of deep fulfilment that my vision of going global has truly become a reality. As well as assisting the WHO as a member of their roster of experts for digital health, in 2021 I was pleased to be able to share our telemedicine model with EMRO, their regional office serving twenty-two countries in the Middle East, North Africa, the Horn of Africa and central Asia, as they explore workable and efficient solutions in that territory. I was also delighted to agree to a request from the oldest and largest humanitarian organization in the world – the International Federation of Red Cross and Red Crescent Societies, which boasts an impressive 15 million volunteers – to model our work for their international communications.

For so much to have come from such dire beginnings may seem incredible. But I truly believe that every one of us, whoever we are, has the potential to realize our dreams. We only need to be given a chance, to have faith in ourselves and to find the courage to fight for those dreams. As a refugee child that was all I had: one big dream.

Epilogue

'THEY ARE IN KABUL bro. Guns firing. And people are escaping.'

It was 15 August 2021. The text was from my brother Farid.

Everyone knew that the Taliban were coming. During the summer they had swept across Afghanistan seizing power in key cities. As part of an agreement made in Qatar with their leaders, the USA were already proceeding with a staged withdrawal of their forces from Afghanistan. But the speed with which the Taliban arrived in Kabul caught the world by surprise.

In Chester, I was catapulted back thirty years to the outbreak of civil war. Memories surged up from deep within me. I could hear the gunfire; feel myself tripping blindly over bloody, broken bodies in the mud as we fled Kabul. To Davina my face appeared blank, emotionless. But she had seen me this way before and understood what was happening inside. Her eyes brimming with tears, she hugged me and soothed our bewildered kids.

The whole family was now calling or texting. I was trying to calm people down left, right and centre. For my sisters, too, history was repeating itself. 'What shall we do? Where can we go this time? Pakistan? Logar?' My dad said nothing. He no longer had any answers. Neither did I. 'Just stay indoors, and stay as calm as you can,' I told them. 'Hopefully, everything will be OK.'

On my television screen, I was watching panicked crowds descending on Kabul airport, clutching assorted documents they could only hope would get them on to one of the military evacuation flights while it was still possible.

Some would make it; most would not. Amid the pandemonium on the tarmac the following day, five people died. One of them was seventeen-year-old Zaki Anwari, an undocumented member of the national youth football team, who fell from the sky while trying to cling to a departing aircraft – a boy much like the boy I had been, for whom this latest chapter in Afghanistan's tragic story spelled the end of all dreams and opportunities. The only difference between us was that I had succeeded in breaking free to pursue mine and he had not. I imagined hanging on to that plane, focused on saving my life and my future, only to feel them slipping from my grasp. I watched, weeping, as parents passed babies over barbed-wire fences into the hands of soldiers, desperate to get them to safety.

On 26 August, a suicide bomber walked into the crush of families at the airport gates, killing more than 180 people and injuring over 150. Among those who narrowly escaped becoming part of that death toll were Farid and his wife and baby daughter.

It was only a couple of days earlier that they had learned their names were on a family list drawn up by Farid's brother-in-law which gave them the chance to seek asylum abroad. Javid was already gone. Thanks to his job with an international NGO, he had been evacuated in July and was trying to carve out a life for himself in America.

Farid had rushed straight round to talk to my dad. He didn't want to leave his home or his life. He was just completing a masters in science and his specialist training in paediatrics at the Indira Gandhi Children's Hospital and, as the only son still in Afghanistan, he saw it as his responsibility to take care of Dad and the rest of the family. But he had a family of his own to support and all his hopes of a future practising medicine in Kabul had been dashed.

The city was in chaos. For weeks displaced families from the provinces had been pouring into the capital, which they had seen as the last bastion of safety, and were sheltering in mosques and living rough in the parks. Staples such as rice and beans had already run out and food prices were soaring. International sanctions were in operation against the Taliban and national assets of nearly $10 billion had been frozen by the World Bank. At a stroke, the struts supporting Afghanistan's fragile economy had been pulled out and everything came crashing down. The president and government ministers had fled abroad. Shops, offices and banks were closed. Neither public services, 75 per cent of which had been financed by foreign aid, nor private companies could function.

In twenty years, the Afghan government had failed to develop a system founded on international funding to a level where it could be sustained without external support. Beyond the ivory tower of the Presidential Palace, the problems had always been apparent. Too often the money had been used merely to plug holes and not enough had been done to prevent large sums going into the pockets of corrupt individuals.

My dad listened to Farid in silence. 'If you think it's best to get out, son, go for it while you can,' he said eventually. When the news reached my sisters, they begged Farid to take one of their boys with him. 'I don't know what to do!' my brother said to me, distraught. 'Don't take anybody,' I urged him. 'They are not on any list and they have no papers. They won't get on a plane.' The prospect of one of my nephews meeting the same fate as Zaki Anwari was unthinkable.

The message summoning Farid and his wife to the airport gave them just two hours' notice to pack some essentials and join the jostling multitude at the gates. Their first attempt to leave was frustrated by an error in the list held by an official at the airport. They had to fight their way home through the gridlocked streets and watchful, gun-toting Taliban foot soldiers to sort things out before returning the next day. At last, in a torment of fear, pain and guilt, they found themselves crammed in the bowels of an overloaded military plane bound for Qatar.

In Kabul, a family still struggling to stabilize without my mum at its centre was torn apart, with all of its sons scattered abroad and Gululai, whose husband had held a senior post with a European NGO, anxiously poised to flee at any moment. My other sisters were afraid and suffering. Three of my brothers-in-law had been civil servants. Zari, widowed as a young woman, had four children to support. Nazifa's husband was selling their possessions in the streets to feed his kids. For older Afghans, all security was gone. For the younger generation, it was the death of hope. Of the dreams and ambitions of my nephews and nieces, all with educations that would, in the short term, at least, be of no practical use to them.

My dad's rental income from the house at Shahre Naow had already vanished. Now his modest social life disintegrated as well. The shop-keeper who used to put a chair out front for him, where he could sit and put the world to rights with his mates, had locked up his shop and fled. So had Dad's doctor, through whom both Farid and I had been able to monitor his health. In the autumn – dangerously ill, it turned out, with pneumonia and sepsis – our father collapsed in the street trying to make his way to a clinic. After that episode, it was clear that he could not manage on his own and Mahvash moved in to keep an eye on him. When I asked her to show me what meds he was taking, she produced some antibiotics. 'Where is the rest of it? The regular meds for his thyroid? His anti-depressants?'

'Son, how are anti-depressants going to make me feel any better?' said my dad. 'What is the point in taking pills to keep myself alive? I am tired of running and I don't know how to protect my daughters. Your mum would have known what to do.'

The ebbing away of his famous optimism was perhaps the saddest thing of all. In tears, he talked to me of the sights he'd seen in the mar-ket: the educated man, dressed in a beautiful suit, begging for small change to buy bread. The people trying to sell their kidneys. The man with a sign round his neck reading 'Child for sale'. 'That might be one of my grandchildren,' he sobbed. 'I don't think there is any hope for our country any more.' This is the reality for so many elderly Afghans. They have spent a lifetime moving heaven and earth to keep their families safe and now they simply have nothing left in the tank.

Shabana and Mahvash were pleading with me for help to get them out. I did some research and it was clear there was no chance. Even though their lives were under some level of threat because of their husbands' former jobs, making an asylum application from Kabul would take years. The UK's resettlement scheme wasn't even up and running.

Their only other option was terrifying, dangerous and arduous: moving by stealth over land in the backs of lorries, and, ultimately, across the sea, paying people-smugglers at every stage. It would also cost enormous amounts of money that none of us had. And yet they were seriously considering it. I spelled out the harsh truths: the lives lost en route; the men, women and children who had drowned in the Channel trying to reach the UK.

The one saving grace was that, although there were some attacks under the radar, there had been no street-by-street fighting in Kabul and the bloodbath we had all feared had not materialized. And, while Afghanistan was very different from the country the Taliban had conquered in the 1990s, and nobody yet knew what their rule might mean now – especially for women and girls – once again, their strict attitude to law and order was seeing crime levels drop dramatically.

'Give it some time. Things may settle down,' I advised. 'We don't have time!' my sisters said. 'We're dying of hunger here. We don't know how we will last the winter.'

'I can't get you out, but we can help you survive in Kabul,' I promised. Davina and I went through our accounts and pledged a regular sum to help with food, medical costs, clothes for the children. And

Perveen, who could not even afford firewood, was persuaded that, for both their sakes, it made sense for her to move in with Dad.

It felt as if we were right back where we'd started. As the stress and emotional exhaustion brought my PTSD to the surface, I fought to keep despair at bay with my longstanding coping mechanisms and support from Davina, from friends and colleagues and from our Arian Wellbeing psychologists. It was a huge reassurance to know that they had my back. I just could not – cannot – let go of hope. It is what helped me to survive.

I channelled my energies into the twin missions of galvanizing humanitarian aid for Afghanistan and advocating for refugees. The plight of the Afghan people is hard to overstate. On top of decades of conflict, misery and poverty – compounded in 2021 by looming famine due to the worst drought in nearly thirty years – they were facing the deadliest winter in living memory, all in the midst of the collapse of their government and economy, mass displacement and a global pandemic.

I was receiving numerous requests from national and international media to speak about the situation. I responded to as many as I could: it gave me a vital platform to put out the message that the world had to draw the distinction between the politics and the humanitarian emergency. It was essential that a mechanism was put in place to get help directly to the people.

By the beginning of 2022, the catastrophe the UN had been predicting for six months was happening. The Disasters Emergency Committee estimated that 98 per cent of Afghans were not getting enough to eat. Twenty-three million were already on the brink of starvation. Almost 40 million people, innocent pawns in international agendas and power struggles, could not just be left to die.

I had been campaigning for some time to challenge the narrative that politicizes, dehumanizes, criminalizes and weaponizes refugees. Nobody chooses to be a refugee. Uprooting your life and leaving your loved ones to start again in a strange land is invariably traumatic, whatever the circumstances of your arrival. After the departure of the Americans and their allies from Afghanistan, a flight had been arranged out of Islamabad for Gululai and her family. They had to make their own way to Pakistan, which was by no means easy, but at least, unlike most Afghans, they already possessed the necessary passports and visas.

A home had been provided for them in Sweden. They are safe in this welcoming country, and full of gratitude to their hosts, but for months Gululai cried every day for what she had lost: her tight-knit Afghan family network, the beautiful house in which she had taken such pride and the privileged life she had led in Kabul. Here she knew nobody. Their apartment was in a complex occupied by immigrants from many different parts of the world. She could do little more than exchange nods and smiles with her neighbours as they shared no common language. She mourned the separation of her children from the cousins they were raised with, fretted about their adjustment to school and lamented that her baby girl would grow up never knowing her homeland.

Javid, on his own on another continent, as I once was, had been accommodated by a host family in Texas. His permanent residency, driving licence and permission to work were quickly granted and before long he was juggling three jobs. He is ambitious, business-minded and has big plans for the future, but working so relentlessly has also been his way of coping. He tired himself out every day, falling asleep at night in his clothes, for fear that taking time off would force him to face his loneliness and homesickness. He badly missed my dad, and the two Pomeranian dogs he had inherited from a departing colleague, known at home as 'Javid's posh dogs', who were now keeping my dad company in Kolula-Pushta.

Farid and his family had spent the best part of a week in Qatar with other refugees in a large, open-sided communal tent in broiling heat, the sun beating down mercilessly on the canvas. There was no fan, only one meal a day, just some kind of biscuits and juice, and all they had for the baby, so vulnerable in these conditions, was what remained of the milk they had brought from Kabul. Then they were flown to an airbase in Germany, where they shivered in the sharp, autumnal weather. After a few days undergoing COVID-19 quarantine, medicals and form-filling, they were transferred to a vast refugee camp at a military facility in the eastern United States, one of several such holding centres across the country.

Here they would remain in limbo for five months, accommodated within partitioned industrial-sized tents, with no indication of where in America they might end up, or when. Bureaucratic delays were apparently worsened by the hasty and chaotic evacuation. By early 2022, some 37,000 refugees were still waiting in these camps, with more arriving every week from the overseas airbases of US allies.

They were safe, well fed and had access to healthcare, and people were kind to them, but there was little to do, no opportunity to work and no authorization to venture beyond the boundaries of the base. Farid was battling to cope. In Kabul he had been a respected doctor. In America he was, suddenly, nobody. Just another refugee. Haunted by guilt at abandoning my dad, he began to question whether he should ever have left.

The refugee experiences of my brothers and sister resonated so strongly with mine. They brought back the unbearable heat of the Pakistan camps of my childhood; the profound disorientation, social isolation and seesawing emotions of my first years in London, when, without warning, all the excitement of a new life in a new land of opportunity would be overcome by a wave of grief for what I had left behind. Compared with so many displaced people, Javid, Farid and Gululai have been blessed. But their difficulties illustrate just how deeply identity is rooted in our families and communities and how hard it is to start again from zero.

Down in Texas, Javid, spotting an advertisement for translators at the medical centre in Farid's refugee camp, successfully applied for a job there and moved some 1,700 miles north-east to be close to our brother. With around 11,000 refugees living on the high-security site, Javid had a busy role but being able to meet up with him in his breaks was a lifeline for Farid.

Javid was seeing at first hand the untreated PTSD suffered by so many refugees. The people routinely handed sleeping pills that can't possibly alleviate their trauma-induced nightmares; the young widow who broke down in the canteen, assailed in the middle of eating her lunch by flashbacks of her husband being shot in the eye and dying in front of her. 'I was there, the kids were there . . . I just can't get it out of my mind,' she sobbed. 'Can you send me home? I just want to go home.'

The medical centre provided paediatric and dental care and had a lab, X-ray machines and a pharmacy. What it didn't have was psychologists. Of course, anyone deemed a risk to themselves or others would be whisked off to hospital, but otherwise, all the nurses here could do was soothe and console. 'You are safe now. You will soon have a new home.' This is not an adequate treatment for PTSD.

With under-resourcing of mental healthcare a major problem everywhere, refugees are, not surprisingly, meeting with a similar response in the UK. As well as a proper, humane policy for admitting refugees we need a coherent system for resettling them efficiently once they are here. The compassion and practical help offered by local communities has been heart-warming but, as we have been seeing for years, so many aspects of the process – lengthy, tortuous and baffling Home Office procedures, entire families being cooped up for months in small hotel rooms – serve only to exacerbate conditions like anxiety, depression and PTSD.

Initial health assessments, currently geared too narrowly to physical health, should cover body and mind so that such conditions can be diagnosed and treated appropriately. I had been in the UK for ten years before my own PTSD was detected. Poor mental health, as I know to my cost, inhibits social integration. People need homes; they need and want to be able to work, to fulfil their potential and contribute to society. Refugees bring with them the talents, skills and innovative ideas they possess already and many more that can be developed through education and training. It benefits neither them nor their host country if they are left for months, even years, demoralized and reliant on the state, while their right to remain is finalized.

My Arian Wellbeing digital platform, now in its final stages of development, is designed to help everyone experiencing difficulties with their mental health, whatever their background. Since the pandemic, levels of depression in the UK have almost doubled. The mental health of young people and children is of particular concern – suicide is the UK's biggest killer of under thirty-fives – and we are already seeing an increase in quick-fix therapy services that do not comply with medical ethics and may do more harm than good. There is no assessment by a qualified psychologist; indeed, probably no human oversight at all. More often than not, users are matched by a bot to a therapist who may be practising in a completely different area of mental health, or merely presented with a long list of semi-qualified practitioners.

The number and range of highly qualified professionals who have already become a part of the Arian Wellbeing project is very encouraging. Treating the whole person also involves understanding how social diversity can affect mental health and reflecting cultural influences and family structures in our assessments and management plans. Creating opportunities tailored to particular demographics – for people to bake together, for example, or make music together – can alleviate social isolation and hopelessness and we are collaborating with local communities to provide them.

In Afghanistan, while charities reliant on boots on the ground have been forced to leave, Teleheal has seamlessly continued its emergency support, through COVID, through the short-lived war with the Taliban in the provinces and through the humanitarian disaster. The physical, mental and emotional strain on medical staff has been severe and, with almost all of the country's basic healthcare run by the World Bank, hospitals were out of even rudimentary medication and supplies as the government crumbled. Many staff went months without being paid. And yet, somehow, they have soldiered on. The use of simple tech and direct communication with the front line that underpins the daily operation of our partnership kept it going independently in the absence of any functioning health ministry, until such point as there might be a health ministry with which we could try to connect. It was further proof of the robustness of our telemedicine model in crisis situations.

Just a few short months after Afghanistan foundered, Russian president Vladimir Putin launched his ferocious military attack on Ukraine, displacing over 10 million people in the biggest refugee crisis seen in Europe since the Second World War. The destruction of Kyiv and Kharkiv – the tanks rolling into residential streets, the jets screaming overhead, the shelling – echoed the scenes of the Kabul and Logar of my childhood during the Soviet occupation and brought fresh waves of remembered terror and despair.

As these massive humanitarian calamities unfolded in quick succession, Teleheal was approached by the UN refugee agency's Global Compact on Refugees and various other international organizations keen to explore ways of using our network, experience and proficiency in the virtual arena to engage and assist both Afghanistan and Ukraine. We were brought on board by Professor Tony Young, NHS national clinical lead for innovation, to spearhead the humanitarian telemedicine response in Ukraine on behalf of the NHS and the UK government. Teleheal has started working with the international Ukraine Medical Association and the charity British

Ukrainian Aid towards rapidly replicating and adapting our tele-medicine model to support doctors in Ukrainian hospitals, and those serving the displaced population, in just the same way as we began it in Afghanistan: connected from the top down, with the agreement of the ministry of health and in direct communication with medics on the ground.

In the spring of 2022, I was invited to share our expertise – particularly in achieving access in emergency, displacement and disaster situations – with national heads of state and health ministers as one of the main speakers at a high-level WHO political summit on world migration and health issues held in Istanbul.

While my vocation has always been its own reward, public recognition of our work during this turbulent time for me came as a welcome boost to my morale. In the autumn of 2021, I had the unexpected honour of being named Doctor of the Year in the *Sun*'s NHS Who Cares Wins Awards, especially humbling in a year when doctors and healthcare professionals throughout the NHS had shown such exceptional heroism in the fight against COVID. Congratulating me backstage at the star-studded ceremony, David Beckham, who, as a Goodwill Ambassador for UNICEF, has worked with kids in refugee camps, encouraged me to keep doing what I'm doing, and there were uplifting words, too, from Prince William, who spoke to me of how inspirational he found my story. That December, I was chosen by *The Times* as one of their people of the year, alongside such icons as the footballer Marcus Rashford, who has done so much to combat child hunger and homelessness in the UK, and Her Majesty the Queen, no less.

This meant more than a pat on the back for my personal contribution, as a former refugee, to my adopted home, and to the people who had offered me a new life, by helping to save lives on the NHS front line during the pandemic. It was an acknowledgement of the potential benefits all refugees, and all those in our country who don't have the best of starts, can bring to our society. If these awards have inspired others, that will be their real worth.

As my family sought to adjust to its new dynamics, I found myself providing practical and emotional support for relatives on three continents. I kept on top of my dad's health and medication as best I could. Concerned by his appearance on a video call one day, I asked my sister to check his oxygen levels. They were worryingly low. I told her she must get him to a hospital as quickly as possible.

My dad had COVID. In a country where only 11 per cent of the population had been vaccinated, he was fortunate to have received two jabs of some sort, though I had no way of knowing what they were. However, with his multiple pre-existing health conditions, which included COPD, he was extremely vulnerable. The clinic that admitted him delivered increasing levels of oxygen, up to the maximum their appliances could handle, but his oxygen saturation stubbornly continued to drop. They had no equipment or training to provide continuous positive airway pressure (CPAP), which would be the next step, no ventilators and no intensive care facilities. If I did not do something my dad was going to die.

In the middle of the night I called a colleague at Wazir Akbar Khan Hospital in Kabul, one of those supported by Teleheal, just praying that he would be there. I was in luck. He told me that they had one free bed in ICU, which he booked immediately. He brushed aside my grateful thanks. 'You have been helping us for seven years,' he said. 'It is an honour to serve you back. We will treat your father like our own and do everything in our power to save him.'

Now we had to get him there. The clinic had no ambulance and my brother-in-law had to find one himself. As it was not equipped with oxygen, he then had to beg the clinic to sell him a cylinder to keep my dad alive on the journey. Online with the ICU doctors at Wazir Akbar Khan, I snapped into A&E case-leader mode. Only this time, I was acutely aware that every single decision I took could make the difference between life and death for my own father. 'Throw everything at it,' I said.

We upped his oxygen, then connected him to a CPAP machine, but still his oxygen levels were falling. Our only remaining option was to ventilate. This is the last roll of the dice for doctors treating COVID anywhere, but in Afghanistan, the outcome is particularly poor because the support systems needed to provide optimum care just aren't there. At Wazir Akbar Khan, one of Kabul's best hospitals, only around 10 per cent of patients survive post-ventilation. Somehow my dad was holding up and he remained mentally alert. We decided to stay with CPAP for just a little longer.

I asked if I could have a video call with Dad. I knew it might well be the last time I ever spoke to him. We had already discussed, in an emotional conversation, his final wishes, to be buried with my mum and for me to take care of our family, wherever they are. 'I'm too tired. I can't breathe. I can't carry on,' he said. I was in tears. It was he who had taught me I must never give up. 'Remember what you used to say to me when I had TB in the refugee camp?' I told him. '"Come on, you can't stop breathing." Well, neither can you.'

Miraculously, Dad's oxygen levels began to pick up at long last. To my joy and relief, he had turned a corner. There was damage to his lungs and the longer-term impact on his health was uncertain but, for the time being, he was back with us, along with his fighting spirit.

My amazing sisters took it in turns to sit with him in the ICU each day, tending to his every need; my brothers-in-law and nephews slept outside the ward each night. Our exiled siblings were on the phone constantly, in great distress. Thankfully, it was not too long before my dad was telling anyone who would listen that he was fine, insisting from his ICU bed that he would be leaving the hospital 'tomorrow' and demanding his phone to contact his grandchildren on Facebook. The day my sisters were finally able to bring him home from hospital was one of rare happiness in these bleak times.

Thanks to Teleheal, my dad had received the basic care unavailable to most Afghans. Everyone deserves that care. Our humanitarian telemedicine network, which strives to help make it accessible to as many people as possible, owes its existence to the family love that surrounded my dad. Love that began with my parents and grew into compassion for my wounded community, and then for the rest of the world. It gave me a real sense of achievement to experience that love coming right back to its source to save the father who had saved me. Who had bundled me into that bread oven and shielded me with his own body from the bombs; who had refused to give up on me when I nearly died of TB.

The same love and compassion had come back to me, too, countless times over. So many others across the globe need it now, including my own siblings.

Farid, his wife and their daughter were eventually relocated to a hotel in Virginia while a home was found for them to rent. For some weeks they remained entangled in the red tape so often encountered by refugees: still waiting for their food stamp card and the social security card Farid would need before he could find a job to pay that rent. But he was already looking to the future, researching the qualifications he will require to pursue his medical career in the States once he is on his feet.

Gululai's children are doing their best to adapt to their changing realities, managing well at school and rapidly learning Swedish. They go with her to the supermarket to translate while she gets to grips with the language. Her eldest son, Wasim, has his sights set on becoming a doctor, too.

Refugees have always been with us and, with no country immune to conflict, they always will be. By opening our hearts to those seeking sanctuary and trying to build new lives, and to the millions of others in need in their homelands, we can play our part in healing our world.

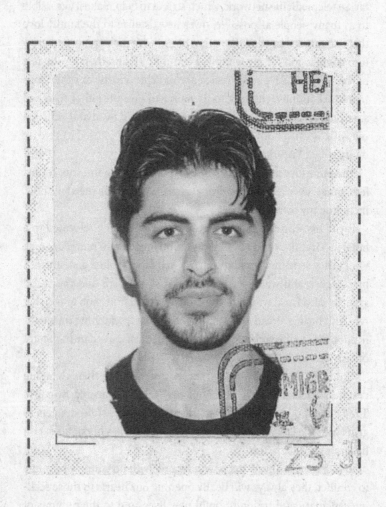

Acknowledgements

Creating a book is a team effort and I owe much to the many dedicated and talented people who have shared their time and expertise with me.

Caroline North McIlvanney, my writer and trusted friend, embraced my mission, took my hand and walked back with me through my life with patience, sensitivity and unflinching attention to detail. Little did either of us realize as we embarked on this book that we would not be able to meet for many months. Instead, with the world in the grip of COVID-19, she lived alongside me in video calls through the dark days of the pandemic and became part of our family, sharing our domestic ups and downs and the excitement of each new development with our global digital health partners. She focused every waking hour on this project. Thank you, Caroline, for your magical weaving together of all the strands of my story and for your incredible commitment.

My terrific agent, Carly Cook, and her team, and our marvellous editor, Andrea Henry, have been unwavering in their belief in my vision to inform and inspire and a driving force in distilling it into this book. Caroline and I are grateful to Andrea and to Stephanie Duncan, our editor on the paperback, for their clear-sighted direction. Thanks, too, to the whole team at Penguin Random House, especially Viv Thompson for her editorial management, Marianne Issa El-Khoury and Phil Lord for the design, Tom Hill for publicity and Lilly Cox for marketing.

As well as a personal memoir, *In the Wars* is a salute to Teleheal's amazing specialist medical volunteers, who give so freely of their time, week in, week out, day and night, to help save lives across the world, and to our international colleagues, who co-operate with us to improve our model while trying to do their jobs in extremely challenging circumstances. They are my constant inspiration, and I thank them from the bottom of my heart.

My thanks, too, to the leaders of all our national and international partners and their teams, and in particular to the various UN agencies, who have enabled us to trial, roll out and scale our support worldwide.

Our charity could not function without the generous pro bono advice and assistance of our volunteers in other professional capacities, from our trustees, Dr Sami Khan, Dr Masood Soorie and Dr Fazale Wardag, to the students who have devoted months of their time to admin and data. I am indebted to Priya Nagpal and her legal team at Simmons & Simmons, to our tech guru, Andy Ward, to Pamela Mooney and Ellen Gangani for their management skills and to Fin McNicol for his deft handling of media communications, and so much more, since Teleheal's inception. We greatly appreciate the work of the journalists and media who have amplified our message.

Our fundraisers and donors make our work possible and an army of unsung heroes has helped in countless ways, large and small, on a personal level as well as from a wider perspective. While respecting their wish to remain anonymous, I would like to make specific mention of philanthropic friends from the US whose practical generosity – such as the loan of their apartment in New York for my visits to promote my vision there – has been invaluable. They have given over part of their home in France to a family of Syrian refugees. That is humanitarianism in action.

The guidance of teachers, tutors and trainers, friends, former fellow students and colleagues, past and present, has been a godsend as I have fought to achieve my goals. It has been one of the privileges of my life to work in our wonderful NHS. My thanks to Tony Young, national clinical lead for innovation, and to all of those among the NHS leadership and management who have supported me as a doctor and the work of the charity. And, of course, to all the dedicated NHS health professionals I am honoured to serve alongside.

As well as having their own stories of hardship and resilience to relate, my sisters, brothers, their spouses and children, aunties, uncles and other relatives, are all a part of mine. We continue to provide a loving, tight-knit support network for each other through good times and bad. I would like to pay tribute, too, to Davina's parents, Graham and Vivianne Pickford, for raising their daughter to become such a strong and giving woman and for all they have done for our family.

When I look back over my life, I realize just how many compassionate and committed people have been there for me, ready to extend a helping hand to move my mission forward. They are testament to the truth that when we work together, there is nothing we cannot achieve. Although there is not space to include you all by name in these pages, every one of you has my heartfelt gratitude.

For more information, and to find out how you
can support us, please visit www.arianteleheal.com
or www.arianwellbeing.com. News of my
current activities is available on my website,
www.drwaheedarian.com, or you can
follow me on social media.

About the Author

Dr Waheed Arian is an NHS A&E doctor and founder of the pioneering charity Arian Teleheal, which works directly with clinicians on the ground in low-resource and war-torn countries. As an adviser, he helps global organizations and governments with the development of their healthcare and education systems. Dr Arian is an NHS Innovation Mentor and was appointed in 2019 to the WHO Roster of Digital Health Experts. Recognized as a UNESCO Global Hope Hero and a UN Global Goals Goalkeeper, in 2021 he was named Doctor of the Year in the Who Cares Wins Awards and chosen by *The Times* as one of their people of the year. In 2022 he was the winner of the Achievement Through Adversity category in the 23rd GG2 Leadership and Diversity Awards. He is a sought-after speaker at national and international conferences and events.

www.drwaheedarian.com

@DrWaheedArian
Instagram: @drwaheedarian
Facebook: @DrWaheedArian